MEMORY AND COVENANT

MEMORY AND COVENANT

THE ROLE OF ISRAEL'S AND GOD'S MEMORY IN SUSTAINING THE DEUTERONOMIC AND PRIESTLY COVENANTS

BARAT ELLMAN

Fortress Press
Minneapolis

MEMORY AND COVENANT

The Role of Israel's and God's Memory in Sustaining the Deuteronomic and Priestly Covenants

Cover design: Alisha Lofgren

Library of Congress Cataloging-in-Publication Data is available

Print ISBN: 978-1-4514-6561-7

eBook ISBN: 978-1-4514-6959-2

The paper used in this publication meets the minimum requirements of American National Standard for Information Sciences — Permanence of Paper for Printed Library Materials, ANSI Z329.48-1984.

Manufactured in the U.S.A.

This book was produced using PressBooks.com, and PDF rendering was done by PrinceXML.

For my mother, on her twelfth yartzeit
2 Iyar 5773

וְהָיָה אִם־שָׁכֹחַ תִּשְׁכַּח אֶת־ה׳ אֱלֹהֶיךָ וְהָלַכְתָּ אַחֲרֵי אֱלֹהִים אֲחֵרִים וַעֲבַדְתָּם
וְהִשְׁתַּחֲוִיתָ לָהֶם הַעִדֹתִי בָכֶם הַיּוֹם כִּי אָבֹד תֹּאבֵדוּן

If you indeed forget Yahweh your God and walk after other gods and serve them and worship them, I swear to you this day that you will surely perish.

—Deut. 8:19

וְזָכַרְתִּי אֶת־בְּרִיתִי יַעֲקוֹב וְאַף אֶת־בְּרִיתִי יִצְחָק וְאַף אֶת־בְּרִיתִי אַבְרָהָם
אֶזְכֹּר וְהָאָרֶץ אֶזְכֹּר

I will remember my covenant with Jacob and also my covenant with Isaac and also my covenant with Abraham I will remember, and the land I will remember.

—Lev. 26:42[1]

1. All translations and renderings of the Hebrew text are my own except where otherwise indicated.

CONTENTS

PREFACE

This book is a substantial revision of my dissertation, "Memory and Religious Praxis: The Meaning and Function of Memory in Deuteronomic and Priestly Religion," written under the supervision of Dr. Stephen Geller at the Jewish Theological Seminary. As its title indicates, the dissertation was concerned with mapping the semantic field of memory in deuteronomic and priestly literature, and, by applying the Theory of Divergent Modes of Religiosity developed by Harvey Whitehouse, with demonstrating the relationship between memory and the religious programs of these two traditions as put forth in the Pentateuch. The present book shifts the focus to explore the relationship between memory and *covenant* as each concept is understood by the authors behind D and P. The shift is not as wide as it might appear, for I maintain that "covenant" in both its priestly and deuteronomic manifestations is conceived of as a lived experience. For this reason, the religious programs envisioned and promulgated in deuteronomic and priestly literature remain central to this work. The principal changes I have made in this version are to condense the analysis of the two memory lexicons, and to develop an idea that I sketched at the end of the dissertation, namely the degree to which the employment of memory in the deuteronomic and priestly traditions is typologically anticipated in the two creation stories that begin Genesis. In other words, this book attempts to integrate deuteronomic and priestly conceptions of memory, the lived covenant, and cosmology, an ambitious undertaking, but one that I believe is justified by the importance the two traditions give to memory as a feature of the covenantal relationship between God and Israel.

The centrality of the covenant idea has been long recognized in connection to Deuteronomy, so much so that its theology is sometimes defined as "covenant theology." Likewise, the importance of creation in priestly theology is well remarked upon. I hope to show that both ideas have currency in both traditions, albeit to different degrees. The authors behind the Pentateuch, after all, came from the same place. Social location and periodicity may differentiate one tradition from another, but I believe it is safe to presume they shared some basic tenets. Among these are the certainty of the special relationship between God and Israel and the conviction that to maintain that relationship demanded a high degree of mindfulness, whether on God's part or Israel's.

I have been exceedingly fortunate to have been guided in my work by a superior scholar of biblical religion. Every meeting with my advisor Stephen Geller brought me new insights. If his learning is cited more frequently than others, I hope it testifies to the sensitivity of his reading of the Hebrew Bible and his ability to relate disparate elements under the rubric of theology.

In addition to Dr. Geller, there are many others to thank. In certain ways, this book reflects the advice, encouragement, suggestions, and insights of all the teachers of Bible with whom I have been privileged to study, my students at the Jewish Theological Seminary and Fordham College, my adult students in the Me'ah and Context programs, and the many groups of individuals whom I have been fortunate to teach. Some out of this group must be identified by name. I am very grateful to my readers, Susan Ackerman, David Marcus, Amy Kalmanofsky, and David Kraemer, and to Edward Greenstein, Shalom Paul, Adriane Leveen, Saul Olyan, David Carr, Ronald Hendel, Carol Newsom, and Michael Carasik, each of whom spurred my work forward in different ways. I also wish to acknowledge the ongoing support provided by the Graduate School at the Jewish Theological Seminary, and in particular Stephen Garfinkel, its Dean while I was a student there.

Scholarship also depends on financial support. The dissertation behind this book was made possible (in part) by funds granted through a fellowship program sponsored by the Charles H. Revson Foundation. As well, my thanks go to the editorial staff at Fortress Press, in particular Marissa Wold who saw the production of this book through, and Neil Elliott who took a chance on a proposal for a book considerably different from the dissertation that preceded it. Last, but hardly least, I want to thank my family: my daughters Emma and Sophie, who are an unending source of joy and a constant cheering section for me; and my husband Jay, who has stood by me though this entire process, read every word, and supported my work emotionally and intellectually. I am deeply indebted to them all.

Abbreviations

AB	Anchor Bible
ABD	*The Anchor Bible Dictionary*. Edited by D. N. Freedman. 6 vols. New York: Doubleday, 1992.
AJSR	*Association for Jewish Studies Review*
ANET	*Ancient Near Eastern Texts Relating to the Old Testament.* Edited by J. B. Pritchard. Princeton: Princeton University Press, 1969.
AOTC	Abingdon Old Testament Commentaries
ATANT	Abhandlungen zur Theologie des Alten und Neuen Testaments
BA	*Biblical Archaeologist*
BASOR	*Bulletin of the American Schools of Oriental Research*
BDB	Brown, F., S. R. Driver, and C. A. Briggs. *A Hebrew and English Lexicon of the Old Testament with an Appendix Containing the Biblical Aramaic.* Boston: Houghton Mifflin, 1907.
BHQ	*Biblia Hebraica Quinta.* General Editor, Adrian Schenker et al. Stuttgart: Deutsche Bibelgesellschaft, 2004–.
BHS	*Biblia Hebraica Stuttgartensia.* Edited by K. Elliger and W. Rudolph. Stuttgart: Deutsche Bibelgesellschaft, 1983.
BR	*Biblical Research*
BSac	*Bibliotheca sacra*
BTB	*Biblical Theology Bulletin*
BWL	*Babylonian Wisdom Literature.* Edited by W. G. Lambert. Oxford: Oxford University Press, 1960.
CAD	*The Assyrian Dictionary of the Oriental Institute of the University of Chicago*. Edited by I. J. Gelb, B. Landsberger, and A. L. Oppenheim. Oriental Institute. Chicago: University of Chicago Press, 1956–.
CAP	Cowley, A. E., ed. *Aramaic Papyri of the Fifth Century B.C.* Oxford: Clarendon, 1923.
CBQ	*Catholic Biblical Quarterly*
COS	*The Context of Scripture*. Edited by W. W. Hallo. 3 vols. Leiden: Brill, 2003.
DJD	*Discoveries in the Judaean Desert*. Editor in Chief: Emanuel Tov. 31 vols. Oxford: Clarendon, 1955–.

EA	El-Amarna tablets. According to the edition of J. A. Knudtzon. *Die el-Amarna-Tafeln.* Leipzig: J. C. Hinrichs, 1908–1915. Reprint. Aalen: Otto Zeller, 1964. Continued in A. F. Rainey, *El-Amarna Tablets, 359–379.* 2nd revised ed. Kevelaer: Butzon und Becker; Neukirchen-Vluyn: Neukirchener, 1978.
ER	*The Encyclopedia of Religion.* Edited by M. Eliade. 16 vols. New York: Macmillan, 1987.
Even-Shoshan	Even-Shoshan, A., ed. *A New Concordance of the Bible: Thesaurus of the Language of the Bible, Hebrew and Aramaic Roots, Words, Proper Names, Phrases and Synonyms.* Jerusalem, Kiryat-Sefer, 1988.
FAT	Forschungen zum Alten Testament
FOTL	Forms of the Old Testament Literature
GKC	*Gesenius' Hebrew Grammar.* Edited by E. Kautzsch. Translated by A. E. Cowley. 2nd ed. Oxford: Clarendon, 1910.
HALOT	*The Hebrew and Aramaic Lexicon of the Old Testament.* L. Koehler, W. Baumgartner, and J. J. Stamm. Translated and edited under the supervision of M. E. J. Richardson. 5 vols. Leiden: E. J. Brill, 1994–99.
HUCA	*Hebrew Union College Annual*
Interpretation	*Interpretation: A Journal of Bible and Theology*
JAOS	*Journal of the American Oriental Society*
Jastrow	Jastrow, M. *A Dictionary of the Targumin, the Talmud Babli and Yerushalmi, and the Midrashic Literature.* 2nd ed. New York: G. B. Putnam, 1903. Repr., New York: Judaica, 1971.
JBL	*Journal of Biblical Literature*
JNES	*Journal of Near Eastern Studies*
Joüon	Joüon, P. *A Grammar of Biblical Hebrew.* Translated and revised by T. Muraoka. 2 vols. Subsidia biblica 14/1–2. Rome: Editrice Pontificio Istituto Biblico, 1991.
JPS	*The JPS Torah Commentary.* Philadelphia: Jewish Publication Society, 1991–96.
JQR	*Jewish Quarterly Review*
JR	*Journal of Religion*
JSOT	*Journal for the Study of the Old Testament*
JSOTSup	Journal for the Study of the Old Testament: Supplement Series
JSS	*Journal of Semitic Studies*

LXX	*Septuaginta: Vetus Testamentum Graecum.* Auctoritate Academiae Scientiarum Gottingensis Editum. Edited by J. W. Wevers. 21 vols. Göttingen: Vandenhoeck & Ruprecht, 1977.
Maarav	*Maarav*
MT	Masoretic Text
NICOT	New International Commentary on the Old Testament
NJPS	*Tanakh: The Holy Scriptures: The New JPS Translation according to the Traditional Hebrew Text*
NRSV	New Revised Standard Version
OJPS	The Holy Scripture: Old JPS Translation
OTL	Old Testament Library
Proof	*Prooftexts: A Journal of Jewish Literary History*
RB	*Revue biblique*
RSV	Revised Standard Version
Sam. Tg.	*Samaritan Targum of the Pentateuch: A Critical Edition.* 3 vols. Edited by A. Tal. Tel-Aviv: Tel-Aviv University Press, 1981.
SBL	Society of Biblical Literature
SBLSymS	Society of Biblical Literature Symposium Series
SBT	Studies in Biblical Theology
TDOT	*Theological Dictionary of the Old Testament.* Edited by G. J. Botterweck and H. Ringgren. Translated by J. T. Willis, G. W. Bromiley, and D. E. Green. 14 vols. Grand Rapids: Eerdmans,1974–.
Tg. Neof.	*Targum Neofiti*
Tg. Onq.	*Targum Onqelos*
Tg. Ps.-J.	*Targum Pseudo-Jonathan*
TLOT	*Theological Lexicon of the Old Testament.* Edited by E. Jenni with assistance from C. Westermann. Translated by M. E. Biddle. 3 vols. Peabody, MA: Hendrickson, 1997.
TOTC	Tyndale Old Testament Commentaries
VT	*Vetus Testamentum*
VTSup	Vetus Testamentum Supplements
Vulg.	Vulgate
WestBC	Westminster Bible Companion
WBC	Word Biblical Commentary
YOS	Yale Oriental Series

PART I

Theoretical Underpinnings

1

Introduction

What did "memory" mean to the Israelite authors behind the Pentateuch? The question assumes, first of all, that memory was a meaningful concept for them, an assumption unlikely to be challenged by the mainstream ever since 1982 when Yosef Hayim Yerushalmi published *Zakhor: Jewish History and Jewish Memory.* Yerushalmi identified memory as "a religious imperative to an entire people" of biblical Israel. He wrote,

> Its reverberations are everywhere, but they reach a crescendo in the Deuteronomic history and in the prophets. "Remember the days of old, consider the years of ages past" (Deut 32:7). "Remember these things, O Jacob, for you, O Israel, are My servant; I have fashioned you, you are My servant; O Israel, never forget Me" (Isa 44:21). "Remember what Amalek did to you" (Deut 25:17). "O My people, remember now what Balak king of Moab plotted against you" (Micah 6:5). And, with a hammering insistence: "Remember that you were a slave in Egypt. . . ."[1]

Yerushalmi further observed that the Pentateuch concretizes the religious imperative of remembering in religious practice:

> Memory flowed, above all, through two channels: ritual and recital. . . . [T]he great pilgrimage festivals of Passover and Tabernacles were transformed into commemorations of the Exodus from Egypt and the sojourn in the wilderness. . . . A superlative example of the interplay of ritual and recital in the service of memory is the ceremony of the first fruits ordained in Deuteronomy 26. . . ."[2]

1. Yosef Hayim Yerushalmi, *Zakhor: Jewish History and Jewish Memory* (Seattle: University of Washington Press, 1982), 9–10.

As his biblical references suggest, Yerushalmi's comments on memory in biblical religion are based almost entirely on deuteronomic literature. In other words, he equates "memory" in biblical literature with the way "memory" is understood in Deuteronomy, as a religious obligation for the Israelite nation. Because Yerushalmi was looking for the origins of the modern idea of Jewish memory in the foundational text of Judaism, it likely did not occur to him to question whether that literature represents the whole of the Bible with respect to memory. Nor did he find it necessary to distinguish between different biblical conceptions of memory or to investigate how the biblical authors spoke about memory. These distinctions have remained largely unexamined in treatments of memory and the Bible by biblical scholars, with the result that both the particular ways in which memory is conceptualized in different religious traditions in the Bible and the possibility of a meaningful connection between memory and the religious programs of individual traditions within the Bible have been overlooked and unexplored.[3]

A salutary exception comes in an offhand comment by Moshe Greenberg in his commentary on Ezekiel:

> Israel's duty to always remember YHWH's redemptive and sustaining deeds (particularly in her prosperity) as the chief motive of obedience to his commandments is a Deuteronomic commonplace. . . . The priestly writings, on the other hand, extol YHWH's remembrance of his covenant as a feature of his trustworthiness.[4]

What Greenberg remarks upon is what this book seeks to demonstrate and develop. Both of the two principal traditions of the Pentateuch, one deuteronomic (D) and the other priestly (P), identify memory as the most instrumental guarantee of covenantal fidelity.[5] Nevertheless, they diverge

2. Ibid., 11–12.

3. To a great extent, this critique applies to almost all work on memory in the Bible as the review of scholarship below will illustrate. Some examples are Joseph Blenkinsopp, "Memory, Tradition, and the Construction of the Past in Ancient Israel," *BTB* 27 (1997): 76–82; Marc Zvi Brettler, "Memory in Ancient Israel," in *Memory and History in Christianity and Judaism*, ed. M. A. Signer (Notre Dame: University of Notre Dame Press, 2001), 1–17; Anto Popović, "The Bible as a Book of Memory," *Antonianum* 79 (2004): 441–43.

4. Moshe Greenberg, *Ezekiel 1–20*, AB 22 (Garden City, NY: Doubleday, 1983), 305.

5. The designations D and P derive from the Wellhausen-Graff "Documentary Hypothesis," which Julius Wellhausen presented in 1886 in his *Prolegomena zur Geschichte Israels* (*Prolegomena to the History of Israel*). Wellhausen postulated four "sources" underlying the Pentateuch: a Yahwistic source (J), an Elohistic source (E), the deuteronomic source (D), and a priestly source (P). Although it is no longer

significantly over what memory is, how memory serves its vital purpose, and as Greenberg observes, whose memory serves it. As Greenberg states, in the deuteronomic tradition, *Israel*'s fidelity to the Sinai/Horeb covenant—expressed through the fulfillment of its terms (commandments)—depends on Israel's continually remembering its obligation to Yahweh. In a slight, but significant, alteration of the second half of Greenberg's statement, in priestly literature, it is *God* who must be reminded of his "eternal covenant" (*b^{e}rît ʿôlām*) with Israel and of his particular commitment to his people.

The possibility that God forgets, except when deliberately and mercifully, is not readily acknowledged by readers of the Hebrew Bible, yet the priestly tradition clearly recognizes it. The most obvious example comes in the beginning of Exodus when, after 400 years, God remembers his covenant with the patriarchs and is thus prompted to intervene on behalf of their descendants. But further confirmation comes from God himself in Genesis 9, when God places his bow in the sky to remind him of his covenant with the world.

So it is that in both traditions, memory—that of Israel on the one hand and God on the other—must be induced or sustained, and the religious programs envisioned provide for that necessity. The different mechanisms used in each tradition reflect their radically different conceptualizations of what memory is. In Deuteronomy, memory tends to be semantic in content: that is to say, it is the acquisition and retention of information and doctrine. Israel's memories are formed verbally, through speech, and they are sustained and transmitted verbally, through recitation or oral instruction. Memory in priestly literature is more of a sensory phenomenon and is "episodic" in content.[6] In this tradition,

generally held that four distinct narratives underlie the Pentateuch as we now have it, these designations continue to be employed to refer to units of textual material that exhibit linguistic and ideational commonality. Because that material may come from several historical periods, I choose to use the term "traditions" rather than "sources" in connection to D and P. On the priority of these two traditions, see Gerhard von Rad, *Old Testament Theology*, trans. D. M. G. Stalker, 2 vols. (New York: Harper & Row, 1963) and Stephen A. Geller, "The Religion of the Bible," in *The Jewish Study Bible*, ed. M. Z. Brettler and A. Berlin (New York: Oxford University Press, 2004), 2121–40. Scholarly consensus attributes the final redaction of the Pentateuch to P. D's role is mainly limited to Deuteronomy, though deuteronomic elements (sometimes called "proto-deuteronomic") can be identified in Genesis–Numbers. See, for example, Anthony Phillips, "A Fresh Look at the Sinai Pericope," Parts 1 and 2, *VT* 34 (1984): 39–53 and 282–94; Casper J. Labuschagne, "The Pattern of Divine Speech Formulas in the Pentateuch: The Key to Its Literary Structure," *VT* 32 (1982): 268–96; and Yair Zakovitch, "The Book of the Covenant Interprets the Book of the Covenant: The 'Boomerang Phenomenon,'" in *Texts, Temples and Traditions: A Tribute to Menahem Haran*, ed. M. V. Fox et al. (Winona Lake, IN: Eisenbrauns, 1996), *59–64 [Hebrew].

6. The terms "episodic memory" and "semantic memory" come from the field of cognitive psychology. Each has its own cognitive underpinnings. Episodic memory concerns specific events—usually, but not

God's awareness of a specific circumstance or obligation is provoked through sensory cues, particularly visual, but also olfactory and aural. In the main, the priestly tradition regards Israel's memory as suspect, but it nonetheless appreciates the power of memory to promote the fulfillment of specific, punctual duties, and to warn about improper behavior. For either purpose, Israel's memory, like God's, is induced through sensory means. In one respect Israel's memory, though of secondary importance relative to God's, plays handmaiden to the task of sustaining God's memory. In another, more intriguing respect, the priestly treatment of Israel's memory illuminates a fundamental yet often obscured tension in priestly religion between a dominant theology authorized by creation and a subordinate theology authorized through revelation.

In addition to assigning to memory a crucial part in their covenant theologies, both the deuteronomic and priestly traditions situate memory's covenantal importance in terms of a divinely authorized worldview. The two versions of creation that open the book of Genesis describe two visions of a "right order."[7] Each creation account is succeeded by a narrative describing the failure and, consequently, the destruction of that right order. The sequence concludes with the resumption of life, but under new terms. In these two versions of the creation–destruction–restoration paradigm, the deuteronomic and priestly traditions each establish the necessity of the particular partnership for God that is realized in God's covenant with Israel.

The claim made in this book is that for the deuteronomic and priestly traditions, these three elements—covenant, cosmogony, and memory—are intricately related. In both traditions, Israel's covenant with God is an answer to the reality of life in a world less perfect than the one conceived originally by God. It offers a way of life to restore as closely as possible the primeval ideal, a way of life in which memory is essential. The identification of Israel's

exclusively, personally experienced—that are preserved as images or sensations and are generally triggered by sensual stimuli. Semantic memory refers to information that is stored in the mind. This can be "how to" information, such as "how to ride a bicycle," content information (the capitals of the states in America; the Boy Scout code of ethics; the Ten Commandments) or propositional or normative tradition. "Episodic memory," rather like the "storehouse" model (see Chapter 3), is the recall of specific events that are filed in the mind as images or experiences. Triggered by sensual stimuli—a song from one's college years, or Proust's *madeleine*—it is experienced in a temporally limited way. Semantic memory is retained and thus has a durative quality.

7. The first creation story (Gen. 1:1—2:4a) is nearly universally attributed to the priestly author(s). The second story (Gen. 2:4b—3:24) is attributed to the Yahwist (J) source, but I suggest, based on analysis I give in Chapter 2, that it resonates with the authors of Deuteronomy, who allude rather directly to it in their literature.

covenant with the reclamation of the right order of the world lends urgency to the religious programs through which Israel's covenant is lived. Israel's covenant with God, whether the conditional covenant known to D or the unconditional covenant of P, must be maintained. For both the deuteronomic and priestly traditions, memory—in the particular way each understands it—is the mechanism to ensure this. Put differently, how each tradition understands Israel's covenant with God and how each conceptualizes memory undergirds the religious programs imagined by D and P.

A considerable body of scholarship has been devoted to clarifying the distinctive theologies of the deuteronomic and priestly traditions,[8] but none has really explored the role of memory in terms of the totality of these traditions: the religious programs that each envisions, their ideational elements, their theologies and cosmologies, and the narrative strategies that each employs to promulgate its programs. As I hope the following investigation will demonstrate, the manner in which memory is conceptualized and used in deuteronomic and priestly literature correlates integrally with most, if not all, aspects of the religious programs that each imagines. Hence, a focus on the meaning and function of memory, particularly its relationship to Israel's covenantal bond with God, can yield important new insights into these traditions, the religious programs they prescribe, and their relationship to one another.

The support for this claim will come in three stages. First, I will attempt to demonstrate the salient relationship between the cosmogonies that open Genesis and the covenant as conceived of in deuteronomic and priestly

8. For example, von Rad, *Old Testament Theology*, and Geller, "The Religion of the Bible," in *The Jewish Study Bible* as referenced in note 5. Geller expands upon the general comments in his essay in a number of articles, including, "God, Humanity, and Nature in the Pentateuch," in *Gazing on the Deep: Ancient Near Eastern and Other Studies in Honor of Tsvi Abusch*, ed. J. Stackert, B. N. Porter, and D. P. Wright (Bethesda, MD: CDL, 2010), 421–65; "Manna and Sabbath: A Literary-Theological Reading of Exodus 16," *Interpretation* 59 (2005): 5–16; "Sabbath and Creation: A Literary-Theological Analysis," *Interpretation*, forthcoming; and the essays "Fiery Wisdom: The Deuteronomic Tradition," and "Blood Cult: An Interpretation of the Priestly Work of the Pentateuch," in Geller, *Sacred Enigmas: Literary Religion in the Hebrew Bible* (New York: Routledge, 1996), 30–61, 62–86. Michael Fishbane's essay on the "sign" is another comparison of the two traditions' treatment of a particular idea ("On Biblical Omina," *Shnaton Ha-Miqra'* 1 [1976]: 213–34 [Hebrew]). Other important contributions are von Rad, *Studies in Deuteronomy*, trans. D. M. G. Stalker, SBT 9 (London: SCM, 1953); Menahem Haran, *Temples and Temple Service in Ancient Israel: An Inquiry into Biblical Cult Phenomena and the Historical Setting of the Priestly School* (Oxford: Clarendon, 1978; repr., Winona Lake, IN: Eisenbrauns, 1985); Jacob Milgrom, *Leviticus*, 3 vols., AB 3–3B (New York: Doubleday, 1991–2001), and Moshe Weinfeld, *Deuteronomy and the Deuteronomic School* (Oxford: Clarendon, 1972; repr., Winona Lake, IN: Eisenbrauns, 1992).

literature. Second, I will clarify how the deuteronomic and priestly traditions each conceptualize memory by analyzing the language each uses to speak of it. For the third leg of my argument, I will analyze the literary representation of the religious programs—the rituals and practices imagined or prescribed in Deuteronomy and in priestly literature—to illustrate how these two traditions make use of memory as each understands it to sustain and preserve Israel's covenant with God.

It should be clear by now that this exploration of memory and covenant is primarily an investigation of biblical theology and biblical literature. I am interested in how the idea of Israel's covenant with God is expressed in the literary representations of the religious programs imagined by D and P, and in how these representations reflect their understanding of Israel's place in God's world. That being said, I wish to state at the outset my belief that this literature has a practical dimension, and that it responds to or is based on, if only to a minimal degree, actual First Temple practices.[9] While the final form of the Pentateuch most likely dates from the postexilic period (539–400 BCE), I contend that both traditions worked with a known religious system that they sought to amend or reinterpret.

The Provenance and Context of D and P

The compositional history of the Pentateuch and of its constituent sources and literary corpora is both complicated and subject to near continuous debate. At one end of the spectrum of opinions is a body of scholars, sometimes referred to as the Copenhagen School, who consider the entire biblical text, including the Pentateuch, to be a Hellenistic product dating to the late fourth century BCE. At the other end are those who argue that the Pentateuch is entirely or mostly of preexilic (i.e., pre-586 BCE), or possibly early Babylonian (i.e., early–mid sixth century BCE) provenance. In the middle ground are scholars who maintain that the Pentateuch is the work of a postmonarchic[10] priestly editor(s) who either in concert with, or in response to, deuteronomic authors, reworked preexilic traditions and texts, including traditions associated with the preexilic priesthood and Deuteronomy, to produce the final form before us

9. On the complexities of using texts to analyze rituals and religious practices, see David P. Wright, "Ritual Theory, Ritual Texts and the Priestly-Holiness Writings in the Pentateuch," in *Social Theory and the Study of Israelite Religion: Essays in Retrospect and Prospect*, ed. S. M. Olyan (Atlanta: Society of Biblical Literature, 2012), 195–216.

10. I borrow the term "postmonarchic" from Lauren Monroe, who uses it to refer to both exilic and postexilic material. *Josiah's Reform and the Dynamic of Defilement* (New York: Oxford University Press, 2011).

now. I align myself with this middle position, and therefore with the belief that we can speak of D and P as the two principal traditions in the Pentateuch. To be clear, by D, I mean both the deuteronomic law code (Deuteronomy 12–26) and the material surrounding it (Deuteronomy 1–11, 27–34) represented as Moses' address to the Israelites in Moab.[11] There are also occasional passages in Genesis–Numbers (e.g., Exod. 13:5, 20:21, 34:10–16) that exhibit markedly deuteronomic features. I do not necessarily attribute these passages to the authors of Deuteronomy itself. But I maintain that, in their final form, they evince deuteronomic influence or editing.[12] By P, I mean priestly material as a whole without distinguishing between strands or periods.[13] Within that corpus, significant differences distinguish the Holiness writers (H) that are germane to this study, including on the matter of whose memory is at stake (see below). When there is reason to differentiate between priestly and holiness material (for instance, in Chapters 5 and 7), P denotes priestly material other than that of the Holiness writers (H).[14] With respect to how memory is conceptualized, however, P and H are similar to one another and distinct from D.

The Deuteronomic Tradition

The identification of the deuteronomic law code with the scroll discovered in the temple during its repairs (2 Kings 22:8-20) is widely accepted as a

11. Many scholars concur with Martin Noth's attribution of the historical introduction (Deuteronomy 1–3) and the narrative about the transfer of leadership from Moses to Joshua (34) to the author of the Deuteronomistic History (i.e., Joshua–2 Kings) who used it as an introduction to that larger history. See *The Deuteronomistic History*, trans. E. W. Nicholson, JSOTSup 15 (Sheffield: JSOT, 1981; trans. of pp. 1–110 of *Überlieferungsgeschichtliche Studien*, 2nd ed. [Tübingen: Max Niemeyer, 1957]), 12–17). The remaining material includes late First Temple contributions (the introductory paraenesis [4:44—11:32], the covenant ceremony on Mt. Ebal and Mt. Gerizim [27–29, 31]; late monarchical or early exilic material [the poems of 32:1-43 and 33]; and a late exilic addition [Deuteronomy 30]). See Moshe Weinfeld, *Deuteronomy 1–11*, AB 5 (New York: Doubleday, 1991), 2–4, 9–13; Frank Moore Cross, *Canaanite Myth and Hebrew Epic: Essays in the History of the Religion of Israel* (Cambridge, MA: Harvard University Press, 1973), 285.

12. See note 5.

13. The difficulty arises because "P" has a number of meanings in the literature. It can refer to one of the four sources posited by the Documentary Hypothesis; the priestly redactor of the Pentateuch in opposition to D; or to priestly material other than that of the Holiness tradition.

14. H's contribution was initially recognized as being limited to Leviticus 17–24, but is now believed to pervade P more widely. See Israel Knohl, *The Sanctuary of Silence: The Priestly Torah and the Holiness School* (Minneapolis: Augsburg Fortress Press, 1995; repr., Winona Lake, IN: Eisenbrauns, 2007); Christophe Nihan, *From Priestly Torah to Pentateuch: A Study in the Composition of the Book of Leviticus*, FAT 2:25 (Tübingen: Mohr Siebeck, 2007); Jeffrey Stackert, *Rewriting the Torah: Literary Revisionism in Deuteronomy and the Holiness Legislation* (Tübingen: Mohr Siebeck, 2007).

foundation for dating a significant portion of Deuteronomy to the late seventh century BCE.[15] According to one view (and one that I share), both the law code and the material surrounding it (Deuteronomy 4–11, 27–29) date from roughly that time. Another view pushes the law code back to the eighth century BCE in the context of Hezekiah's reforms while attributing much of the frame to the Josianic period.[16] An early exilic date for the material surrounding the law code is also possible, as is the possibility of "double redaction."[17] In some respects, the reforms that Josiah is said to have undertaken in c. 622 BCE, particularly abolishing all cultic shrines outside of Jerusalem and centralizing worship in Jerusalem (cf. 2 Kings 22, 2 Chronicles 35), conform to the ethos of the law code, in particular its restriction of sacrifice to only "the place Yahweh has chosen to let his Name reside" (cf. Deut. 12:5; 14:23; 15:20; 16:2, etc.) and the ban on all foreign altars, shrines, and images (Deut. 12:2-5).[18] Many of the

15. See the discussions in Weinfeld, *Deuteronomy and the Deuteronomic School*, 1–9; Haran, *Temples and Temple Service*, 132–40; Marvin Sweeney, *King Josiah of Judah: The Lost Messiah of Israel* (Oxford: Oxford University Press, 2001), 137–69; Andrew D. H. Mayes, "Deuteronomistic Ideology and the Theology of the Old Testament," *JSOT* 82 (1999): 68–69. A minority associates the law code with Hezekiah. See Jack R. Lundbom, "The Law Book of the Josianic Reform," *CBQ* 38 (1976): 292–302. Both positions depend, to some extent, on the historicity of the Josianic reforms themselves, which not all scholars accept. At a minimum, Michael LeFebvre's claim that "[f]or the *Deuteronomic* Josiah, the law code is a basis for official action" is fair. LeFebvre, *Collections, Codes and Texts: The Re-characterization of Israel's Written Law* (New York: T. & T. Clark, 2006), 58 (italics mine).

16. Jonathan Rosenbaum, "Hezekiah's Reform and the Deuteronomistic Tradition," *HTR* 22 (1979): 23–43.

17. The latter is the position of the so-called "American School" of Frank Moore Cross and his students. Cross identifies a preexilic (seventh century BCE) author (Dtr1) who took a version of Deuteronomy consisting of the law code and the material immediately framing it, added a historical introduction (Deut. 1:1—4:43) as well as 31:1—32:44 to serve as the introduction to a history (Deuteronomy–2 Kings). A second redaction of the history was done in exile by Dtr2. Cross, *Canaanite Myth and Hebrew Epic*, 274–85. An alternative division comes from the Göttingen School, which posits three redactions, each reflecting a different orientation—historical, prophetic, and legal. For good recent summaries of scholarship on this topic, see Nathan MacDonald, "The Literary Criticism and Rhetorical Logic of Deut. I–IV," *VT* 56 (2006): 203–12; and Thomas C. Römer, *The So-Called Deuteronomistic History: A Sociological, Historical and Literary Introduction* (London and New York: T. & T. Clark, 2005), 21–37; Sandra L. Richter, *The Deuteronomistic History and the Name Theology:* ləšakkēn šəmô šām *in the Bible and the Ancient Near East* (Berlin and New York: Walter de Gruyter, 2002), 1–7; Steven L. McKenzie, *The Trouble with Kings: The Composition of the Book of Kings in the Deuteronomistic History*, VTSup 42 (Leiden and New York: E. J. Brill, 1991), 1–19; and idem, "Deuteronomistic History," *ABD* 2:160–68.

18. Some comparisons of Josiah's actions as reported in 2 Kings 22–23 and the law code undermine the notion of a direct relationship between the law code and Josiah's reforms. See for instance Monroe, *Josiah's Reform and the Dynamics of Defilement*; John J. Collins, "The Zeal of Phinehas and the

themes expressed in the framing material, including the importance attached to the verbalization of memory, may also be explained in connection to the political exigencies of Josiah's reign or as a theological response to Judah's newfound prominence in the aftermath of the fall of the northern kingdom a generation earlier, in 722 BCE.[19]

The elimination of all extra-urban shrines likely left a vacuum in the religious life of people in outlying areas of the kingdom.[20] In the absence of opportunities to participate in sacrificial rituals, the requirement that doctrine be continually rehearsed, taught, and learned may have served a compensatory function. Josiah's geopolitical objectives may also have been served by the new religious program. Second Kings 23:19 and 29 tell of Josiah's expansionist campaign into Samaria. That being the case, his annexation of portions of the former kingdom would have introduced a new population that had to be integrated into Judah.[21] By establishing a shared, collective memory in the form of the official history as the primary ingredient of liturgy and as something that Israel is required *covenantally* to learn and inculcate, the deuteronomic program offered a way to ease and sustain the incorporation of communities into the religious polity that was Judah. In the same way the story of the first Thanksgiving was popularized as a foundational story for all Americans, the recitation required by Deuteronomy "preserves the store of knowledge from which a group derives an awareness of its unity and peculiarity."[22] Finally, in the sense that it promotes "intellectual religion," the investiture of memory as

Legitimization of Violence," *JBL* 122 (2003): 11; James W. Watts, "Ritual Legitimacy and Scriptural Authority," *JBL* 124 (2005): 401–17.

19. Various motives have been adduced for Josiah's reforms, among them his wish to assert the hegemony of Jerusalem and right of royal imprimatur over temple practices, and his desire to demonstrate Judah's release from Assyrian domination following the death of Assurbanipal in 627 BCE by ridding the kingdom of foreign ritual material. As well, Josiah appears to have taken advantage of Assyria's decline by undertaking an expansionist campaign to annex the southern part of the foreign kingdom of Israel into Judah. Alternatively, some argue that centralization became a *de facto* position in the wake of the Assyrian destruction of most of Judah in 701 BCE.

20. Possibly the loss was felt less keenly by women. See Susan Ackerman, "Cult Centralization, the Erosion of Kin-Based Communities, and the Implications for Women's Religious Practices," in *Social Theory and the Study of Israelite Religion: Essays in Retrospect and Prospect*, ed. S. M. Olyan (Atlanta: Society of Biblical Literature, 2012), 19–40.

21. The exact nature of the relationship between the two kingdoms prior to Israel's defeat is something at which we can only guess. According to the biblical account, at least, whatever common history the two kingdoms shared does not appear to have promoted strong feelings of unity or kinship. See for instance 1 Kings 12:16-17; 15:16-21; 2 Kings 14:8-14; 16:5-6. Cf. Isa. 7:1-2. Furthermore, after its conquest by Assyria, Samaria was repopulated by foreign peoples who had no shared background with Judah (2 Kings 17:24).

a central religious observance comports with Deuteronomy's abstract theology of a transcendent deity, whose "name" (*šēm*) alone dwells in the temple.[23] In sum, the deuteronomic liturgical program could serve both far-flung populations—that of Judah beyond the Jerusalem environs and that of Samaria. In place of ritual activity, both populations are provided with an "intellectualized" religion that entailed speaking about its unique relationship to Yahweh.[24]

The Priestly Tradition

The Hebrew Bible provides no *terminus ante quem* like that of the scroll of Second Kings from which to date priestly literature.[25] Further complicating the matter, as I alluded above, priestly literature includes several literary strata reflecting different periods and even different priestly schools. For the purposes of this project, I recognize three layers of priestly writing: a preexilic priestly corpus dating to the end of the monarchical period or the very beginning of neo-Babylonian conquest of Judah (i.e.,+/– 600 to 550 BCE); the Holiness school (H) from the early exilic period; and a postmonarchical priestly corpus (P).[26]

22. See Jan Assmann and John Czaplicka, "Collective Memory and Cultural Identity," *New German Critique* 65 (1995): 130. Their characterization of cultural memory is instructive: "[C]ultural memory is characterized by its distance from the everyday. Distance from the everyday (transcendence) marks its temporal horizon. Cultural memory has its fixed point; its horizon does not change with the passing of time. These fixed points are fateful events of the past, whose memory is maintained through cultural formation (texts, rites, monuments) and institutional communication (recitation, practice, observance)." Ibid., 129. Elsewhere, Assmann explains how such rites both sustain identity in the present and ensure their transmission in the future. Through "formative" and "normative" rites and texts, "cultural memory disseminates and reproduces a consciousness of unity, particularity, and a sense of belonging among members of a group." Formative rites and texts establish and "transmit identity-confirming knowledge by narrating stories that are shared." Normative rites and texts "transmit practical knowledge and point the way to right action." See *Religion and Cultural Memory: Ten Studies*, trans. Rodney Livingstone (Stanford: Stanford University Press, 2006), 38.

23. A religion that privileges verbalized historical narrative is, moreover, a logical consequence of the increased intellectualization and spiritualization of theology, which, it has been argued, was a characteristic of the so-called Axial Age (800 BCE to 200 CE). Such a theology goes hand in hand with an emergent self-consciousness also associated with that period. On the Axial Age itself, see Karl Jaspers in *The Origin and Goal of History* (New Haven: Yale University Press, 1954); Shmuel Noah Eisenstadt, ed., *The Origins and Diversity of Axial Age Civilizations*, SUNY Series in Near East Studies (Albany: State University of New York Press, 1986); and David Brakke, Michael L. Satlow, and Steven Weitzman, eds. *Religion and the Self in Antiquity* (Bloomington: Indiana University Press, 2005)

24. Cf. Hos. 6:6, 1 Sam. 15:22, and Prov. 21:3 where sacrifice is subordinate to pious behavior.

25. There has been an effort to establish such a benchmark by demonstrating either P's familiarity with, or ignorance of, deuteronomic legislation, but neither position is conclusive.

As indicated earlier, I will refer to the non-H material as P pointing out when necessary if the preexilic or postmonarchical stratum is intended.

There is ample evidence, I believe, to claim that the author(s) responsible for the preexilic layer of P were familiar with First Temple ritual. The meaning and function it had *in situ* may not have been identical to that of the priestly writers, but they worked with known practices, simultaneously reinterpreting them in terms of their theology of divine immanence.[27]

Writing in exile, the Holiness writers presuppose that priestly material, which they explain, supplement, revise, and reinterpret. Although the Holiness tradition conceives of memory, as P does, in sensory and episodic terms, it exhibits some characteristics that distinguish it from the rest of priestly material. Foremost for the purposes of this study is its concern for Israel's memory over that of God's. This shift in emphasis comports with the Holiness tradition's notion of what Israel Knohl terms "inclusive sacredness" and from its reinterpretation of Israel's covenant in bilateral terms. The latter is likely evidence of the influence of Deuteronomy on H.[28]

The influence of H can be seen in subsequent priestly material, which was likely composed in anticipation of the restoration of the temple in Jerusalem. In this stratum, a late exilic, or possibly postexilic, priestly author(s) reworked and/or added to the older material (early P and H) to shape it in terms of a thoroughgoing creation theology. In their representation, the cult assumes cosmic significance, and the transformative capacity of ritual is reinterpreted in terms of that significance. The cosmic significance of the cult also means that its performance must be perfect, and this in turn underscores the essential role of the priests. For this reason, the priestly writers use narratives to create memories

26. There are some scholars who dismiss the possibility of a preexilic P, among them Philip Davies, Thomas L. Thompson, and Niels Peter Lemche. A sizable cohort of scholars dates the composition of P to the Persian period, but concedes that it draws on preexilic traditions (for instance, Joseph Blenkinsopp, David M. Carr, and Kenton Sparks). A few scholars such as Jacob Milgrom, Israel Knohl, and Avi Hurvitz locate all of P in the preexilic period. Knohl maintains that H was active from the eighth century BCE through the exile, when it functioned as the Pentateuch's redactor. Jeffrey Stackert also locates a priestly stratum in the pre-exilic period. H, in his view, interprets and revises P while trying to displace deuteronomic and Covenant Code legislation.

27. See Chapters 5 and 8.

28. Knohl, *The Sanctuary of Silence*, 180–86. On the relationship between H and Deuteronomy, see Stackert, *Rewriting the Torah*; "The Holiness Legislation and its Pentateuchal Sources: Revision, Supplement, and Replacement," in *The Strata of the Priestly Writing: Contemporary Debate and Future Directions*, eds. S Shectman and J. S. Baden, ATANT 95 (Zürich: Theologischer, 2009), 187-204. Nihan, *From Priestly Torah to Pentateuch.*

powerful enough to keep unauthorized persons from intruding into the sacred precincts and practices.

Review of Scholarship

Considerable work has been done both on biblical notions of covenant and on memory in connection with the Bible, but almost no investigation of their relationship to one another or of the theological significance of that relationship has been carried out to date. There is also a growing body of work on ritual and memory from the field of social anthropology, but again almost none of that work examines their relationship in connection with biblical religion.[29] Nor has the growing body of work on ritual and biblical religion given attention to the topic of memory.[30] It is my hope that this book will advance a synergistic understanding of these vital themes in biblical scholarship.

Memory and Biblical Scholarship

Scholarship around the idea of memory in the Bible can be grouped under three general rubrics: lexical studies; discussions of biblical historiography in which memory is considered a contributive element; and examinations of memory in ideological or religious terms focusing on a discrete corpus of work. The two most important lexical studies to date are Brevard Childs's *Memory and Tradition in Israel* (1962) and Willy Schottroff's 1967 dissertation, *"Gedenken" im Alten Orient und im Alten Testament: Die Wurzel* zākar *in semitischen Sprachkreis*.[31] Each purports to "discover what the Old Testament understands by memory, and what is the scope of its meaning,"[32] and does so through careful examination of

29. An exception is Gilbert Lewis, "Religious Doctrine or Experience: A Matter of Seeing, Learning, or Doing," in *Ritual and Memory: Toward a Comparative Anthropology of Religion*, ed. H. Whitehouse and J. Laidlaw (Walnut Creek, CA: AltaMira, 2004), 155–72. Lewis addresses the issue of "orthopraxy" in Leviticus, in the context of a collection of essays responding to Harvey Whitehouse's Divergent Modes Theory (see below).

30. Recent examples include Saul Olyan, *Biblical Mourning: Ritual and Social Dimensions* (Oxford: Oxford University Press, 2004), *Rites and Rank: Hierarchy in Biblical Representations of Cult* (Princeton: Princeton University Press, 2000); Roy Gane, *Cult and Character: Purification Offerings, Day of Atonement and Theodicy* (Winona Lake, IN: Eisenbrauns, 2005); Frank Gorman, *The Ideology of Ritual: Space, Time and Status in the Priestly Theology* (Sheffield: JSOT, 1990); and Watts, "Ritual Legitimization and Scriptural Authority."

31. Brevard Childs, *Memory and Tradition in Israel*, SBT (Naperville, IL: Allenson, 1962). Willy Schottroff, *"Gedenken" im Alten Orient und im Alten Testament, Die Wurzel* zākar *im semitischen Sprachkreis* (Neukirchen-Vluyn: Neukirchener, 1967).

32. Childs, *Memory and Tradition*, 6.

the core root *zkr*. Schottroff's comprehensive taxonomical study analyzes both Hebrew *zkr* and its Akkadian and Canaanite cognates. Childs, too, begins with a lexical analysis of *zkr*, its semantic range and distribution in terms of subject (divine or human), and then proceeds to relate its usage to the theological idea of "actualization."[33]

As lexical studies, these works have the virtue of allowing biblical language rather than some externally imposed concept of "memory" to determine the parameters of study. That virtue is also their weakness. As John F. A. Sawyer shows in his study of Hebrew words for "salvation," it is not easy to subsume even a solidly biblical concept under a single modern English lexeme.[34] Concentrating exclusively on *zkr*, neither work considers the full complement of biblical terms and expressions relating to memory. Furthermore, they overlook the possibility that the meaning of *zkr* for one author may have a different semantic range than when used by another. As we shall see in Chapter 3, the memory lexicons of D and P are considerably large and *zkr*, though a core term, does not account for the entire conceptual field of memory in the Bible.[35]

33. Ibid., 63–73, 81–89. The concept of "actualization" (*Vergegenwärtigung*) with respect to biblical theology was introduced by von Rad, who used the term to explain Israel's reinterpretation of agrarian cultic traditions in terms of a historically determined religion. This allowed the historical acts through which God established Israel to be contemporized (*Old Testament Theology*, 2:103–5). In this original sense, "actualization" presumes a diachronic approach to the Bible. For Childs, however, it is inextricable from his view of canonical Scripture as transhistorical. The canonical Bible becomes universal, and its theological meaning transcends historical particularity. "Within the Old Testament Israel is portrayed both as a concrete, historical nation, as well as a transhistorical, even ideal reality. It has both a political past and an eschatological future." *Biblical Theology of the Old and New Testaments: Theological Reflections on the Christian Bible* (Minneapolis: Augsburg Fortress Press, 1992), 442. In short, for Childs through "actualization," events in Israel's past become part of a universal narrative of redemption, no longer tied to Israelite practice (law) or nationhood.

34. John F. A. Sawyer, *Semantics in Biblical Research: New Methods of Defining Hebrew Words for Salvation*, SBT 2/24 (London: SCM, 1972). Sawyer uses the term "concept field" to refer to the overlapping semantic ranges of terms related to a broad concept such as "salvation" or, for the present purposes, "memory."

35. More recent language studies of *zkr* take the broader semantic field into consideration. See for instance H. Eising, "זָכַר *zākhar;* זֵכֶר *zēkher;* זִכָּרוֹן *zikkārôn;* אַזְכָּרָה *'azkārāh,*" *TDOT* 4:64–82, and Michael Carasik, *Theologies of the Mind in Biblical Israel*, SBL 85 (New York: Peter Lang, 2006), 54–91. On the problem of semantics in general, see Michel Bréal, *Semantics: Studies in the Science of Meaning, with a new introduction by Joshua Whatmough* (New York: Dover, 1964), 109–14, 115–21; repr., of *Semantics: Studies in the Science of Meaning*, trans. Mrs. H. Cust (New York: Henry Holt, 1900); John Lyons, *Introduction to Theoretical Linguistics* (London: Cambridge University Press, 1968), 408, 412–14. For its application to biblical literature, see Edward Ullendorff, "Thought Categories in the Hebrew Bible," in *Is*

A second weakness in Childs's work derives from his theological commitment to the idea of "actualization." In his reading of Deuteronomy, memory allows Israel to "actualize" its *Heilsgeschichte* or "salvation history."[36] Because the cult was no longer relevant yet could not be abandoned, Deuteronomy "relativized" its practices, interpreting them as mechanisms enabling later generations of Israelites to participate in the redemptive history of their ancestors.[37] The Israelites are to observe the Sabbath (or pilgrimage festivals or care for the indigent and the stranger) *so that* they will recall the experience of slavery and remember their deliverance by God. Actualization of the history is the ultimate object rather than observance of the law:

> Israel is commanded to be obedient to the commandments *in order to* remember the redemptive history . . . memory in this case assumes the meaning of actualization. By keeping the Sabbath holy, later Israel remembers or participates in the redemptive history of her past. (Italics in original.)[38]

Childs mainly applies the concept of "actualization" to Deuteronomy, but it influences his interpretation of memory in priestly literature as well. Thus Childs—mistakenly in my view and that of many scholars—finds the priestly tradition to profess a "theology of history," and on God's memory in P, he concludes, "[t]he use of the verb *zkr* reflects the Priestly writer's concern to

Biblical Hebrew a Language? Studies in Semitic Languages and Civilizations, ed. E. Ullendorff (Wiesbaden: Otto Harrassowitz, 1977).

36. The concept of *Heilsgeschichte* underlies Childs's notion of "actualization." He regards salvation as the essence of deuteronomic (and biblical) religion over the particular covenant between God and Israel with its mandates to fulfill commandments. Privileging Israel's emotional connection to its past over a physical, concretizing tie fits well with the Christian, in particular Protestant, emphasis on "faith" over "works," a prioritization that has its roots in the New Testament (e.g., Rom. 3:27-28; 4:13-16; Gal. 2:15-16; 3:21-26; Hebrews 11) and in Protestant theology more generally. Childs is not alone in this perspective. Referring to memory in the introduction to his commentary on Deuteronomy, J. A. Thompson writes, "[t]his active recall, not merely by those who had participated in the exodus, but by all the future members of Israel, was designed to enable the continuing Israel to participate in the great acts of redemption wrought by Yahweh in the course of their own history. Such a recollection and identification in memory and *by faith* would stimulate both gratitude and love in the Israelite of every age." He adds in a footnote to this statement, "[t]he Christian worshipper will recall at once the Lord's Supper, which provides an opportunity to 'remember' the Lord's death. Such an act of remembrance leads to an *identification with Christ* and a response of *faith*, love and gratitude." Thompson, *Deuteronomy: An Introduction and Commentary*, TOTC (London: InterVarsity, 1974), 77 (italics mine).

37. Childs, *Memory and Tradition*, 79.

38. Ibid., 78–79.

present history as a witness to the unfolding of the purpose of the covenant God who is active in Israel's midst. This history is merely a working out of the one eternal act of divine grace."[39]

While Childs regards memory of the redemption history as the chief object of ritual and fulfillment of commandments, Moshe Weinfeld and Jeffrey Tigay see it the other way around. Memory of slavery and the exodus serves the humanitarian aim of stirring empathy that leads to just treatment of the disenfranchised. Weinfeld locates the function of memory emphatically within the context of the humanistic orientation characteristic of Deuteronomy, but he also associates that orientation with Israel's feelings of gratitude for its deliverance. The empathy and gratitude that are stirred result from the memory of both slavery and deliverance. Their combined force motivates the Israelites to obey the commandments. The end objective, however, is fulfillment of the commanded act.[40] Tigay makes a similar claim in his comments on four verses invoking memory of slavery and exodus (Deut. 5:15; 15:15; 16:12; and 24:18). He writes (commenting here on Deut. 16:12): "[T]he memory of slavery is invoked to motivate extending the benefits of this prescription to servants and other poor individuals."[41] It should be noted that these readings also evidence the influence of theology, in this instance the search for rational explanations for the commandments (*ṭeʿamê miṣwôt*), which has deep roots in the Jewish exegetical tradition.

Like the majority of scholars, Childs, Weinfeld, and Tigay principally address Deuteronomy in their discussions of memory and the Bible. They are aware that P speaks of memory and makes use of its terminology (Childs gives some attention to P's use of the noun *zikkārôn* but does not discuss other

39. Ibid., 43.

40. Cf. Moshe Weinfeld's comments on Deuteronomy's reformulation of cultic observance and of the Sabbath commandment in the Decalogue. *Deuteronomy and the Deuteronomic School*, 222. Weinfeld argues that the author of Deuteronomy reconceptualizes cultic observance as a means for providing for the poor and disenfranchised, a practical object that necessarily emphasizes the performative aspect of the commandment. With respect to the Sabbath, the author of Deuteronomy does more than provide an alternative rationale for this commandment; he shifts "[t]he stress . . . from cause to purpose (cf. למען): the purpose of the Sabbath is, to be sure, that man shall rest, but not because God himself rested on this day" (ibid.). On the Sabbatical year, see ibid., 233; on the laws of tithes and firstlings, 290.

41. Jeffrey Tigay, *Deuteronomy*, JPS (Philadelphia: Jewish Publication Society, 1996), 157. In a similar vein, see Tigay's note to 24:18, ibid., 228. In his comment on Deut. 5:15, Tigay notes that among traditional commentators, opinions are divided regarding the underlying purpose of memory's motivational power, with some stressing empathetic treatment of servants and strangers and others maintaining that its purpose is to affirm God's authority and Israel's corresponding obligation and fealty to God. Ibid., 69.

terms in P's memory lexicon[42]), but because they assume memory to be only a cognitive process, they fail to recognize its reference or employment elsewhere in the Bible. The study of experiential (episodic) or "imagistic" memory and the Bible is a scholarly lacuna.

A second avenue of biblical scholarship looks at memory as a contributive element in biblical historiography. Moving away from the issue of the Bible's "historicity," scholars have looked at Israel's "collective" or "cultural" memory as a valid alternative. Books like John Van Seters's *In Search of History*, Marc Zvi Brettler's *The Creation of History in Ancient Israel*, Baruch Halpern's *The First Historians*, and Jens Bruun Kofoed's *Text and History: Historiography and the Study of the Biblical Text* seek to establish criteria for determining the reliability of biblical historiography.[43] Some concept of "history" motivates this work, but what Israel remembered rather than *wie es eigentlich gewesen* ("how it actually happened") becomes the object of inquiry.

A different emphasis can be observed in the work of Ronald Hendel and Mark Smith, who shift the historiographic enterprise away from the search for the history of ancient Israel to the question of how the Israelites used their history. In *Remembering Abraham: Culture, Memory, and History in the Hebrew Bible*,[44] Hendel explores how biblical Israel makes use of a remembered past to construct its identity as a distinct people. A similar objective drives Smith's *The Memoirs of God: History, Memory, and the Experience of the Divine in Ancient Israel*.[45] Smith wants "to advance the claim that the academic study of collective memory offers important intellectual help for understanding the biblical representations of Israel's past."[46] How the Israelites remembered and transmitted their national stories reveals as much about them as it does about their past. In effect substituting "memory" or "collective memory" for "history,"

42. Childs, *Memory and Tradition*, 43, 68.

43. John Van Seters, *In Search of History: Historiography in the Ancient World and the Origins of Biblical History* (New Haven: Yale University Press, 1983; repr., Winona Lake, IN: Eisenbrauns, 1997); Marc Zvi Brettler, *The Creation of History in Ancient Israel* (London and New York: Routledge, 1995); Baruch Halpern, *The First Historians: The Hebrew Bible and History* (San Francisco: Harper & Row, 1988); Jens Bruun Kofoed, *Text and History: Historiography and the Study of the Biblical Text* (Winona Lake, IN: Eisenbrauns, 2005).

44. Ronald Hendel, *Remembering Abraham: Culture, Memory, and History in the Hebrew Bible* (Oxford: Oxford University Press, 2005).

45. Mark S. Smith, *The Memoirs of God: History, Memory, and the Experience of the Divine in Ancient Israel* (Minneapolis: Fortress Press, 2004).

46. Ibid., 125. See as well Smith, "Remembering God: Collective Memory in Israelite Religion," *CBQ* 64 (2002): 631–51.

Smith does away with the accuracy requirement with respect to biblical narrative. He remains interested in reconstructing the past, only now the centerpiece of that past is the Israel that is remembering rather than the remembered Israel.

David M. Carr's *Writing on the Tablet of the Heart: Origins of Scripture and Literature* provides a somewhat different exploration of memory and biblical literature. Carr makes the case for a function of written texts as memory aids for the performance of traditional material, presumably by scribes already familiar with the texts they declaim, as a vital instrument of cultural transmission or "enculturation." His discussion of how written texts participate in the larger "cultural project of incising key cultural-religious traditions—word for word—*on people's minds*" sheds light on the deuteronomic reliance on written support for the formal recitations this tradition mandates.[47] Four times in Deuteronomy (6:7, 9; 11:19–20; 31:9–13 and 31:19) the injunction to recite the teaching is accompanied by the instruction to write down the teaching in some form. This may reflect the very integration of the two forms of enculturation that Carr describes.[48]

The performance aim underlying written texts, which Carr presumes, may also elucidate an aspect of the priestly manipulation of memory. As I shall demonstrate in Chapter 6, the priestly tradition incorporates narratives of trauma to incise memories and the lessons they teach on the minds of their audience. If, as Carr suggests, "the aim of the educational process was ultimately the scribe's memorization of the cultural tradition and cultivation of his (and occasionally her) ability to perform it," the written format of these narratives need not preclude their dramatization through oral performance where the trauma they recount can take on a more experiential quality.[49]

A few scholars have worked on how the idea of memory is used in particular contexts of biblical literature. John Barton, for instance, looks at "memory" in the context of what he terms the "theology of divine forgetting" in the Hebrew Bible.[50] Barton observes that "a belief in the forgiving mercy of God is deeply connected with the idea of divine forgetfulness, in a way that is unfamiliar from Christian language about forgiveness."[51] He writes, "God

47. David M. Carr, *Writing on the Tablet of the Heart: Origins of Scripture and Literature* (New York: Oxford University Press, 2005), 8. (Italics in original.)

48. See Chapter 4.

49. Carr, *Writing on the Tablet of the Heart,* 9. Carr himself, it must be noted, does not attribute this objective to the performance of text.

50. John Barton, "Forgiveness and Memory in the Old Testament," in *Gott und Mensch im Dialog*, ed. M. Witte (Berlin: Walter de Gruyter, 2004), 987–95.

forgets, we might say, only after he has remembered, so that there is no 'cheap grace' as we may put it, in the Old Testament."[52] Divine forgetfulness, however, is in dialectic tension with the necessity for human remembrance of sin: "God forgets, but we have to remember."[53] Barton does not identify this dialectic in terms of a specific theological tradition in the Bible. His interest is in explaining a foreign conceptualization of divine memory and forgetfulness to a Christian audience committed to the twin ideas of God's omniscience and graciousness. Barton places the subject of biblical memory in the context of religion and ideology. His consideration of memory, however, deals with a very small corpus and he does not relate that corpus to the larger question of memory in the various religious traditions in the Bible.

Like Barton, Edward Greenstein's reading of Psalm 78 situates the subject of memory and the exercise of memory in the context of biblical religion. For Greenstein, the exercise of memory undertaken by the psalmist is done "not to recount the past, but to prompt the kind of remembrance that leads to change."[54] The psalmist uses "strategies of remembering" as "a rhetorical move" to educate the reader. Greenstein concludes,

> The psalm, as I read it, is not about history; it deals in memory. It is not about something called memory; rather, through the rhetoric adopted by the psalmist for jogging the people's recollection, he exercises their memory by exercising his own. I read the psalm as a process of remembering. . . . The psalmist does not ruminate on the past; he addresses the present and, like a prophet, seeks to transform the future.[55]

Greenstein is exceptional in linking narrative strategy, theme, and ideology in his reading of the psalm. His interpretation argues for the integrative role of memory in biblical religion as a meaningful religious concept and as an instrument of religious practice.

Two recent investigations into the uses of memory in particular biblical traditions are Adriane Leveen's work on Numbers[56] and Jerry Hwang's on Deuteronomy.[57] Leveen's *Memory and Tradition in the Book of Numbers* argues

51. Ibid., 989.

52. Ibid., 990.

53. Ibid., 994.

54. Edward L. Greenstein, "Mixing Memory and Design: Reading Psalm 78," *Proof* 10 (1990): 197.

55. Ibid., 209.

56. Adriane Leveen, *Memory and Tradition in the Book of Numbers* (New York: Cambridge University Press, 2008).

that memory is both a theme and an instrument in the priestly editors' construction of the history of the wilderness period.[58] The priestly editors of the book, she maintains, attempted to shape Israel's collective memory to justify their particular vision of life after exile under the authority of the priesthood.[59] This agenda defines both the shape of Numbers and its texture. With descriptions of the proper organization and regulation of the community framing the rebellion narratives, the overall structure of the book demonstrates the destabilizing potential of memory as well as the need for a formal structure to control it properly.[60]

With her main interest the political uses of memory as an instrument of control and authority, Leveen illuminates how the theme of memory serves the redactional project of the priestly editors. Priestly agenda rather than priestly theology drives her discussion. The same emphasis guides her representation of three commemorative objects introduced in Numbers: the fringes; the plating on the altar; and Aaron's rod—which, she writes, "are designed to remind the people of God and the commandments, leading to the proper conduct and the proper deference to God's chosen leaders."[61]

As the most recent entry to the memory field, Hwang revives Childs's theology of actualization and a timeless, universal covenant. Hwang proposes that Deuteronomy's references to the patriarchs and the promises made to them are an intentional rhetorical device employed not only to express Israel's transgenerational corporate solidarity but also to harmonize the Israelite (conditional) and patriarchal (unconditional) covenants. Deuteronomy's use of the "fathers," he maintains, provides "a timeless symbol of every generation of God's people that receives YHWH's promise but still awaits their fulfillment,"

57. Jerry Hwang, *The Rhetoric of Remembrance: An Investigation of the "Fathers" in Deuteronomy*, Sifrut 8 (Winona Lake, IN: Eisenbrauns, 2012).

58. Leveen, *Memory and Tradition*, 22. "[T]he editors of Numbers not only have created a usable past on behalf of a later community but have left behind sustained reflections on such an attempt."

59. Leveen is mainly interested in how the priestly editors "organized the various stories of the wilderness period, some of which dated from much earlier times, into a coherent whole while creatively editing or adding other materials to the mix, including their own comments, in order to ensure the success of their endeavor. A variety of agendas powered this project. Explain the past. Shape collective memory. Ensure the means of transmission. Prevent recurrence of disaster." Ibid., 3.

60. Ibid. The opening and closing sections of the book, she says, are "a frame in which the rest of the book is placed" (ibid., 33). "[C]hapters 1–10 understand memory as a stabilizing force, used to forge Israel's identity as a collective with a shared past dominated by God's saving acts. Such memories oblige the people to serve God and Moses and to submit to priestly regulation, successfully preventing dissent and ensuring harmony in the camp." Ibid., 67.

61. Ibid., 98.

while the synthesis of the two covenants transforms the law into "a gift rather than a burden for Israel."[62] Like Childs, Hwang is foremost interested in the covenant concept, and like Childs, he conceives of the covenant apart from its essential feature, namely the laws and commandments that obligate Israel. This, I believe, distorts the biblical perspective. The reason memory is so crucial to Deuteronomy, however, is precisely because of the law. Israel is exhorted to remember so that Israel will fulfill its obligations.

Barton, Greenstein, Leveen, and Hwang begin to situate the study of memory and the Bible in the context of biblical ideology and religion, yet there is still work to be done. Outside of Barton's article, there is little exploration of God's memory and almost no work on God's memory in the Pentateuch. A second lacuna, as mentioned earlier, is any exploration of the dynamics of memory in its various forms and conceptualizations. Memory is a complex topic and can be understood in a number of ways. The attention given to the historiographic memory reflected in Deuteronomy has not been matched by work on sensory and experiential memory, which priestly literature seeks to exploit. I hope to address these lacks first in Chapter 3, which deals with memory theory and the memory lexicons of D and P, and subsequently in Part II of this book.

The Deuteronomic and Priestly Covenants

That ancient Israel enjoyed a particular relationship with its God is an article of faith for both D and P. The precise nature of this relation differs for the two traditions, but behind them, and behind all the traditions in the Pentateuch, is the certainty that no matter how universal is Yahweh's authority, reign, or scope, Israel ranked most important in the divine mind. The biblical authors express this certainty through the idea of "covenant." For Deuteronomy, as stated at the outset of this chapter, this covenant requires Israel's obedience and loyalty in return for God's benevolent care. The priestly covenant is more in the nature of a boon. If Israel provides God with a *miqdāš*—a "place of holiness"—God promises to dwell (*šākantî*) with his people (Exod. 25:8). Israel's only obligation is to maintain the holiness of God's dwelling place, an obligation that justifies the laws of purity.

The Pentateuch refers to a great number of covenants, and the literature on covenant is likewise extensive. While a complete review exceeds the limits of the present study, a brief review may be useful.[63] Studies of the covenant concept analyze it from a wide range of perspectives: in terms of its historical

62. Hwang, *The Rhetoric of Remembrance*, 233.

and ideational background, particularly ancient Near Eastern land-grant and sovereign–vassal treaties; the etymology of the term *b^erît* and the semantics of "establishing" (*hēqîm*) or "cutting" (*kārat*) a covenant; and the age and evolution of the covenant idea in the Bible.[64]

Another avenue of scholarship considers the individual covenants in the Pentateuch and their relationship to one another.[65] Genesis, for instance, knows three divine covenants: the eternal covenant with Noah and all living beings (Genesis 9) and the eternal covenant with Abraham (Genesis 17), both of which are priestly. The third is an alternative version of the covenant with Abra[ha]m, this one sealed through a ritual ceremony, and is attributed to the J source (Genesis 15). The covenant between God and Abraham is presumed to extend to the patriarch's descendants (cf. Exod. 2:22; 6:4-5), but it is not certain the patriarchal covenant is the same as the "eternal covenant between me and the Israelites" referenced in Exod. 31:16.[66] A different covenant idea is introduced in Exodus 24. Exodus 24:5-8 describes a covenant ceremony

63. For an excellent and relatively brief discussion of the biblical concept of "covenant," see Walter Brueggemann, *Theology of the Old Testament: Testimony, Dispute, Advocacy* (Minneapolis: Augsburg Fortress Press, 1997), 414–34. Among the surveys of research on covenant in the Hebrew Bible are Scott Hahn, "Covenant in the Old and New Testaments: Some Current Research (1994–2004)," *Currents in Biblical Research* 3 (2005): 263–92; Steven L. McKenzie, *Covenant* (St. Louis: Chalice, 2000); Frank Crüsemann, *The Torah: Theology and Social History of Old Testament Law*, trans. A. W. Mahnke (Minneapolis: Fortress Press, 1996); Robert Davidson, "Covenant Ideology in Ancient Israel," in *The World of Ancient Israel: Sociological, Anthropological and Political Perspectives*, ed. R. E. Clements (Cambridge: Cambridge University Press, 1989), 323–47; Delbert R. Hillers, *Covenant: The History of a Biblical Idea* (Baltimore: Johns Hopkins University Press, 1969). On the etymology of *b^erît*, see James Barr, "Some Semantic Notes on the Covenant," in *Beiträge zur Alttestamentlichen Theologie: Festschrift für Walther Zimmerli zum 70. Geburtstag*, ed. H. Donner, R. Hanhart, and R. Smend (Göttingen: Vandenhoeck & Ruprecht, 1977), 23–38, and Moshe Weinfeld, "בְּרִית, *berîth*," *TDOT* 2:253–79.

64. For ancient Near Eastern sources for the covenant see George Mendenhall, *Law and Covenant in Israel and the Ancient Near East* (Pittsburgh: Biblical Colloquium, 1955); Moshe Weinfeld, "The Covenant of Grant in the Old Testament and Ancient Near East," *JAOS* 90 (1970): 184–203; Klaus Baltzer, *The Covenant Formulary in Old Testament, Jewish and Early Christian Writings*, trans. D. E. Green (Philadelphia: Fortress Press, 1971); Dennis J. McCarthy, *Old Testament Covenant: A Survey of Current Opinion* (Richmond, VA: John Knox, 1972). Examples of work exploring the covenant relationships in different literary traditions include Jon D. Levenson, *Sinai and Zion: An Entry into the Jewish Bible* (San Francisco: HarperCollins, 1985); Claus Westermann, *The Promises to the Fathers: Studies on the Patriarchal Narratives*, trans. D. E. Green (Philadelphia: Fortress Press, 1980. Originally published as *Die Verheissungen an die Väter*, Göttingen: Vandenhoeck & Ruprecht, 1976); S. David Sperling, "Yahweh's *Berît* (Covenant): Which Came First—Sex or Politics?" in Sperling, *The Original Torah: The Political Intent of the Bible* (New York: New York University Press, 1998).

65. Hwang's book, mentioned earlier, is a very recent exemplar.

associated with the Sinai revelation that requires Israel to acquiesce to and observe all the laws binding it. Developing that idea, Deuteronomy refers to a covenant between God and Israel that was sealed at Horeb and that bound Israel to God's commandments. Deuteronomy tells of a second covenant as well, which Israel enters into on the plains of Moab, and of the ceremony for its ratification when the Israelites enter the Promised Land. Finally, there are two somewhat anomalous covenants, one associated with the Bread of the Presence (Lev. 24:5–9), and the "covenant of well-being . . . an eternal covenant of priesthood," which God bestows on high priest Eliezar's son Pinchas (Num. 25:12–13). Each of these may represent a different articulation of an underlying concept of Israel's relationship to God.

A different line of research examines biblical covenant as a theological idea. Ernest Nicholson's monograph *God and His People: Covenant and Theology in the Old Testament* is an example, and one especially fruitful for the present study.[67] Nicholson borrows from social anthropology the interpretation of religious ideas and systems as constructs to "legitimize" a social institution:

> One way of describing religion is that it is part of a society's endeavor to impose meaning upon its experience of the world. Among the nations of Israel's environment religion performed this role in an all-embracing manner. As a microcosm is related to a macrocosm, the humanly perceived "right order" of the social world was seen as a reflection of the cosmic order created and willed by the gods. . . . Society's structures and institutions were in this way believed to be grounded in the sacred order of the cosmos and were accordingly seen as being divinely legitimized.[68]

Drawing on social anthropology, Nicholson considers the function of creation myths to provide a model of "the 'right order' of the world [which] informed all activities of a society's life, the total well-being of which depended upon upholding it."[69] The authorizing function of creation myths for ancient Near Eastern societies spilled over into Israel, Nicholson maintains: "Israel too

66. Blenkinsopp makes the observation that in terms of P, the covenant with Abraham in Genesis 17 "does not emerge . . . as structurally very significant." "The Structure of P," *CBQ* 38 (1976): 278.

67. Ernest W. Nicholson, *God and His People: Covenant and Theology in the Old Testament* (Oxford: Clarendon, 1986).

68. Ibid., 193–94. On this see also Mircea Eliade, *The Sacred and the Profane: The Nature of Religion*, trans. W. R. Trask (New York: Harcourt Brace Jovanovich, 1959).

69. Nicholson, *God and His People*, 194.

understood itself, its structures and institutions *sub specie aeternitatis*, as we may put it; religion in Israel performed a legitimizing role no less than the religions of other nations at the time."[70]

The mythic background of the priestly strand of biblical literature has not gone unremarked by scholars. The priestly conception of the tabernacle as a microcosm of creation, for instance, is widely recognized, as is its perception of the sacred calendar as a replica of divine time.[71] In fact, the creation underpinnings of Israelite worship are among the defining characteristics of the vision represented by postmonarchical P.[72] The possibility of an analogous cosmogonic background for Deuteronomy's covenant theology has received less attention, but should, I believe, be explored. If, as Clifford Geertz has famously explained, religious systems are "models *of* and models *for*" reality, the religious system that the deuteronomic tradition promotes rests on a foundational conception of reality that transcends history to be operative at all times. Grounded in such a foundational conception of reality, the deuteronomic religious system, like that of the priestly tradition, reflects a divinely authorized "right order."[73]

Religious Practice and Memory

The role of memory in religious practice has gained some attention in the last few decades, principally in the work of Harvey Whitehouse.[74] Whitehouse

70. Ibid., 200.

71. See, for instance, Mark Smith, *The Priestly Vision of Genesis 1* (Minneapolis: Fortress Press, 2010), 92–93, 107–12; Blenkinsopp, "The Structure of P"; Nihan, *From Priestly Torah to Pentateuch*, 54–55; Nahum M. Sarna, *Exploring Exodus: The Origins of Biblical Israel* (New York: Schocken, 1986), 213–15; and Umberto Cassuto, *A Commentary on the Book of Exodus*, trans. I. Abrahams (Jerusalem: Magnes, 1997), 477.

72. M. Smith, *The Priestly Vision of Genesis 1*, 111–12.

73. David Carr expresses this well in his remarks on "cultural memory": "Though . . . cultural memory often consists in large part of recollection of various narratives in the group's past, it can also include behavioral norms and visions of the future. Within the ancient world, however, such behavioral norms and visions usually *are embedded in memories of the distant past, with this past having powerful associations of goodness and normativity. Indeed, that past is never 'past' in the way we might conceive it but stands in the ancient world as a potentially realizable 'present' to which each generation seeks to return.*" (*Writing on the Tablet of the Heart*, 11 [italics mine]). On the relationship between theology and ideology in Deuteronomy, see Mayes, "Deuteronomistic Ideology and the Theology of the Old Testament," 73–78.

74. Harvey Whitehouse, "Apparitions, Orations, and Rings: Experiences of Spirits in Dadul," in *Spirits in Culture, History and Mind*, ed. J.M. Mageo and A. Howard (New York: Routledge, 1996), 173–94; *Arguments and Icons: Divergent Modes of Religiosity* (Oxford: Oxford University Press, 2000); *Inside the Cult: Religious Innovation and Transmission in Papua New Guinea* (Oxford: Clarendon, 1995); *Modes of*

maintains that there is a salient relationship between memory and religious systems. His theory of Divergent Modes of Religiosity correlates the kind of memory a given society privileges and the nature of its ritual or religious practice.[75] With some caveats, Whitehouse's theory is suggestive for the study of memory and the religious programs envisioned in the Pentateuch. Before it can be applied to the Bible, however, two things must be clarified: What is meant by ritual practice, and to what extent can a literary description represent it?

The literature on ritual is both extensive and heterogeneous, and the difficulty of coming up with a definition inclusive enough to account for the variety of material and ideological contexts in which ritual is found is readily acknowledged by anthropologists.[76] Most taxonomies of ritual tend to dichotomize thought and action,[77] explicit expression and symbolic communication, and utilitarian and non-utilitarian objectives, with ritual representing the second part of each pair. This polarization makes immediately apparent the insufficiency of such descriptions for pentateuchal religion. They work well for the practices mandated in priestly literature, but are of no use to those of deuteronomic literature, for which thought, explicit communication, and clear functional objectives are intrinsic to prescribed religious practices.

Approaches that map more generous parameters within which to identify ritual are also problematic, as the following quote from Catherine Bell's *Ritual: Perspectives and Dimensions* demonstrates:

> [W]hat sort of practice is ritual? Clearly, ritual is not the same thing everywhere; it can vary in every feature. As practice, the most we can say is that it is [*sic*] involves ritualization, that is, a way of acting that distinguishes itself from other ways of acting in the very way

Religiosity: A Cognitive Theory of Religious Transmission (Walnut Creek, CA: AltaMira, 2004); "Rites of Terror: Emotion, Metaphor and Memory in Melanesian Initiation Cults," in *Religion and Emotion: Approaches and Interpretations*, ed. J. Corrigan (New York: Oxford University Press, 2004), 133–48 [repr., from *Journal of the Royal Anthropological Institute* 2 (1996): 703–15].

75. The term "religiosity" refers to such features as ritual practice, the transmission and dissemination of religion, and the social/political organization of religious systems, which collectively describe their "mode."

76. For a review of theories of ritual see Jack Goody, "Religion and Ritual: The Definitional Problem," *The British Journal of Sociology* 12 (1961): 142–64; Catherine Bell, *Ritual Theory, Ritual Practice* (New York: Oxford University Press, 1992); and idem, *Ritual: Perspectives and Dimensions* (New York: Oxford University Press, 1997).

77. Goody, "Religion and Ritual," 147. "Generally [ritual] has been used to refer to the action as distinct from the belief component of magico-religious phenomena."

> it does what it does; moreover, it makes this distinction for specific purposes.[78]

Bell's statement tells us as much about the difficulty of identifying ritual as it does about the character of ritual itself. The definition suggested by Evan Zuesse in the *Encyclopedia of Religion* is only somewhat more specific. Rituals, he writes, are

> conscious and voluntary, repetitious and stylized symbolic bodily actions that are centered on cosmos structures and/or sacred presences. (Verbal behavior such as chant, song, and prayer are of course included in the category of bodily actions.)[79]

In the face of such little clarity, the analysis of priestly and deuteronomic ritual may be aided by two approaches: Bell's "practice approach," which considers "how a particular community of culture ritualizes (what characteristics of acting make strategic distinctions between these acts and others) and then address[es] when and why ritualization is deemed to be the effective thing to do,"[80] and Geertz's conception of ritual as enactment, dramatic rendering, materialization, or realization of ideology.[81] The virtue of Bell's approach is that it permits deuteronomic and priestly religion to define the salient practices in their respective traditions. Geertz's enactment idea integrates the dichotomous poles of ritual taxonomy listed above so that both deuteronomic practice and priestly practice can fall under the rubric of ritual. Both the cultic practices of priestly literature and that of Deuteronomy, in which verbalization has both theological and utilitarian value, can be understood as enactments, or models, of and for theological reality.[82]

Of course the Pentateuch is not an anthropological field report. Although it is possible, as I suggested earlier, that the text describes rituals that were meant to be enacted or were based on actual practices, what the Pentateuch principally offers are theological statements whose relationship to actual practice can neither be determined nor assumed.[83] This reality does not greatly disturb

78. Bell, *Ritual: Perspectives and Dimensions*, 81.

79. Evan M. Zuesse, "Ritual," *ER* 12:405b.

80. Bell, *Ritual: Perspectives and Dimensions*, 81.

81. Clifford Geertz, *The Interpretation of Cultures* (New York: Basic Books, 1973), 114.

82. Ibid., 93.

83. A utilitarian purpose for Leviticus has been argued by scholars but cannot be proven definitively. That ancient Near Eastern cultures produced guiding documents for the enactment of ritual seems certain based on Hittite and Akkadian documents. See *COS*, 1:160–63, 1:427–36, and 3:61–65. However,

the exploration of deuteronomic and priestly theology, nor of how each tradition conceptualizes memory, but it does complicate the analysis of deuteronomic and priestly worship and practice as represented, and of the literary presentation of those practices. As *represented*, prescribed practices must be imagined as if taking place in the reality constructed by the narrative. Their literary *presentation*, however, is directed to a reading or listening audience, for not only do both traditions offer visions of religious life, they also seek to involve the audiences reading or listening to their writing in that religious life. As David P. Wright says with respect to priestly literature (and I would add, for D as well),

> the socialcultural [*sic*] world in which PH was created, whatever that may have been has to be considered as a factor in its formulation. The corpus has been written in dialogue with that environment and in reaction to it. As such it is probably not merely descriptive but prescriptive in the larger ideological sense in that it seeks to shape opinion and motivate response.[84]

In Deuteronomy, the gap between religious practice as represented and the presentation itself is not so great, since both the text and the practices it prescribes have a pedagogic purpose and rely on narrative. For instance, Deuteronomy 26 not only contains a liturgy for offering the first fruits, it also contains introductory material that sets the scene with allusive language that reinforces the ideas recited in the liturgy. The religious practices represented in P, however, are more problematic. First, and perhaps most obviously, because P's rituals are directed to God, the text cannot provide much information on how they are received or experienced.[85] Moreover, because these rituals rely on sensory experience, the presumed enactment and effect of ritual on the one hand, and its textual representation on the other hand, are asymmetrical. One is experiential; the other is cognitive.

The engagement of Israel's memory in P also poses difficulties. To demonstrate: in an episode to be taken up later, the two rebellions in Numbers 16–17, two different appeals to Israel's memory are involved. One, represented

with regard even to documents such as these, the precise relationship between document and actual practice is something at which we can only guess.

84. D. Wright, "Ritual Theory, Ritual Texts, and the Priestly-Holiness Writings of the Pentateuch," 207.

85. As we will see in the next chapter, however, one function of P's cosmogony is to illustrate God's reception to ritual.

in the narrative, makes use of commemorative objects to remind the people of Aaronide authority. The second appeal is achieved through the presentation of the event.[86] On the second level it seeks to ensure that the audience remembers the consequence of flouting God's choice. It provides what Wesley Bergen calls "imaginative performance" of an event meant to create a terrifying experiential memory.[87] To the extent that the experience of reading or hearing the text has ritual significance, the rhetorical and literary strategies to engage the audience's memory are worthy of investigation.

Organization of This Project

This work is organized into two parts. Part I provides the theoretical underpinnings for the analysis of the religious programs that occupy Part II. The theoretical work begins in Chapter 2, where I show how the deuteronomic

86. Such compensatory participation may also take the form of ritual, namely the ritualized reading, hearing, or recitation of the text, which, as the rabbis of the *Mishna* understood, could substitute for experience and be regarded, therefore, as a kind of religious activity. Consider, for instance, the statement of Rabbi Gamliel: "Anyone who does not say these three things has not fulfilled his [Passover] obligation, and they are: *pesaḥ maṣṣah* and *maror." M. Pesaḥ* 10:5. The statement is included in the Passover Haggadah, where it invites participants at the *seder* to fulfill their obligation by saying the three words in lieu of actually sacrificing the Passover offering and eating with unleavened bread and bitter herbs as required according to Exod. 12:8. See Mordechai Leib Katzenellenbogen, ed., *Haggadah Shel Pesach, Torat Chaim* (Jerusalem: Mosad Harav Kook, 1998), 143.

87. Wesley Bergen uses the model of Monday-night football to explain that rituals involve four levels of participants: the direct participants in the ritual (level 1); those who make the game possible (level 2); the spectators at the game (level 3); and the audience that watches from a distance spatially and perhaps temporally as well. He correlates levels 1–3 with the characters in the biblical text (i.e., the individuals who bring sacrifices, the officiating priests, and the Israelites of the biblical world, respectively) and level 4, with the readers of the biblical text: "Like the fourth-level participants in Monday Night Football, the reader of the text is far removed from the events described in the text. . . . In fact, the text very carefully removes any illusion of direct participation by locating the event in the 'Tent of Meeting,' a building that did not exist even in the writer's own time. So not only does the existence of the text create the possibility of the fourth-level participant, but the text deliberately creates readers who recognize that their participation in the act of reading the text involves their *imaginary* participation in a dead ritual" (italics mine). Wesley J. Bergen, *Reading Ritual: Leviticus in Postmodern Culture*, JSOTSup 417 (London and New York: T. & T. Clark, 2005), 31. The model is useful; however, if Israelites (and later, Jews) are indeed reading or listening to the text and recalling its content, then "dead" is probably too strong a word. Indeed, the detailed expositions of temple ritual in the *Mishna* were recorded long after the temple itself was destroyed and the rituals were made obsolete. As two examples among numerous such passages, see the detailed description of the Day of Atonement in *M. Yoma* (e.g., 1:1-2, 4:1-3) and of the Passover sacrifices in *M. Pesaḥ* 5:5-10. The authors of the *Mishna* write as if describing a living institution, although it is also possible that the texts reflect messianic preparation for a new temple in the future.

and priestly covenant ideas reflect worldviews as encapsulated in the creation stories that open Genesis (Gen. 1:1—2:4a and Gen. 2:4b—3:24). I offer a close reading of the two creation stories and (in connection with Genesis 1), the flood narrative in Genesis 6–9, and correlate them with passages in Deuteronomy and in priestly material to show how they respectively reflect deuteronomic and priestly theology. Through this process, I demonstrate that each of the two stories endows Israel's covenant as conceived in each tradition with cosmogonic purpose and establishes memory as a key covenantal instrument.

In Chapter 3, I turn to the subject of memory. Here, I clarify how D and P each conceptualize memory by analyzing the language each tradition uses to speak of it. I also coordinate the two conceptualizations of memory with the worldviews expressed in the creation stories to establish memory's participation in the thought complex informing D's and P's respective worldviews. The privilege Deuteronomy accords semantic memory and its faith in the verbalization of memory are shown to be matched by the concern for the proper use of human intellect evinced in Genesis 2–3. Loyalty and obedience to God should be the object of the thinking Israelite. The foundation of that loyalty and the means by which it is sustained and transmitted are the verbalization of authorized versions of the past. In contrast, priestly terminology and the way it is used reveal this tradition's preference for the sensory and experiential over the intellectual and doctrinal. According to the priestly tradition, memory is awakened through sensory cues, and its primeval history proves that sensory instruments can be used to keep God attentive and mindful of Israel.

In the second half of this book (Chapters 4–8), I analyze the literary representation of the religious programs—the rituals and practices imagined or prescribed in Deuteronomy and in priestly literature—to illustrate how these two traditions make use of memory. Chapter 4 analyzes the several recitations mandated in Deuteronomy to keep covenantal obligation and loyalty firmly and continually in mind. These include parental instruction (and Moses' modeling of it in the historical retrospect that opens Deuteronomy), the sabbatical recitation of the Law, the creedal recitations associated with offering the first fruits and the third-year tithe, and the song that Moses teaches the Israelites.

Chapter 5 looks at the tabernacle instruments and practices that serve God's memory according to the priestly tradition. I explore the mnemonic function of the various instruments and garments that God instructs Moses to have made as "reminders" (*zikkārôn*) and the sacrifices, particularly the *ʾazkārâ* of the meal offering which provides a "pleasing fragrance" for God.

Israel's memory returns for consideration in Chapters 6 and 7. In Chapter 6 I relate the priestly conception of memory and its use in connection with the Israelite laity. Although Israel's memory is not its primary concern, the priestly tradition nonetheless makes use of memory to regulate the behavior of the non-priesthood. The necessity for this is not only in support of the political objectives of the priesthood as Leveen suggests, but derives from a theological urgency as well. From that perspective, I discuss not only the commemorative objects associated with wilderness rebellions, but the priestly use of dramatic narratives and overall literary structure to teach the Israelites of the danger of encroachment on the sacred.

Chapter 7 turns to the Holiness school and memory in the context of exile. As mentioned earlier, the Holiness school shares the basic conceptualization of memory as sensory and experiential found in the priestly tradition, but it places greater emphasis on Israel's memory than on God's. In this chapter, I demonstrate how the Holiness writers transform divine mnemonics into memory tools for Israel, and how they reinterpret priestly terminology to give new meaning to unviable practices, while maintaining a connection to the ritual life of the past. Chapter 8 focuses on the priestly use of the term "sign" (*'ôt*), arguably the most important term in the priestly memory lexicon. I discuss the "signs" introduced in priestly literature and their transformation from concrete markers to symbolic cues for God's memory. Chapter 9 concludes this investigation with some thoughts about the relationship between deuteronomic and priestly literature, the kind of religiosity each promotes, and the integrative model that the Pentateuch provides by their combined presence in the text.

2

Two Worldviews: Creation–Destruction–Re-Creation

Readers familiar with the book Genesis know that the book starts with two stories of creation, one (Gen. 1:1–2:4a) a seven-day schema culminating in God's rest on the seventh day, attributed to P, and a second (Gen. 2:4b—3:24), the story of Adam and Eve in the Garden of Eden, attributed to J. The second story describes not only creation, but (in Genesis 3) the events that bring about the loss of primeval paradise. There is also a priestly account of destroyed creation—the flood story of Genesis 6–9. This story concludes with renewal and the promise of re-creation sustained. The resolution of Genesis 3 is only partial. Its fulfillment comes with God's selection of a partner to live in his land.

The biblical text supplies a number of creation accounts outside of Genesis 1–9, and doubtless, many versions were known to Israel.[1] But as Mark Smith writes in his book on Genesis 1, "[t]he positioning of Genesis 1 arguably represents the claim that it is to be seen as *the* creation story, not simply one more among many."[2] This argument, however, begs the question: Why include the second creation story as well?[3] Was it kept for its etiological contributions? Does it simply "make explicit what P merely implies"?[4] Without discounting additional purposes that are served by Genesis 2–3, I wish to suggest first that, in analogy with the priestly creation and flood stories, Genesis 2–3 provides another primeval model of creation and destruction that sets up the conditions for re-creation. Second, again in analogy with the P version, Genesis 2–3 provides a conceptual introduction for Deuteronomy. This does not mean that

1. For a review, see Claus Westermann, *Genesis 1-11: A Commentary,* trans. J.J. Scullion (Minneapolis: Augsburg Press, 1984–86), 19–25; Mark Smith, *The Priestly Vision of Genesis 1* (Minneapolis: Fortress Press, 2010), 11–37.

2. Smith, *Priestly Vision of Genesis 1,* 136.

3. For a summary of opinions, see ibid., 117–38.

4. See discussion of the flood story below.

the authors of Deuteronomy were responsible for the composition of Genesis 2–3.[5] Rather they found in that material a perspective on the reality of human life that deeply resonated with both their values and their understanding of the proper position of humanity in God's world.[6]

If Genesis 2–3 supplies an etiology for the divine–human relationship reflected in Deuteronomy, it then turns out that the Pentateuch opens with typological creation accounts for each of its two primary traditions. That is precisely what I wish to demonstrate in this chapter. The creation portion of each narrative presents a model for the world, a model authorized by God by virtue of being that which God originally sought. The two models not only define the ideal relationship between God and humans; they establish a set of principal values. At the same time, the totality of the two narratives indicates that God's ideal plan for the world ultimately cannot be sustained. Nevertheless, even though in both accounts humans are responsible for the loss of the creation ideal, God gives up on neither them nor on the world. Instead God devises a new system for sustaining an imperfect world. In short, each of the stories that open Genesis exhibits a creation–destruction–re-creation pattern. In either version, whether by means of the design of the re-created world (for P) or by explaining the cause of destruction (for D), the two narratives provide a model, a divinely ordered background, for the covenants as conceptualized in Deuteronomy and the priestly tradition.

Both traditions consider Israel, as God's covenantal partner, to have a crucial role in the re-created world. P is more explicit with respect to the design of the re-created world, and as we shall see, it provides abundant foreshadowing of Israel's place in it. For this reason, I will discuss it first. That being said, Genesis 2–3 also contains numerous details in which the deuteronomic authors may have found *illo tempore* anticipation of the concerns and values supporting its covenant idea.

5. That the legends recounted in Genesis 2–3 were surely known in Israel prior to their incorporation into the biblical text must certainly be true. P. E. S. Thompson makes the argument that "the J 'creation story' has been subjected to considerable editorial activity since the original myth was taken over by J and then later by P," i.e., the Pentateuch's final editor. Thompson, "The Yahwist Creation Story," *VT* 21 (1971): 201.

6. Cf. Umberto Cassuto's observation about the pericope: "[F]rom this section: we learn of the necessity of discipline founded on God's statutes; of man's innate conscience; of the law of Divine reward and punishment. . . ." Umberto Cassuto, *A Commentary on the Book of Genesis. Part 1—From Adam to Noah: A Commentary on Genesis I—VI 8*, trans. I. Abrahams (Jerusalem: Magnes, 1998), 71. Although features like the anthropomorphisms of Genesis 2–3 are contrary to deuteronomic sensibilities, the moral underpinnings of this creation story in its final form speak directly to Deuteronomy's concerns, as will be demonstrated below.

The Priestly Creation Account (Gen. 1:1—2:4a; 6–9)

Creation (Gen. 1:1—2:4a)

The priestly version of creation (Gen. 1:1—2:4a) describes a harmonious universe systematically unfolding over six days. Beginning with the cosmos, God speaks into being all the elements of world: the heavens, the earth, the seas, plant life, animal life, and finally man on the sixth day. Each element is defined by its boundaries. God divides (*wayyabdēl*) light from darkness (Gen. 1:4-5), earth from the heavens (Gen. 1:6-7), water and dry land (Gen. 1:9-10), and creates animals appropriate to water, land, and air (Gen. 1:20-25) as well as plant life on the earth (Gen. 1:11-13). The world is also organized according to divine time, with the sun, moon, and constellations created to organize the calendar and its set days (*môʿădîm*). At every stage, God looks (*wayyarʾ*) at the day's creation to evaluate it and declares it to be "good" (Gen. 1:4, 12, 18, 21, 31).

The world God creates appears to be self-maintaining. Grasses "sow their own seed" (*mazrîaʿ zeraʿ mônēhû*) while "trees produce fruit which contains their seed" (*ʿēṣ ʿōśēh pᵉrî ʾăšer zarʿô-bô lᵉmînēhû*).[7] To be steward of the whole, God creates "man, in our form and in our likeness" who will subdue and rule over the land (Gen. 1:26-28):

> God blessed [the man and woman] and God said to them: "Be fruitful and multiply and fill the earth and subjugate it. Rule over the fish of the sea, and the birds of the heavens and every living thing that creeps on the earth." (1:28)

With the work completed, set up to run continuously, and managed by his human surrogates, God can now rest (*wayyišbōt*) as God indeed does on the seventh day, a day God blesses and sanctifies "because on it he desisted (*šābat*) from all of his work that God created to make."

As God's creation, the "good" world of Genesis 1 can be understood as a priestly ideal, the world God desires.[8] As many scholars have argued, priestly

7. The use of the cognate accusative (*mazrîaʿ zeraʿ*) in Gen. 1:11 and 1:12 grammatically expresses their self-perpetuating ability. The same idea is conveyed in the English translation (fruit trees that make fruit).

8. It is reflected in priestly literature both in terms of style (for instance the frequent use of chiasm as a structuring device), and in terms of the religious program promulgated (for instance, the realms of holiness described in the dietary laws in Leviticus 11 and the arrangement of the tribes around the tabernacle in Numbers 1–4). See Philip Peter Jenson, *Graded Holiness: A Key to the Priestly Conception of*

religion is founded on the idea of clear delineation between degrees of access or contact with the holy (*qôdeš*). That ideal can only be sustained if there are clear and intractable structures to separate that which is pure from the impure. Without such a system, the ideal—and therefore the original world—is unsustainable. The earth's becoming corrupt and filled with violence, so God decides to destroy it.

DESTRUCTION (GENESIS 6–7)

An ancient tradition with parallels in ancient Near Eastern literature, including *Atrahasis*, *Gilgamesh*, and *Enuma Elish*, the flood story in Genesis is widely assumed to be a composite text shaped by a priestly writer who incorporated a variety of extant traditions including material from the J source.[9] And while many analyses of Genesis 6–9 focus on identification of the individual literary strands, more recently scholars tend to advocate for a synchronic reading that pays attention to how the different voices interact to produce a richly textured text.[10] According to this view, the act of weaving involves a degree of selection from older material that is used for strategic rhetorical purposes.[11]

According to P, because the world "becomes corrupt" (*nišḥātâ*) and filled with "violence" (*ḥāmās*) (Gen. 6:12),[12] God declares intent to destroy (*šḥt*) everything God has made by flooding the earth (Gen. 6:13). The only exception is Noah, who alone in the world is deemed "righteous and free

the World, JSOTSup 106 (Sheffield: Sheffield Academic Press, 1992). On the examples noted, see Jacob Milgrom, *Leviticus*, 3 vols., AB 3–3B (New York: Doubleday, 1991–2001), 1:39–42, 718–31; Milgrom, *Numbers*, JPS (Philadelphia: Jewish Publication Society, 1990), 376–70; Baruch Levine, *Numbers*, 2 vols., AB 4A–B (New York: Doubleday, 1993–2000), 1:142–44, 150–51; and Levine, *Leviticus*, JPS (Philadelphia: Jewish Publication Society, 1989), 243–48.

9. Some scholars suggest P and J drew on different traditions of the ancient myth, and that this explains differences between their two versions. In addition to the divine name used by each (Yahweh or Elohim), the two versions exhibit such inconsistencies as the number of animals brought into the ark (2 of each in P [6:19-20] or, distinguishing between clean and unclean, seven of the former and two of the latter in J [7:2-3]); the cause of the flood, and its duration, as well as some doublets (e.g., 6:5-8 and 6:9-12).

10. See, for instance, Bernhard W. Anderson, "From Analysis to Synthesis: The Interpretation of Genesis 1-11," *JBL* 97 (1978): 23–39; Yair Lorberbaum, "The Rainbow in the Cloud: An Anger Management Device," *JR* 89 (2009): 498–540.

11. B. Anderson, "From Analysis to Synthesis," 37.

12. Among the meanings of *ḥāmās* are murderous violence (Gen. 49:5) and bloodshed (through parallelism with, e.g., Judg. 9:24; Ps. 72:14; Ezek. 7:23). See H. Haag, "חָמָס, *chāmās*," *TDOT* 4:478–86. According to Num. 35:33, bloodshed corrupts the land.

of blemish" (*ṣaddîq tāmîm*) and his family. God makes a covenant with Noah (6:14), promising to spare his household.

While P's juxtaposition of the earth's corruption and Noah's purity might imply that the flood is a form of purification, neither P nor J makes its purpose explicit.[13] P does make clear that the overall effect of the flood is to obliterate the order established at creation and return the world to primeval chaos.[14] In P, the flood is caused by both the heavenly waters and waters of the deep (7:11) which mingle together, dissolving the separation of Gen. 1:6-7. The waters themselves erase the boundary dividing water and dry land.[15]

Re-Creation (Genesis 8–9)

After 150 days of watery disorder, God acts upon the covenant and "remembers" Noah (Gen. 8:1). God's memory leads to re-creation. God brings a wind (*wayyaʿăbēr ʾĕlōhîm rûaḥ*) on the water and causes it to recede.[16] On the first day of the first month, the water dries up and Noah leaves the ark (Gen. 8:13). Recapitulating his instruction to the first humans at creation, God instructs Noah to "be fruitful and multiply" (Gen. 9:1). The recreated world in which Noah is to reproduce, however, is not identical to the original. God redefines humanity's place in the world. Instead of ruling (*kbš*) the animals of the earth as formerly, now they will merely inspire dread (*môraʾăkem*), this possibly because God permits man to eat meat (Gen. 9:2-4). Meat-eating itself represents an alteration. The rules governing meat-eating suggest that God grants it as a concession to the human tendency to violence, for they forbid not only consumption of blood but the shedding of human blood. The *ḥāmās* that corrupted the world will not disappear, so instead God limits and channels it. There is, of course, still the possibility that violence may again corrupt the earth and a second flood may be required. To protect the world against that

13. This possibility is set forth by Tikva Frymer-Kensky in "The Atrahasis Epic and Its Significance for Our Understanding of Genesis 1-9," *BA* 40 (1977): 147–54.

14. B. Anderson, "From Analysis to Synthesis," 37. "Clearly the priestly trident sought to rework the received tradition of a violent forty-day rainstorm into his own conception of the *mabbûl* as a cosmic catastrophe which threatened the earth with a return to primeval chaos."

15. As a remedy for the corrupted earth, the flood presages particular priestly programs for mediating the relationship between imperfect human and the divine. Washing one's clothes is the final step in the process of purification from uncleanliness. By wiping out all living beings, the flood also bears remarkable similarity to the exile as described in Lev. 26:43, which allows the land to "requite its Sabbaths." Once the land has been cleansed of its impurity, Israel can return (Lev. 26:43, 44-45).

16. As Bernhard Anderson points out, the echo of Gen. 1:2 (*wᵉrûaḥ ʾĕlōhîm*) in Gen. 8:1 relates the restoration of the world following the flood to the original creation. "From Analysis to Synthesis," 36.

possibility, God establishes an eternal covenant (*b^{e}rît ʿôlām*) with Noah and all living things. To keep God true to this promise, God places a bow in the clouds as a reminder of the covenant.[17]

> God said: this is the sign of the covenant (*ʾôt-habb^{e}rît*) which I am bestowing, between me and you and all living things with you, for all generations eternally (*l^{e}dōrōt ʿôlām*). My bow I place in a cloud and it will be a sign (*w^{e}hāyĕtâ l^{e}ʾôt*) of the covenant between me and the world. When I cause clouds to cover the earth, the bow will be seen (*w^{e}nirʾătâ*) in the cloud and I will remember (*w^{e}zākartî*) my covenant between me and you and all living beings, all flesh. The waters will never again become a flood to destroy all flesh. (Gen. 9:12-15)

The similarity of the bow in Genesis and the lapis lazuli necklace of flies worn by the goddess Nintu (or Ishtar) in the Mesopotamian flood legends in *Atrahasis*, *Gilgamesh*, and *Enuma Elish* has been recognized as a trope appropriated from the Mesopotamian sources. In the Akkadian versions, the necklace is a reminder that the gods will be without food if they destroy humankind. In the biblical text, however, the "sign" of the bow has a much broader function, nothing short of the continuation of the world.[18] The necessity of the sign raises the theological question: If God places the bow in the sky to ensure that God will remember the covenant, does this mean God could forget God's promise?[19] The question is hardly frivolous, for the text appears to accept that possibility with its report that after 150 days God "remembered" (*wayyizkōr*) Noah, and its

17. The covenant in Genesis 9 is not the same as the one made with Noah in 6:18. As the perfect (*wahăqimōtî*) implies, in Gen. 6:18, God made a one-time promise to Noah. The participle form in Gen. 9:9 describes an ongoing promise: "As for me: Behold I am establishing (*mēqîm*) my covenant with you."

18. The theological import of "signs" in P will be discussed in Chapter 3. On the etymology of *ʾôt*, see F. J. Helfmeyer, "אוֹת ʾôth," *TDOT* 1:167; Michael Fishbane, "On Biblical Omina," *Shnaton Ha-Miqra*ʾ 1 (1976): 213. On the putative Akkadian cognate *ittu/idatu*, see *CAD/I-J:* 304b, 306b–308a.

19. Commentaries disagree over for whom the bow is a sign. Westermann and von Rad see it as an assurance for humanity. For Westermann, it is the infrequent appearance of the [rain]bow "that gives it its function of *confirming* God's assurances," and he suggests it is a sign for humanity. *Genesis 1–11*, 474 (italics mine). More explicitly, von Rad interprets it as "God's gracious will made visible to give mankind, terrified by the chaotic elements, renewed assurance that God will support this aeon and to guarantee the duration of his ordinances." Gerhard von Rad, *Genesis: A Commentary*, OTL (Philadelphia: Westminster, 1972), 133. Gordon J. Wenham, on the other hand, maintains that the sign is to remind God. *Genesis 1–15*, WBC 1 (Waco, TX: Word, 1987), 195.

implication, therefore, that God must have forgotten, or at least failed to attend to him in the interval.[20]

God's reliance on the sign of the bow further implies that God's memory must be sensually induced. As Genesis 1 implied, God is a visual perceiver. It is upon seeing what God has created that God declares it to be good. With respect to the covenantal promise, sight remains key for God's memory as indicated by the repeated use of *rʾh* in Genesis 9. The bow will "be seen" (*nirʾătâ*). God will "see it and remember" (*ur^{e}ʾîtîhâ lizkōr*).

I have shown the P version of the flood to describe the complete creation–destruction–re-creation paradigm. Nevertheless, the priestly editors of this passage chose to include elements of the more archaic J version of the story. Why? What does J add to the primeval story? Many solutions have been offered, but there are two I wish to mention. One is, as Yair Lorberbaum observes, to make "explicit" what "is only implied in P."[21] For example, whereas P rather obliquely attributes corruption and *ḥāmās* to humankind,[22] J explicitly identifies humanity's "evil" nature as the reason for the flood (6:5). God's acceptance of human nature in P, only implied by the permission to eat meat and the laws around blood, is explicit in J when Yahweh acknowledges that postdiluvian man is "evil from his youth" (8:21).

A second, perhaps more significant, contribution made by the J material is to establish the linkage between the primeval history and Israel's cult. In J's account of the immediate aftermath of the flood, Noah offers Yahweh a sacrifice:

> Noah built an altar to Yahweh and he took of all the clean animals and clean birds and made them into a burnt offering on the altar.[23] Yahweh smelled the soothing fragrance (*rêaḥ hannîḥōaḥ*) and

20. Not all scholars concur on this interpretation of Gen. 8:1. Cassuto insists, "[t]he Creator of the world did not forget his creatures. . . . The meaning is not that He remembered at the termination of the hundred and fifty days mentioned in the previous verse." Umberto Cassuto, *A Commentary on the Book of Genesis—Part 2: From Noah to Abraham*, trans. I. Abrahams (Jerusalem: Magnes, 1997), 99. Sarna comments here (and echoes it in his comment on Exod. 2:24) that "'remembering,' particularly on the part of God, is not the retention or recollection of a mental image, but a focusing upon the object of memory that results in action." Nahum M. Sarna, *Genesis*, JPS (Philadelphia: Jewish Publication Society, 1989), 56. Cf. Sarna, *Exodus*, JPS (Philadelphia: Jewish Publication Society, 1991), 13. The alternative view is well presented in Lorberbaum, "The Rainbow in the Cloud," 528.

21. Lorberbaum, "The Rainbow in the Cloud," 520.

22. See note 12.

23. While in P, Noah brings two of every animal into the ark, in the J version he brings seven pairs of each clean animal, thus permitting him to offer clean animals as sacrifices.

> Yahweh said to himself, "Never again will [I] curse the earth because of man for the inclinations of man's heart are evil from his very youth. Never again will [I] cut off all life as I did. For all the days of the earth, sowing and harvesting; cold and hot; summer and winter; day and night will not cease (*lōʾ yišbōtû*)." (Gen. 8:20-22)

Such a passage could not come from P, for sacrifice without a cult, tabernacle, or priesthood is illegitimate from the priestly perspective. But by bringing in J's account of Noah's sacrifice, P is able to show God's receptivity to the *smell* of sacrifice, to olfactory stimuli, and to sensory stimuli more generally.[24] In the context of the immediate post-flood, it is the pleasing smell that reconciles God to human nature and induces God to guarantee by oath the stability and continuation of the world. Most importantly, by prompting Yahweh's oath, the "pleasing fragrance" of Noah's sacrifice performs a function analogous to the mnemonic function of the bow in Genesis 9. It attracts God's attention and reconnects God to his created world. Together, the sign of the bow and the scent of sacrifice paradigmatically anticipate the priestly religious program centered on the tabernacle and illustrate its vital role in terms of God's covenant with Israel.

The connection between the cosmology outlined in Genesis 6–9 and God's covenant with Israel is further implied by two additional elements of the flood story: the date on which re-creation begins, and the term "sign" for the device reminding God. The date on which the earth becomes dry and re-creation begins is the "first day of the first month," a date with two critical resonances. It is the date on which Israel's history begins, and it is the date on which Israel's ritual life commences. Israel's national story begins in Exod. 12:2 when Yahweh says to Moses and Aaron, "This month is the first of the months of the year for you." The announcement that introduces the instructions for the exodus night also signals Israel's transition from a people enslaved to Egypt into a people bound to God. What is more, the declaration ties the new Israel and its calendar to that of the recreated world. The day on which Israel becomes a nation is "first day," the same day as the one on which the post-flood world begins. The rebirth of the world anticipates the birth of Israel.

Not only does Israel come into being on the "first day of the first month," its cult begins on that date as well. The connection between the tabernacle and

24. Despite the anomaly with P in terms of Noah's action, the poetic oath in verse 22 reveals an ideational affinity with P. It expresses a vision of a world that is as ordered and stable as that of Genesis 1. Even more striking is the use of *lōʾ yišbōtû* ("will not cease") at the oath's conclusion, which recalls God's rest in Gen. 2:2-3 at the end of the original creation.

creation as described in Genesis 1 is often remarked upon.[25] Its connection to *re*-creation has received far less attention. The date on which the tabernacle is erected, however, unites it with the start of the post-flood world. This means that the day on which Israel can begin to live its covenant with God, by having the rites associated with the covenant performed, is the anniversary of re-creation. Originating in the same cosmic moment, Israel and Israel's covenant are united into a single ideational complex.

The identification of the bow in Gen. 9:12-17 as a "sign" provides a second foreshadowing allusion to Israel. Israel's signatory role comes into play immediately after its connection to the "first day" has been announced when the Israelites are instructed to provide God with the "sign" of the blood painted on their houses. Like the sight of the bow, the sight of the blood will be a brake on the destruction to be wrought in Egypt. God will "see the blood and rescue" the Israelites and "not let the affliction of the destroyer (*mašḥît*)" affect them when "I strike the land of Egypt" (Exod. 12:13).

Together, the priestly account of the flood story and re-creation explains the world as one that exists through the providence and benevolence of God. It is a world that, despite being faulty and prone to corruption and the impurities that are part of human existence, God has promised to maintain, so long as God remembers. The resonances with the exodus night foreshadow Israel's responsibility to provide the necessary reminders, while the allusions to Israel and its ritual life identify Israel's cult, ritual life, and covenantal relationship with God as paradigmatically one with the world's re-creation and continuation. The creation and flood stories are, to use the term coined by Mircea Eliade, *hierophanies*, representations of divine order that serve as models for Israel's cult.[26] They unite Israel and its cult to re-creation, and they unite the ritual appeals to God's memory with the bow that guarantees God's fidelity to God's covenant with the world.

Deuteronomy's Creation Story (Gen. 2:4b—3:24)

Creation

In contrast to the global scope of the priestly creation and flood stories, Gen. 2:4b—3:24 takes place in a small locale, a garden in Eden. It is there that Yahweh-God plants trees that are "beautiful to behold and good to eat," the

25. See Chapter 1, note 71.

26. Mircea Eliade, *The Sacred and the Profane: The Nature of Religion*, trans. W. R. Trask (New York: Harcourt Brace Jovanovich, 1959), 22.

Tree of Life, and the Tree of Knowledge of Good and Evil (2:9). The larger world is known only from the river whose four tributaries flow to other lands and it seems barely to matter (2:10–14). The setting of this story is limited, and God's relationship to it is intimate as evinced by God's "making" (*wayyîṣer*) Adam from the soil, "blowing" life (*wayyippaḥ bᵉʾappâyw nišmat ḥayyîm*) into his nostrils (2:7), and placing him in the garden (2:8).

Adam's purpose is implied at the story's outset: "Yahweh-God had not brought rain onto the earth and there was no man to work (*laʿăbōd*) the land" (2:5). Unlike the man and woman of Genesis 1 who rule over the land, Adam must serve it. The relationship between Yahweh-God and Adam, while benevolent, is predicated on Adam's dependence on, and inferiority to, God. God sustains the life of the garden, while Adam's job is to work and take care of the garden (*lᵉʿābdāh ûlšomrāh*) (Gen. 2:15). The responsibility is not meant to be onerous, for God provides for Adam. All God requires is that Adam obey:

> Yahweh-God commanded the man saying, "From all the trees of the garden you may surely eat, but from the Tree of Knowledge of Good and Evil, do not eat from it for on the day you eat from it, you will die." (2:16)

Destruction

As scholars have long appreciated, the garden dwelling and the Tree of Life are regular elements in ancient Near Eastern myths.[27] The Tree of Knowledge, however, is unique to the biblical story and accordingly, its introduction is of particular significance. Yet despite the identification with knowledge, the tree is not the source of intelligence.[28] Adam already can discern among the animals and give each a name. The woman is also intelligent. She can appreciate the tree's fruit and she can debate the serpent.[29] It is because they have cognitive ability that Adam and the woman can choose to eat the fruit or not, to disobey God or not, and it is the misuse of that intelligence that causes the garden idyll of Genesis 2 to fall apart. The two humans listen to and are swayed by the

27. See P. E. S. Thompson, "The Yahwist Creation Story," 202, n. 3.

28. Among the interpretations for the "knowledge" obtained from the fruit of the tree are moral discernment, sexual knowledge, omniscience, and wisdom. See the discussion in Westermann, *Genesis 1–11*, 211–51.

29. Possibly Adam's capacity for understanding is limited and he has limited self-consciousness or self-awareness, as the otherwise *non sequitur* that closes this creation account suggests: "The two of them were naked, the man and his wife, but they were not ashamed (*yitbōšāšû*)" (Gen. 2:25). The use of the *hitpaʿel* suggests a reflexive nuance: "They were not ashamed before each other."

wrong guides. The woman heeds the snake, the man heeds the woman, and both disobey God and eat. The price of their disobedience is expulsion from the garden and the loss of a land enjoying God's focused and singular attention.

As with Genesis 1, Genesis 2–3 has parallels in ancient Near Eastern myth, particularly in the creation account that begins *Atrahasis*:

> When the gods like men
> Bore the work and suffered the toil
> The toil of the gods was great,
> The work was heavy, the distress was much.
> Tablet I: 1–4

In the myth, the gods assign their work first to a lower level of deity, but following a rebellion, decide to create humankind for that purpose:

> They summoned and asked the goddess,
> The midwife of the gods, wise Mami
> "You are the birth-goddess, creatress of mankind
> Create *Lullû* that he may bear the yoke . . . .
> Let man carry the toil of the gods."
> Tablet I: 192–97[30]

In a manner similar to Adam of Genesis 2, the human is fashioned from clay and imbued with life by the blood of an intelligent god, "[t]hat god and man/May be thoroughly mixed in the clay."[31]

The connections between Genesis 2–3 and D may not be immediately apparent, but there are a number of points of convergence between them, including the attention to land, the significance of rain, the importance of obedience, and the consequences of disobedience. The singular interest of Yahweh-God in the Garden of Eden in Genesis 2–3 is echoed in God's attitude toward the land the Israelites are to inherit in Deuteronomy. As God explains, that land enjoys God's special providence:

> For the land that you are going into to inherit is not like the land of Egypt from which you came out, that you sowed seeds and watered on foot like a vegetable garden. The land that you are crossing into

30. *Atrahasis*. W. G. Lambert and A. R. Millard, *Atra-Ḫasīs: The Babylonian Story of the Flood* (Winona Lake, IN: Eisenbrauns, 1999), 43, 57.

31. Ibid., 59.

> to inherit [is] . . . a land that Yahweh your God looks over; the eyes of Yahweh your God are on it always, from the beginning of the year to the end of the year. (Deut. 11:10b–12)

It requires little effort on Israel's part, for it is a land of

> great good cities that you did not build, and houses full of all good things that you did not fill, and wells that are dug which you did not dig, of vineyards and olive trees that you did not plant, but you may eat and be satisfied. (Deut. 6:10b–11)

The role of rain as an indication of God's favor in Deuteronomy (cf. Deut. 11:13–17; 28:23–24) is foreshadowed in Gen. 2:5: "Yahweh-God had not sent rain to the land," while the rivers that water the garden when Adam is first made anticipate the rain and dew that will water the land so long as the Israelites are faithful to Yahweh (cf. Deut. 11:13–15).

Most crucially, Genesis 2–3 emphasizes the importance of obedience. Thompson's suggestion that "it was the emphasis on disobedience that suggested [Genesis 2–3's] further use to the priestly redactor"[32] is correct, but only if "priestly redactor" is changed to "deuteronomic interests." Obedience is not a paramount priestly concern. It is, on the other hand, a deuteronomic obsession, and the story's emphasis on it anticipates the essence of the deuteronomic covenant idea. The authors of Deuteronomy were doubtless familiar with the Yahwistic text, for they allude to it in a very direct manner. Speaking to the Israelites, Moses describes who merits life in the land promised by God:

> Your little children of whom you said, "They will be carried off!" and your children who this day *do not know good and evil*, they will go there, and to them I will give it, and they will inherit it. (Deut. 1:39)[33]

As the review of memory terminology in Chapter 3 illustrates, Deuteronomy does not reject intelligence. It simply requires that intelligence be of the right kind and be used properly. The garden story provides evidence of the consequences of its wrong use. Sensually provoked desire drives the woman to disobedience. Because she "saw that the tree was good for eating and was

32. Thompson, "The Yahwist Creation Story," 202.

33. See as well Deut. 29:3.

desirable (*ta'ăwâ*) to the eyes" (3:6) she took the fruit and ate it. Indeed as Steven Weitzman has argued, Deuteronomy evinces an acute distrust of the senses and of sensual perception, and it concertedly seeks to defend against the danger of yielding to either. Referring to Deuteronomy 1–11, he proposes,

> it is possible to read these chapters as a sustained history of the senses in Israel's religious life, the ways in which its eyes, ears, and mouth threatened its covenant with God, and the solutions that Moses contrives to counter this threat.[34]

Adam too uses his senses incorrectly: "Because you listened to the voice of the woman and ate from the tree about which I commanded you saying 'do not eat from it . . .'" (3:17). Adam's crime resonates with a possibility warned against in Deuteronomy. The Israelites must not intermarry with the Canaanites, "because they will turn your sons away from me and they will worship other gods" (Deut. 7:1-4).

So it is in both the primeval condition and the legend concerning it, as represented in Genesis 2–3, that the deuteronomic writers found a model for their view of Israel's proper relationship with God. Like Adam, Israel is the body about which God is occupied and attentive. All God asks is that Adam follow God's instruction. The benefit to Adam is clear: he is given a fertile land watched over by God in which to live. Adam is exiled from this paradise because of the woman's acquiescence to mere desire, and his own attention to the wrong voice. Both are misuses of the intelligence they possess. The possibility of a humanity incapable of misusing its cognitive faculties is attractively illustrated by Jer. 32:39-40 and Ezek. 36:26, but D takes a starker and more realistic position on the human mind. Being human, Israel has intellect. That intellect can be turned to infidelity, apostasy, hubris, and the like. The challenge is to harness intelligence in the service of devotion to Yahweh.

In contrast to the unconditional, eternal covenant envisioned in P, the deuteronomic covenant imposes obligations on Israel in return for which Yahweh will ensure life and fertility in the land of Israel. The result is an exclusive relationship, but one that requires constant and total loyalty on the part of the subordinate party (Deut. 4:32-36). From D's perspective, the world beyond Israel and Judah exists as a place of exile. Only Israel and the land given it have Yahweh's complete attention (4:31). But this must not be taken for granted. Israel must strive to remain worthy of Yahweh's attention and

34. Steven Weitzman, "Sensory Reform in Deuteronomy," in *Religion and the Self in Antiquity*, ed. D. Braake, M. L. Satlow, S. Weitzman (Bloomington: Indiana University Press, 2005), 126.

protection, and this requires vigilance in the fulfillment of the law. Vigilance is the essence of Moses' instruction to the Israelites on the plains of Moab. Constant and continual mental attention must be paid to what Yahweh commands. The Israelites must constantly and continually remember.

Deuteronomy may not ground its covenant idea in a cosmic foundation as does P, but it does make use of a cosmogony that provides a model for what Israel's life should be like and what is needed to ensure it. Though parochial in scope, Deuteronomy's covenant provides Israel with a way to restore as fully as possible the ideal divine–human relation established by God at creation. It is to Israel, not all of humanity, that God chooses to offer the possibility of redemption. As a consequence of that choice, Israel is the obligated party. Deuteronomy assumes Yahweh's fidelity, for Yahweh is the one "who keeps his covenant" (7:9) and who "does not forget" it (4:31). Israel is the one whose faithfulness is less certain.

Genesis 2–3 further shows intelligence to be the wild card in human behavior. From that story, Deuteronomy concludes that if Israel is to remain true to its covenant with Yahweh, its obligation to Yahweh must constantly occupy its thought. This requires the exercise of memory: memory of what is required (i.e., the law) and memory of why it is required (i.e., the history). It requires that Israel continually speak, learn, and teach about God and God's law. In order that the people do so, Deuteronomy offers a religious practice based on the verbalization of memory.

Conclusion

The two grand narratives of creation, destruction, and re-creation reflect the essential theologies and anthropologies underlying the deuteronomic and priestly traditions. Each reveals a God whose original hopes can be uncovered, but whose plan was thwarted by the reality of human nature. Each also reveals the possibility for a return to the primeval ideal—in both cases, by means of a covenant secured by memory.

In the priestly version, the maintenance of re-creation depends on God's remembering the covenantal promise, and God calls upon Israel to induce God to do so. The cultic practices overseen by the priesthood are meant to provide God with the crucial reminder of God's obligation. Hence not only must the priests provide God with reminders of the covenant, they must ensure that those reminders are properly presented. The crucial function of the cult in terms of re-creation elevates the consequences of error and encroachment, and the necessity that it be protected from impropriety. To ensure its protection, the priestly tradition takes pains to remind Israel both of its authority and of the boundaries surrounding the tabernacle.

The orbit of Deuteronomy's concern is narrower and the significance of the covenant is smaller. Nevertheless, from D's perspective, creation too provides a model for Israel that illustrates the importance and the rewards of obedience, while warning of the misuse of intelligence. Unchecked, it can lead to defiance. But by means of active memory, intelligence can be harnessed to the service of God.

3

What Is "Memory"?

As stated at the outset of this work, memory is central to the covenant theologies of the deuteronomic and priestly traditions. But what is "memory" for each? Is it recollection or retrospect? Is it retrieval or retention? Does it concern specific episodes or extended events? Is it information or experience, ideas or images? As historians of memory theory know, the question of what is memory has occupied philosophers, theologians, and scientists for millennia. Most chart the consideration of this question from Aristotle (384–322 BCE), whose essentially static view of memory held sway for nearly 2000 years. Both Aristotle and later Augustine (353–430) conceptualized memory as a "storehouse of images" from which intact and immutable pictures of past events could be drawn. This notion of memory as a discrete act of retrieval performed at a particular time held through the Renaissance and Enlightenment, continuing even in the work of Georg Friedrich Wilhelm Hegel (1770–1831).[1] It was Friedrich Nietzsche (1844–1900) who challenged this view by recognizing the personal and subjective aspects of memory and, by implication, the dynamic, imaginative aspect of memory.[2]

The Study of Memory

The modern study of memory begins with Henri Bergson (1859–1941). Bergson's 1896 *Matter and Memory* provided a phenomenology of memory that has profoundly influenced subsequent analysis from both philosophical and psychological perspectives.[3] Bergson's distinction between "image" memory and "habit" memory is the basis of memory taxonomy today. Habit memory is

1. The preceding summary is based on Gerdien Jonker, *The Topography of Remembrance: The Dead, Tradition and Collective Memory in Mesopotamia* (Leiden: E. J. Brill, 1995), 6–21.

2. Jeffrey Andrew Barash, "The Sources of Memory," *Journal of the History of Ideas* 58 (1997): 717.

3. Henri Bergson, *Matter and Memory*, trans. N. M. Paul and W. S. Palmer (Mineola, NY: Dover, 2004).

consciously imprinted on the mind through repetition. It is the acquired skill or the lesson "learned by heart" that is expressed in the present as something acted, such as a ritual or recited liturgy.[4] "Image" memory, constituting "the principal share of individual consciousness in perception [and] the subjective side of the knowledge of things," concerns unique, unrepeatable events.[5]

Bergson's analysis concentrates on memory as an individual experience. A generation later, Maurice Halbwachs (1877–1945) coined the term "collective memory" to explain the participation of socially constructed reality in the formation of memory.[6] In two groundbreaking books, *La topographie légendaire des évangiles en Terre sainte: Études de mémoire collective* and *Le mémoire collective*, Halbwachs investigates aspects of the intersection of memory and religion. In the first, Halbwachs explores the identification of landmarks in Jerusalem, namely the location of each of the Stages of the Cross, to concretize and secure the authorized account of Jesus' passion. In his chapter on "Religious Collective Memory" in *Le mémoire collective*, Halbwachs considers the uses to which religious remembrances are put. Religious movements, he explains, invoke memory to establish origins or to demonstrate continuity with older traditions.[7] Furthermore, and to a greater extent than other categories of collective memory, "religious remembrances" are represented as eternal and immutable. Here is Halbwachs on Catholicism:

> When believers participate in the Sunday Mass, go to church and participate in rites on holy days, recite prayers every day, or fast, they undoubtedly do not think above all of past events of which these practices reproduce certain traits, like an echo resounding across the centuries. Preoccupied with obtaining salvation according to the customary forms and with complying with the rules observed by the same members of their religious group, they indeed know that these

4. Ibid., 89, 91. Bergson's "habit" memory is termed by philosophers "procedural memory" and by psychologists "embodied skill," like riding a bicycle.

5. Ibid., 25.

6. Maurice Halbwachs, *The Collective Memory*, trans. F. J. Ditter and V. Y. Ditter (New York: Harper & Row, 1980), translation of *Le mémoire collective* (Paris: Presses Universitaires de France, 1950). See also *La topographie légendaire des évangiles en Terre sainte: Études de mémoire collective* (Paris: Presses Universitaires de France, 1941).

7. "Society is aware that the new religion is not an absolute beginning. The society wishes to adopt these larger and deeper beliefs without entirely rupturing the framework of notions in which it has matured up until this point. That is why at the same time that society projects into its past conceptions that were recently elaborated, it is also intent on incorporating into the new religion elements of old cults that are assimilable into a new framework." *Collective Memory*, 86.

> institutions existed before them. But these institutions appear so well adapted to what these believers expect of them and the idea that they have of them is so closely linked to all their other thought that these institutions' historical color becomes effaced in their eyes and they are able to believe that these institutions *could be no other than what they are*. (Italics mine)[8]

The sense of eternality that tradition imparts to religion gives both its content and the practices derived from it divine sanction.

From two quite different perspectives, Paul Ricoeur (1913–2005) and Jan Assmann (1938–) further Halbwachs's investigation of collective memory's authorizing capacity. In *Memory, History and Forgetting*, Ricoeur's last publication, the author deals with the mnemonics that societies use to remember or commemorate the past.[9] Ricoeur is interested in the selective aspect of collective memory. As a whole, societies choose to remember some things and forget others. Such vehicles as recitation and commemorative objects or rituals permit societies to "manipulate" or institutionalize some memories, while permitting others to fade into oblivion. The two instruments activate the dialectical relationship between interior act of remembering ("reflexivity") and the cultural context ("worldliness") in which one remembers.[10] The worldly aspect of memory underlies the function of commemorations as instruments to fix memory as a complete and punctual event. Concentrating an event in the past into a single, authoritative experience he terms a commemoration, Ricoeur believes, can be an instrument of control. In a different manner, recitation, whether of liturgy or instruction, facilitates the internalization of an authorized narrative. "Recitation," Ricoeur observes,

> has long constituted the preferred mode of transmission, under the direction of educators, of texts considered, if not as founding words of the culture of instruction, at least as prestigious, in the sense of texts that are authoritative. For it is indeed authority that is at issue in the final analysis, more precisely enunciative authority, to distinguish it from institutional authority. . . . [E]very society has the burden of

8. Ibid., 99.

9. Paul Ricoeur, *Memory, History and Forgetting*, trans. K. Blamey and D. Pellauer (Chicago: University of Chicago Press, 2004).

10. Ricoeur, *Memory, History and Forgetting*, 363. "These situations imply one's own body and the bodies of others, lived space, and, finally, the horizon of the world and worlds, within which something has occurred."

> transmitting from one generation to the next what it holds to be its cultural acquisitions. For each generation, the learning process . . . can dispense with the exhausting effort to reacquire everything each time all over again.[11]

Assmann is interested in the way that cultural memory ensures "'the maintenance of the symbolic universes over the generations,' that is, of tradition in the sense of the continuity of meaning, 'world,' and identity."[12] He speaks of "formative" and "normative" rites and texts as mechanisms through which this is achieved. Formative rites and texts establish and "transmit identity-confirming knowledge by narrating stories that are shared," while normative rites and texts "transmit practical knowledge and point the way to right action."[13]

The mechanisms that Ricoeur and Assmann identify have resonance in the religious programs represented in deuteronomic and priestly literature. The purpose and power of the several liturgical or instructional scripts that D requires be recited, for instance, can be elucidated through reference to Ricoeur's discussion of recitation and Assmann's concept of "formative" texts. Ricoeur's comments on commemorations and Assmann's on "normative" texts have much to offer to our understanding of P's treatment of Israel's memory.

Another dimension to the exploration of the relationship between memory and social (religious) organization comes from the social anthropologist Harvey Whitehouse. Whitehouse's theory of Divergent Modes of Religiosity correlates religious modality with the kind of memory a given society privileges, whether "semantic" or "episodic."[14] "Doctrinal" religions tend to emerge in societies that privilege "semantic" memory. They emphasize verbally based religious practices, such as liturgical recitation, verbal review of religious tenets, or the transmission of "normative" (to use Assmann's term) texts. "Imagistic" religions emerge in societies that privilege "episodic" memory. Such religions make use of emotion-inducing, sensual religious practices to awaken memory, or to stimulate the formation or recall of memory. Visual and other sensory cues, the commemoration of traumatic events, terrifying, or paranormal manifestations of the divine are characteristic of "imagistic" religions.[15]

11. Ibid.

12. Jan Assmann, "Invisible Religion and Cultural Memory," in *Religion and Cultural Memory: Ten Studies*, trans. Rodney Livingstone (Stanford: Stanford University Press, 2006), 37.

13. Ibid., 38.

14. See Chapter 1, note 6.

15. Harvey Whitehouse, *Modes of Religiosity: A Cognitive Theory of Religious Transmission* (Walnut Creek, CA: AltaMira, 2004). Whitehouse characterizes the two modes in terms of the following elements: medium or form of revelation, medium or form of codification, mechanisms of transmission

As Table 1 suggests, these various ways in which memory is understood exhibit some commonalities. Differences in both terminology and explanation are largely a function of what aspect of memory is addressed.

	Generalized	*Particularized*
Psychological term	Semantic memory	Episodic memory
Bergson	"Image" memory	"Image" memory
Ricoeur	Recitation	Commemorations
Assmann	Normative Rites	Formative Rites
Whitehouse	Doctrinal Religion	Imagistic Religion

With their common interest in memory and religion, Ricoeur, Assmann, and Whitehouse make the case in different ways for a salient connection between how memory is understood and how it is implicated and manipulated in religious contexts. Mapping Whitehouse's correlation of memory type to religious modality onto the mechanisms identified by Ricoeur and Assmann for transmitting culture and cultural memory suggests a method for investigating the juncture between memory as conceptualized and memory as manipulated in deuteronomic and priestly religious polemic.

Memory Language of the Pentateuch

To arrive at how each conceptualizes memory, we must look at how each speaks of it.[16] The deuteronomic and priestly traditions have very different ways of referring to memory, and their respective lexicons illustrate this. As we will see, D's largely verbal (in the grammatical sense of the word) lexicon correlates with its trust in verbalized or semantic memory and its faith in the governing power of Israel's verbalization of authorized collective memory. The preponderance of nouns in P's memory lexicon reflects this tradition's reliance on sensory tools—or the verbal representation of them—to awaken

and dissemination, ritual practice and frequency thereof, level of exegesis (i.e., codified or spontaneous; "thick" or "thin"), social organization (diffusive or cohesive; strong or weak level of centralized authority).

16. For a more detailed discussion, see my "Memory and Religious Praxis: The Meaning and Function of Memory in Deuteronomic and Priestly Religion," Ph.D. diss., Jewish Theological Seminary, 2011.

God's memory and, for Israel, both to create and to stimulate the recall of key episodes.

In the Bible generally and D and P specifically, the core root for memory is *zkr*, particularly in the *qal* (*zākar*—"remember") and *nipʿal* (*nizkar*—"be remembered"). In addition to *zkr*, D and P employ a range of terms that evince their distinct perspectives on memory. Privileging verbs, D regards memory as a physical and intentional activity. One neither retrieves nor is overtaken by memory in this tradition. One must keep it in mind continually and constantly, and one does so by speaking. P, in contrast, considers memory to be associated with the senses, and P's memory terminology is overwhelmingly nominal, words describing the sensory instruments that kindle memory or promote its retrieval. (See Table 2.)

Who remembers is another point of contrast between D and P. While the former is obsessed with Israel's memory, P's primary concern is for God's memory. Repeatedly, D employs its rhetoric to exhort Israel to be vigilant about remembering God's deliverance and its own covenantal obligation, i.e., the law. God's memory is assumed in D, as is the certainty that God will never forget, hence D references God's memory very rarely.[17] In P the situation is reversed. Here it is God who both "remembers" (six times) and "takes note" (four times), and God is the one by whom Israel "is remembered" (Num. 10:9). Only once does P refer to Israelite memory, when the people falsely and ungratefully remember the abundant fish and melons they ate in Egypt (Num. 11:5).[18] Rather than recall the past, P expects Israel to "observe" particular rituals and rites. In other words, Israel's awakened memory is put to use in a specific moment for a specific purpose: to circumcise (Gen. 17:9, 10); to observe the Festival of Unleavened Bread (Exod. 23:15; 34:18), or the Sabbath (Exod. 31:13, 14, 16), and to carry out the sacrifices appropriate to the fixed days (Num. 28:2). As we shall see later, the contrast outlined above is somewhat softened in Holiness literature. (See Table 2.)

17. Deuteronomy 4:31 is an assertion of God's constant memory: "For Yahweh your God is a compassionate God. He will neither desert you nor ruin you nor forget you." In Deut. 9:27, Moses quotes his prayer to Yahweh, when he appealed to Yahweh's memory of the patriarchs.

18. See Chapter 6, pp. 123–24.

Table 2: Memory Terms in D and P

	Deuteronomy		P	
	Israel	God	Israel	God
VERBS				
zkr	5:15 7:18 8:2 8:18 9:7 15:15 16:3 16:12 24:9 24:18 24:22 25:17 32:7	9:27	Num. 11:5	Gen. 8:1 Gen. 9:15 Gen. 9:16 Gen. 19:29 Exod. 2:24 Exod. 6:5 (*nip‘al*) Num. 10:9
škḥ	4:9 4:23 6:12 8:11 8:14 8:19 9:7 24:19 25:19 26:13 31:21 32:18	4:31		
nšh/šyh	32:18			
pāqad = “take note [of]” (primarily *pqd*		5:9		Gen. 21:1 Exod. 20:5

means "enlist" or "count").				Exod. 32:34 Num. 14:18
šmr	*(qal)* 15:12 16:1 *(nipʿal)* 4:9 4:23 6:12 8:11 24:8 *šāmar laʿăśôt* 5:1 5:32 6:3 6:25 8:1 11:32 12:1 13:1 15:5 17:10 17:19 19:1 24:8 28:1 28:15 28:58 31:12 31:46	7:9 7:12	Gen. 17:9 Gen. 17:10 Exod. 13:10 Exod. 23:15 Exod. 31:13 Exod. 31:14 Exod. 31:16 Exod. 34:18 Num. 3:10 Num. 18:7 Num. 28:2 *(nipʿal)* Exod. 34:12	Num. 6:24
byn	*(qal)* 32:7	*(poʿal)* 32:10		

	32:29 (*nip'al*) 1:13 4:6			
šnn	6:7			
śym ['al lēb]	11:18 32:46			
yd'	4:39 7:9 8:5 9:6 11:12 29:15 31:13			
NOUNS				
zikkārôn			Num. 17:5	Exod. 17:14 Exod. 28:12 Exod. 28:29 Exod. 30:16 Exod. 39:7 Num. 5:15 Num. 5:18 Num. 10:10 Num. 31:54
'ôt	4:34, 6:8, 6:22, 11:3, 11:18, 13:2 13:3, 26:8, 28:46, 29:2, 34:11 *In Deuteronomy, *'ôt* is always paired with *môpēt* (wonder) and refers to the plagues in			Gen. 9:12 Gen. 9:13 Gen. 9:17 Gen. 17:11 Exod. 12:13 Exod. 13:16 Exod. 31:13 Exod. 31:17

	Egypt. It is not a mnemonic; it forms part of the recalled history.		Num. 17:3 Num. 17:25
mišmeret		**Permanent:** Exod. 16:32–34 Num. 17:25 **Temporary:** Exod. 12:6 (the lamb) Exod. 16:23 (reserved manna) Num. 19:9 (the ashes from the red heifer)	
zēker	25:19 32:26	17:14	
ʾazkārâ			Lev. 2:2 Lev. 2:9 Lev. 2:16 Lev. 5:12 Lev. 6:8 Lev. 24:7 Num. 5:26

Table 3: Memory Terms in the Holiness Code

	Israel	God
Verbs		
zākar	Num. 15:39 Num. 15:40	Lev. 26:42 Lev. 26:45

pāqad		Lev. 18:25 *(hipʿil)* 26:16
šāmar	Exod. 12:17 *šāmar laʿăśôt* Lev. 18:4 Lev. 18:5 Lev. 19:3 Lev. 19:19 Lev. 19:30 Lev. 18:26 Lev. 19:37 Lev. 20:8 Lev. 20:22 Lev. 22:31 Lev. 25:18 Lev. 26:3	
Nouns		
zikkārôn	Exod. 12:14 Exod. 13:9 Lev. 23:24	

The Semantics of Memory: Verbs

zkr (remember)

The root *zkr* is attested in all the Semitic languages: Akkadian (*zakāru*); Ugaritic (*ḏkr*); El-Amarna (*zkr*); Phoenician, Punic, and neo-Punic (*zkr*, *skr*); Samaritan and Aramaic (*dkr*); Ethiopic (*zakara*); Old South Arabic (*ḏkr*) and Arabic (*ḏakara*).[19] Only in Biblical Hebrew, however, does it denote memory, specifically memory tied to action that is motivated by recall.[20] The principal meanings of the Akkadian verb *zakāru* are "to declare," "make a declaration," "declare under oath," "command," "mention," "name," and "invoke."[21] The

19. W. Schottroff, "זכר *zkr*, to remember," *TLOT* 1:381–82.

20. The meaning "remember" does occur in the Amarna Letters, but as a foreign word or to gloss *ḫasāsu*. *CAD/Z*: 22a–b.

21. *CAD/Z*: 16a–22a.

verbal aspect of the Akkadian cognate is present in deuteronomic usage of *zkr* in that "to remember" in D is to speak the memory.

In Deuteronomy, *zkr* is primarily associated with human—that is, Israelite—memory. The constancy of God's memory is largely assumed (cf. Deut. 4:31), but Israel must be encouraged to remember. Repeatedly Israel is exhorted to remember, and the memory commanded must be intentional. Moses not only says to Israel, "remember Amaleq's attack" (Deut. 25:17), but adds as well, "do not forget!"[22] Memory is also intellectual, as illustrated both by the parallelism of *zkr* and *byn* ("be mindful") in Deut. 32:7, and by its association with epistemology. Deuteronomy 8, for instance, recounts memories of the wilderness period to keep the Israelites mindful of their dependency on Yahweh and their obligation, therefore, to remain loyal to his covenant.[23] Elsewhere, the wilderness is used to remind the Israelites of their penchant for rebellion (9:7; 24:9). Most importantly in D, memory is motivational. The six times Israel is exhorted to remember slavery in Egypt (16:12; 24:22); slavery and deliverance (5:15; 15:15; 24:18); or the Exodus alone (16:3), the instruction is tied to fulfillment of a commandment: observance of the Sabbath (5:15); observance of the Festival of Weeks (*Bikkurîm*)(16:12); eating unleavened bread during Passover (16:3); manumission of slaves in the seventh year (15:15); and just treatment of the stranger, widow, and orphan (24:18, 22). Rhetorically, D establishes the connection between remembering and observing the law with the expression *ʿal-kēn* ("for this reason," "therefore"), which grammatically makes the commandment a function of the memory.[24] It makes fulfillment of commandments the logical and inevitable result of memory and underscores D's ideal of a seamless transition from the act of memory (speaking) to the act of fulfilling the law that D demands.

The priestly tradition makes far less use of the verb *zākar* than does D, but when it does so, it is almost exclusively God's memory that matters. God is the grammatical subject of *zākar* six out of seven times in P.[25] Also in contrast to D, memory in the priestly tradition is associated with sensation rather than

22. Note also the structure of Deuteronomy 6. As Walter Brueggemann observes, two appeals to remember (vv. 1-9 and 20-25) frame the central command not to forget (10-[12]-19). *Deuteronomy*, AOTC (Nashville: Abingdon, 2001), 91.

23. Tellingly, Weinfeld titles the section of his commentary covering Deut. 8:1-20, "The Lessons from the Wanderings in the Desert." *Deuteronomy 1–11*, AB 5 (New York: Doubleday, 1991), 384.

24. The expression occurs seven times in Deuteronomy, to introduce a commandment or commandments in general (Deut. 5:15; 15:15; 24:18, 22) or to explain the rationale for a law (Deut. 10:9; 15:11; 19:7). In each instance, the force of *ʿal-kēn* is to make the commandment or rationale implicit and, by implication, logical and inevitable.

the intellect. Not only is Israel's memory provoked by hunger, God's memory is prompted by sensory cues, whether the sight of the bow created after the flood (Gen. 9:15, 16) or the cries of the Israelites in Egypt (Exod. 2:24; cf. Exod. 6:4).[26] In every case, what is remembered is God's covenant and the promises associated with it.

Aspects of both deuteronomic and priestly notions of memory are in evidence in the Holiness tradition's use of *zkr*. Like D, the Holiness writers see a positive role in Israel's exercise of memory, and they attribute to God's memory a level of constancy that resembles the deuteronomic view.[27] No sensory event is involved when God remembers the covenant in Leviticus 26. Rather, it is Israel's repentance that encourages God to remember and reinstate God's covenant with them. In fact, since God claims to have kept the covenant in mind during the period of punishment, God's memory of the covenant is not really newly aroused. Israel, however, requires visual aids to memory—whether the fringes on the garments (Num. 15:37-41) or the symbolic ornaments worn in Exod. 13:9.

škḥ (forget)

Biblical Hebrew alone among the Semitic languages (including epigraphic Hebrew) uses *škḥ* to mean "to forget." In Aramaic, *škḥ* means "to find," and appears, therefore, to derive from a separate root. The root does not exist in Akkadian; Akkadian expresses forgetting with the verb *mašû*, which is cognate to Hebrew *nšh/šyh* a synonym for *škḥ* and parallel to it in Deut. 32:18.

In the deuteronomic tradition, the dangers of forgetting are as important as is the obligation to remember.[28] Israel is warned to "not forget" in Deuteronomy almost as often (twelve times) as it is charged to remember.[29] To

25. Genesis 8:1; 9:15, 16; 19:29; Exod. 2:24; 6:5. The seventh occurrence is Num. 11:5, referenced above and discussed further in Chapter 6.

26. There are two exceptions: Gen. 8:1 and Gen. 19:29. No explicit sensory cue induces God's memory of Abraham, and then Lot. It is possible that the violence of the conflagration at Sodom plays that role, but the text does not make that claim.

27. See Lev. 26:27-45.

28. In pentateuchal and deuteronomic usage, *šākaḥ* nearly always denotes forgetting that is tied to breaking a promise or vow. Rebecca implies that if Esau forgets, he will not enact his sworn vengeance against Jacob (Gen. 27:45). Similarly, the butler fails to fulfill his promise to Joseph because he forgets Joseph (Gen. 40:23). In the deuteronomic history, Israel's forgetting is highly theological, tantamount to turning away from God as in Judg. 3:7: "The Israelites did evil in the eyes of Yahweh. They forgot (*wayyišk*^{e}*ḥû*) Yahweh their God and they served the *Baalim* and the *Asherot*." I addressed the covenantal implications of *šākaḥ* in "Is שכח a Technical Term for Covenantal Disloyalty?" (paper presented at the international meeting of the SBL, London, June 2011).

"not forget" requires care, for Israel shows a marked propensity to do so. The Israelites must "be on guard lest [they] forget" (Deut. 4:9, 23; 6:12; 8:11), must be exhorted to "not forget" (Deut. 31:21), and must "remember not to forget" (Deut. 9:7). The moral consequences of forgetting are made explicit in Moses' elaborate and detailed warning in Deut. 8:11-20:

> Guard yourselves lest you forget (*pen-tiškaḥ*) Yahweh your God and fail to keep his commandments and his statutes and his laws that I am commanding you today. Lest you eat and are satisfied and you build good houses and dwell [in them] and your cattle and your flocks increase and silver and gold increase for you and everything you have increases, and your heart becomes arrogant and you forget (*w^e rām l^e bābekā w^e šākaḥtā*) Yahweh your God who took you out of the land of Egypt, from the house of bondage, who led you through the great and terrible wilderness with snakes, seraphs and scorpions—a parched land with no water—who brought out for you water from the flinty rock . . . and you say to yourselves, "my power and the strength of my hand produced all this wealth for me."

As Moses cautions, forgetting both prompts and is an act of hubristic impiety. Moreover, for D, forgetfulness leads inexorably to neglect of the commandments (Deut. 8:11), idolatry (Deut. 4:9, 6:12 [cf. 6:14]), and breaking the covenant (Deut. 4:23). This use of *šākaḥ* underscores D's belief that memory requires intentionality and vigilance.

Neither the priestly tradition nor H makes use of *škḥ*.

šmr (keep, guard)

In its deuteronomic usage, *šāmar* ("observe," "guard") and especially the expression *šāmar la'ăśōt* ("be careful to do") implies both scrupulous performance of required actions and the thought behind their performance.[30] In almost

29. Deut. 4:9, 23; 6:12; 8:11, 14, 19; 9:7; 24:19; 25:19; 26:13; 31:21; 32:18. Deuteronomy 24:19 should be set apart from these because the forgetting in question is circumstantial. It concerns the hypothetical forgotten sheaf that the Israelites are to leave for the stranger, orphan, or widow. The verb occurs one time with God as subject (Deut. 4:31).

30. The two verbs appear together in Deuteronomy thirty-two times, but the idiom occurs in only eighteen of these: Deut. 5:1, 32; 6:3, 25; 8:1; 11:32; 12:1; 13:1; 15:5; 17:10; 24:8; 28:1, 15, 58, 31:12, 46; and in Deut. 17:19 and 19:9 where the direct object of *šāmar la'ăśōt* separates the main verb from the auxiliary verb. Michael Carasik explains the linkage of *zkr* and *šmr* as the twin elements that form the "retentive mind" in Deuteronomy: "זכר is used to command the retention and preservation of experience, the experience which prompts obedience to God and the inclination to uphold certain

every instance, that which the Israelites are commanded to "be careful to do" is the "laws, statutes and commandments" or "the instruction (*hattōrâ*).[31] Like remembrance, mindfulness is part of the process of fulfilling the obligation, as in the command in Deut. 16:1 to "observe the month of Abib." Followed as it is by detailed instruction for the observance of Passover, this command should be understood as "be sure to fulfill [the laws associated with] the month of Abib." Similarly, the substitution of *šāmôr* for *zākôr* in the deuteronomic restatement of the Decalogue's Sabbath commandment (5:12), puzzling given the centrality of memory in his tradition, may be intentionally underscoring the inextricable link between memory and performance. In the *nipʿal* with the reflexive meaning, "guard yourself," the act of self-guarding is explicitly linked to memory four of the twelve times[32] this form occurs (4:9; 4:23; 6:12; 8:11): Israel is warned: "guard yourselves . . . lest you forget."

With God as the subject, *šmr* denotes ongoing mindfulness. God is called "[He] who keeps (*šōmēr*) the covenant" in Deut. 7:9, and in Deut. 7:12 God pledges that "if you heed these laws and keep them and do them, Yahweh your God will keep (*šāmar*) for you the covenant and the loyalty that he swore to your ancestors."

In priestly writings as well, *šmr* occurs in connection with commandments, but here the "keeping" has more of the sense of preservation than of mindfulness. When the Israelites are instructed to "keep" the key institutions of the Sabbath and circumcision, it means to "perform properly and keep intact." "Keeping" a duty also means carrying it out properly and punctually at the appropriate time, as in Num. 28:2 where the Israelites are to "be careful to offer [the sacrifice appropriate to each festival] to me in its proper time" (*tišmᵉrû lᵉhaqrîb lî bᵉmô ʿădo*).[33]

pqd (take note)

The range of meanings associated with the root *pqd*, a root that occurs in all the Semitic languages, can be illustrated by the Akkadian *paqādu*: "entrust,"

religious and social norms; שמר describes the preservation of these norms." *Theologies of the Mind in Biblical Israel*, Studies on Biblical Literature 85 (New York: Peter Lang, 2006), 195.

31. The other objects are the judgment of the priest in Deut. 17:10, and the priest's instruction concerning leprosy in 24:8. The object of *šāmar laʿăśôt* in 6:3 is unspecified.

32. Deuteronomy 2:4; 4:9, 15, 23; 6:12; 8:11; 11:16; 12:13, 19, 30; 15:9; 23:10.

33. "Keep" takes on a perpetual quality in P only when applied to God or to the priests. Thus Num. 6:24-26, the opening verse of the priestly blessings ("May Yahweh bless you and keep you"), bespeaks the hope for God's constant care, while Num. 3:10 and 18:7 concern observance of priesthood as an ongoing obligation.

"take care of," "provide for," "muster," "check on," "appoint," and "commission."[34] The basic underlying idea carried by this root seems to be "noticing" or "examining closely," both of which imply both cognition (perception) and action.[35] Idiomatically the Akkadian verb can connote note-taking that is both favorable and unfavorable.[36] In religious contexts it may mean to administer or organize offerings at the temple, but it also functions as an attribute of a providential deity. In the latter sense, *pqd* is used in connection with memory in the Pentateuch, primarily by P and once in Deuteronomy (in the deuteronomic version of the Decalogue: Deut. 5:9 = Exod. 20:5).

The root *pqd* occurs frequently and in multiple conjugations in priestly material, mainly in connection with the census, and the organization of the tribes, but only when God is its subject does it imply remembrance or "taking note." With God, the memory described by *pqd* is the realization or fulfillment of divine intent. Positively, God "takes note of Sarah" to fulfill the promise made to Abraham in Genesis 18. More frequently, when God "takes note," it is to carry out punishment for past transgression. There is something haphazard in the way that God's "taking note" occurs: that is to say, no apparent event or experience prompts it. Until God takes note, whatever has been committed, whether for good or for bad, remains stored in a nowhere time of God's mind as yet unrealized promises. Once God "takes note," whatever action is warranted comes to fruition.[37]

lāmad (learn), *limmēd* (teach), *šinnēn* (repeat) *and śām 'al lēb* (place on the heart)

34. *CAD/P*: 115a.

35. According to Baruch Levine, a basic underlying meaning of the root is "'to hand over, deliver, assign,' hence: 'to turn one's thoughts or attention to,'" and he cites 1 Kings 20:15; 1 Sam. 14:17; 18:1; and Zech. 10:3 as evidence. *Numbers*, 2 vols.; AB 4A–B (Garden City, NY: Doubleday, 1993–2000), 1:134–35.

36. *CAD/P*: 122b–123a.

37. In passages attributed to H, God's note-taking is made for its deterrence value. In Lev. 18:25, instead of announcing judgment in the future, the text invokes God's judgment in the past to warn. God reminds the Israelites to keep the land from defilement because that was why the Canaanite nations were expelled. "The land was defiled and I called its iniquity to account (*wā'epqōd 'ăwōnāh 'ālêyhā*), and the land vomited out its inhabitants." While God's exercise in memory is implied in this passage, its main point is that Israel should learn from the example of past punishment. The same is the case in Lev. 26:16 where God declares that if Israel disobeys, God will "bring upon you (*wᵉhipqadtî 'ălêkem*) terror; disease; fever ..." The *hip'il* denotes the imposition of punishment, not the mental process that provokes it. In both these Holiness passages, the terrible past consequences of God's enduring memory are held up for Israel's recollection and reflection. Again, the point is that Israel should remember and be careful.

Deuteronomy makes use of an abundant ancillary vocabulary to represent the acquisition, maintenance, and transmission of memory through instruction, learning, and repetition of canonic lessons. The verbs employed to describe the acquisition of memories indicate that establishing memories is hardly a casual enterprise. The content of Israel's covenantal memory must be deposited and maintained in the site of intelligence and cognition (the heart) through formal recitation and repetition.[38] Repeatedly, Moses charges the Israelites to "teach," "learn," "repeat," and "place in the heart" the laws and lessons God is giving to them.

In the context of the deuteronomic narrative, there is something paradoxical in Moses' instruction. Speaking to the generation following the exodus, Moses makes reference to firsthand memories that they do not have, as if his audience actually remembered the experiences of their parents (Deut. 4:9–13; 11:2–7). On the other hand, it is precisely because his audience did not witness God's saving and revelatory acts in Egypt and Sinai/Horeb that Moses requires them to rehearse the national story again and again. This is because, as Carasik suggests, teaching fulfills a dual function. It reinforces the information (doctrine) that leads to successful life in the land, that is to say, adherence to the commandments. At the same time, the act of teaching "adds the power of continuity and repetition to an otherwise apparently unique and not replicable phenomenon."[39] The doctrine must be spoken and repeated to be learned and transmitted.[40] In their act of teaching, the teachers remind themselves of the formative memories that lead to obedience while supporting their preservation for future generations.[41]

38. Deuteronomy recognizes that wayward and deviant behavior can also be learned, and twice cautions against such instruction: in Deut. 18:9, Israel is warned against learning "to do the abominations of those nations [in those lands]," and in Deut. 20:18, the reason apostate Israelite towns within the land must be put to the ban is so that the people as a whole will not be taught to behave as had the deviants.

39. Carasik, *Theologies*, 181.

40. Ricoeur points out the role of recitation as "the preferred mode of transmission . . . of texts considered . . . authoritative." *Memory, History and Forgetting*, 60.

41. Not all commentators appreciate the reflexive pedagogical function of *teaching* as characterized in Deuteronomy 6. Brueggemann seems to be of two minds on this point. On the one hand he recognizes that the full "embeddedness" of the covenant "takes place only by constant, intentional verbal reiteration (vv. 7–9, 20–25) plus the parents' vigorous obedience (vv. 1–2)." At the same time, he seems to regard the teaching generation as committed to the teaching and concerned only with its transmission: "The teaching community is in a life-or-death struggle for the heart, commitment, and imagination of the younger generation." Brueggemann, *Deuteronomy*, 92. But Deuteronomy's insistence that the present generation, those present "today," is its audience means that those who are directed to teach are as much in need of the exercise of recitation as are their children.

The expression "place on the heart" adds a yet more physical dimension to memory. When Moses restates the instruction of Deut. 6:7 ("repeat them to your children") with "place these words on your heart" in Deut. 11:18, he implies that what is to be remembered must be physically attached to, or inserted into, the mind (heart).

ידע (know)

The verb *yādaʿ* ("to know") occurs forty times D.[42] In seven of these, what must be known are creedal tenets. "Know this day and keep it in your heart that Yahweh is God in the heavens above and on the earth below, there is no other" (4:39; cf. 4:35; 9:3). "Know with your heart that just as a man disciplines his son, Yahweh your God disciplined you" (8:5). "Know that it is not because of your righteousness that Yahweh is giving you this good land to inherit, for indeed you are stiff-necked" (9:6). "Know this day that it is not with your children who did not know and did not see the instruction of Yahweh your God, and his greatness and his strong hand and stretched out arm . . ." (11:2). "Know that Yahweh your God, he is God. He is the faithful God who keeps his covenant and faithful kindness to those who love him and keep his commandments to the thousandth generation" (7:9).[43] Deuteronomy 4:39 makes explicit what such knowing demands: placing it on the heart so it will be perpetually in mind. Knowledge, or rather the lack of it, explains the purpose of reading the law every seven years, so that future generations who do not have firsthand experience of God's care in the desert and "who do not know" (Deut. 31:13) will learn the history (4:9). In short, knowing and remembering are twin pillars of the relationship between Israel and God. To know Yahweh, Israel must remember Yahweh. Apostasy, the consequence of forgetting God, is to worship "other gods whom you do not know" (Deut. 11:28; 13:3, 7, 14) or whom "they do not know" (Deut. 29:25; 32:17).

The Semantics of Memory: Nouns

zēker (name)

42. Deuteronomy 1:13, 15, 39; 2:7; 3:19; 4:35, 39; 7:9, 15; 8:2, 3, 5, 16; 9:3, 6, 24; 11:2, 28; 13:3, 4, 7, 14; 18:21; 20:20; 22:2; 28:26, 33, 36, 64; 29:3, 5, 15, 25; 31:13, 21, 27, 29; 32:17; 33:9; 34:10. It also occurs in the *hipʿil* (4:9, 8:3) and *poʿel* (21:1).

43. Deuteronomy makes use of *ydʿ* not only to describe the relationship between Israel and God. It also warns that the worship of "other gods you did not know" will be requited in kind: God will exile Israel to a place where the only option is to worship "other gods that you do not know, nor your ancestors: gods of wood and stone" (Deut. 28:64).

The deuteronomic lexicon incudes only one noun pertaining to memory, *zēker*, which means both "name" and "memory" (Deut. 25:19; 32:26). The two meanings are not unrelated, as demonstrated in Deut. 25:17-19 and the command to blot out Amaleq's *zēker*.[44] As the primary vehicle for the perpetuation of an individual's legacy, names are integrally linked to the idea of memory. A "name" encapsulates the character of its designee. As Martin Rose explains, it serves as its "distinguishing mark" and the aspect of a person that endures beyond the life of the body.[45] Erase the name and nothing of a person endures. Additionally, as a synonym of *šēm* (cf. Exod. 3:15), *zēker* evokes the aspect of God that, in Deuteronomy's theology of transcendence, "dwells" in the place God chooses.[46]

zikkārôn and zikrôn (remembrance, reminder)

The noun *zikkārôn* or its construct form *zikrôn* occurs twenty-two times in the Hebrew Bible,[47] but in the Pentateuch it is found only in priestly literature (P and H).[48] The word *zkrn* is also attested in Aramaic papyri from Elephantine where it means "memorandum," the meaning it has in Esther and its cognate has in Ezra.[49] In P, *zikkārôn* is a mnemonic device, usually of a concrete nature, and always sensory. Most are housed in the tabernacle or

44. Although the word *zēker* does not appear in it, the brief reference to Absalom's monument in 2 Sam. 18:19 further illustrates the conceptual link between memory and name.

45. Martin Rose, "Names of God in the OT," *ABD* 4:1002a–b. "The 'distinguishing mark' (name) is not quite identical with what is designated; this little difference allows one to think and to hope that the name will endure. This hope also indicates an aspect of the salutary significance of the name: it juxtaposes the experience of human transience with hope of durability."

46. Deuteronomy 32:26 mingles two aspects of the meaning of *zēker*, "name" and "memory," to convey the idea of an enduring record of existence. God declares that it is only the fact that other nations would claim the destruction of Israel for themselves (Deut. 32:27) that keeps God from erasing its memory. The word *zēker* in Deut. 32:26 clearly refers to Israel's memory, that is, to the preservation of the record of Israel. But Deut. 32:27 demonstrates that the *zēker* really at stake is God's. Cf. Hos. 14:8, which compares Israel's *zēker* to wine of Lebanon. Interest in Israel's memory, which is the literal sense of the text, is ultimately subsumed within the theme of God's works (14:6-9). It is God's providence that enables Israel to be fertile and blossoming, and the successful preservation of Israel's memory redounds to God's reputation.

47. Exodus 12:14; 13:9; 17:14; 28:12 (2×); 28:29; 30:16; 39:7; Num. 5:15, 18; 10:10; 17:5; 31:54; Josh. 4:7; Isa. 57:8; Zech. 6:14; Mal. 3:16; Job 13:12; Qoh. 1:11; 2:16; Esth. 6:1; Neh. 2:20. The Aramaic cognate is found in Ezra 4:15 (*dokrānayyā'*, 2×) 6:2 (*dikrônā*).

48. On *zikkārôn* as a cultic term, see Gerhard von Rad, *Old Testament Theology*, 2 vols. (London: SCM, 2012), 1:242–43.

49. See CAP 32:1, 2, and 61:10. The word also appears in CAP 62:4; 63:10, 12; and 68:11 obv. However, these last three letters are fragmentary, and the precise sense of *zkrn* can only be inferred.

associated with its rituals, and most are directed to God's memory. These are the stones of remembrance on the ephod (Exod. 28:9-12); the stones on the breastplate of judgment (Exod. 28:16-21, 29) worn by the high priest; the half-shekel payment (Exod. 30:16); the booty from the battle with the Midianites (Num. 31:54); the blast of the silver trumpets (Num. 10:10); and the meal offering of remembrance in the trial for the woman suspected of adultery (Num. 5:11-30). The plating on the altar (Num. 17:3-5) is anomalous among these remembrances in that its memorial function is directed to the Israelites. The plating is made to remind them of the consequences of encroaching on priestly prerogative.[50] Unrelated to the tabernacle, the written text regarding Amaleq (Exod. 17:14) is also termed a "remembrance."[51]

The meaning of *zikkārôn* in H is taken up in Chapter 7.

ʾazkārâ ("that which recalls")

The grammatical explanation of *ʾazkārâ* is not certain; it may be a denominative derived from the Aramaic *apʿal*, hence causative.[52] Thus the noun could be taken to mean something like "the part which reminds one of the whole." It is sometimes translated as "memorial portion"[53] or "token portion."[54]

50. The plating is also a "sign," on which see below and see Chapter 7.

51. The term is used here in the very way attested extrabiblically in mid-first millennium BCE Aramaic papyri, and as in Esth. 6:1 where Ahasuerus's "Book of Reminders" prompts him to reward Mordechai. This "memorandum" will remind God to execute his promise at the proper time, namely when the Israelites are settled in their land (cf. Deut. 25:19; 1 Sam. 15:2). In this case, God instructs Moses to write a memorandum to remind God of his pledge to annihilate the memory of Amaleq which, according to Exod. 17:14 and 17:16 (and in contrast to Deuteronomy 25), will be carried out by God.

52. See Levine, *Numbers*, 1:199.

53. Haran, who uses this translation, has observed that the Septuagint and Vulgate translate *ʾazkārâ* as μνημόσυνον ("memorial, record") or ανάμνησιν ("calling to mind") and *memoriale*, respectively. (μνημόσυνον is the preferred term in the LXX everywhere but in Lev. 24:7, where the Greek uses ανάμνησιν.) He suggests that the root *zkr* has a specific meaning in this context and denotes the fragrant, noncorporal part of the grain offering: "ואפשר שהשורש זכר בא כאן בהוראה מיוחדת והאזכרה מציינת את החלק הריחני ומבושם שבמנחה." Menahem Haran, "Minḥa," *ʾEnṣîqlōppedia Miqraʾît* 5:26b [in Hebrew]). See also *Temples and Temple Service in Ancient Israel: An Inquiry into Biblical Cult Phenomena and the Historical Setting of the Priestly School* (Oxford: Clarendon, 1978; repr., Winona Lake, IN: Eisenbrauns, 1985), 230, 242.

54. Milgrom, *Leviticus*, 3 vols. AB 3–3B (New York: Doubleday, 1991–2001), 1:181–82. Levine, *Numbers*, 1:199. Both Milgrom and Levine offer this as an alternative interpretation, based on a secondary meaning of Akkadian *zikru:* "image" or "replica" (cf. *CAD/Z*: 116B), but neither seems convinced. Milgrom provides three traditional explanations of *ʾazkārâ*, all of which have support in biblical parallels: "memorial," "burnt portion," and "fragrant portion," as well as Schottroff's suggestion, "invocation portion." Ultimately, however, he dismisses these and concludes "provisionally" that *ʾazkārâ* should be

Found six times in priestly texts, *'azkārâ* is the name given to the portion of the grain offering brought to the tabernacle, either in analogy to the burnt offering (Lev. 2:2, 9, 16; 6:8), as a sin offering (Lev. 5:12), or as a *minḥat haqq^enā'ōt* of a meal offering (grain offering of jealousy) (Num. 5:25). In these verses, *'azkārâ* is a technical term for the portion of the grain offering that is turned to smoke on the altar (Lev. 2:16). In Lev. 24:7, it refers to the incense associated with the bread of the presence displayed in the inner court of the tabernacle.[55]

mišmeret (safeguard[ed thing])

The primary meaning of *mišmeret* is "guarding,"[56] but in a few instances it denotes an item that is to be preserved for safekeeping.[57] The use of *mišmeret* in the sense of "safekeeping" may be further subdivided.[58] In Exod. 12:6, 16:23,

"related to *zēker* 'remembrance', referring to the fact that the entire cereal offering should really go up in smoke and that the portion that does is *pars pro toto:* it stands in for the remainder." Milgrom, *Leviticus*, 1:182. Somewhat more positively, Erhard S. Gerstenberger asserts that the purpose of the *'azkārâ* is to invoke the deity who is "summoned by name, *hizkîr*." He brings to bear the prominence given to the grain offering in Num. 7:10–83 and the record of the dedication offerings for the altar (*Leviticus: A Commentary*, OTL [Louisville: Westminster John Knox, 1996], 42).

55. Noth regards*'azkārâ* as a Holiness term. Knohl would appear to agree as he attributes all the Leviticus verses to the Holiness school.

56. Etymologically, *mišmeret* is related to *šmr* and in addition to its primary sense, the meanings "supervision," "safekeeping," or "maintaining" occur as well. See Jacob Milgrom, *Studies in Levitical Terminology*, 2 vols., Near Eastern Studies 14 (Berkeley: University of California Press, 1969), 8–15, and *Leviticus*, 1:7, 541; Levine, *Numbers*, 1:141–42. The expression *šāmar mišmeret Yahweh* (cf. Lev. 8:35; Num. 9:19; 9:23) seems to mean "to adhere to Yahweh['s command]," while *šāmar 'et-mišmartî* (cf. Lev. 18:30; 22:9) occurs in connection to prohibitions, i.e., "guarding [oneself] against the violation of Yahweh's commandments." Milgrom, *Leviticus*, 1:7. Milgrom maintains that "משמרת in connection with the Tabernacle/Tent of Meeting means 'guard duty' *and nothing else*" (italics in original). *Studies in Levitical Terminology*, 8. Levine, however, disagrees: "Actually, the term *mišmeret* enjoys several connotations in Numbers. The Hebrew verb *šāmar*, and nominal *mišmeret*, are subject to subtle shifts in meaning that can significantly affect our understanding of the text, as well as of the duties of the Levites." *Numbers*, 1:141.

57. Exodus 12:6; 16:23, 32, 33, 34; Num. 17:25; 19:9.

58. Thomas B. Dozeman's interpretation of *mišmeret* as "observance" or "obligation" glosses over the difference between those objects safeguarded temporarily and those that are to be kept permanently. Dozeman, *Exodus*, Eerdmans Critical Commentary (Grand Rapids: Eerdmans, 2009), 265. He uses it as well to denote the cultic duties of priests in Numbers 3, 4, and 18. Although the translation satisfactorily accounts for the mandatory aspect of "safeguarded objects" as things set apart at God's command to be used in connection with the cult, and is adequate for the three short-term kept items, in my view it insufficiently reflects the affective aspect of the two permanent *mišmārôt*, which are instituted in order to stimulate or perpetuate memory.

and Num. 19:9, *mišmeret* refers respectively to the lamb selected on the tenth day of the first month, the double portion of *manna* provided on the sixth day of the week, and the ashes of the red heifer. Each is to be held onto for a limited period: until the fourteenth day of the month in the case of the lamb and through the seventh day in the case of the *manna*. As for the ashes of the red heifer (Num. 19:9), since they will be used to make the waters of lustration, they too will not be kept in perpetuity. Twice, the *mišmeret* is to be kept forever: in Exod. 16:32-34 (a saved *ōmer* of *manna*) and Num. 17:25 (Aaron's flowering rod). Both times, as we shall see, it is associated with the rituals of the tabernacle, and is, at least in part, for Israel's edification as commemorations of signal experiences: the miracle of the *manna* and the lesson of the Sabbath through the former, and the demonstration of high priests' exclusive and salutary authority through the latter.[59]

ʾôt (sign)

The word *ʾôt* ("sign") occurs seventy-nine times in the Hebrew Bible, and the Aramaic cognate *ʾāt* occurs three times (all in Daniel). It has a wide range of meanings, including "portent" for good or bad (Jer. 10:2; Ps. 86:17), "symbol" (Isa. 20:3; Ezek. 4:3) and "calendar-fixing-celestial-body" (Gen. 1:14), as well as "divine demonstration";[60] "confirmation of a statement";[61] "confirmation of promise";[62] and "enduring reminder."[63] Its etymology is uncertain. Akkadian *ittu/idatu*[64] and Arabic *ʾāyat* may be cognates but are not conclusively so. Although within the Bible *ʾôt* occurs in secular contexts, a theological meaning predominates.[65]

59. The significance of the rod as a "sign" will be taken up in Chapter 8.

60. Exodus 7:3; 10:1, 2; Deut. 4:34; 6:22; 11:3; 26:8; 29:2; 34:11; Josh. 24:17; Jer. 32:20, 21.

61. Exodus 8:19; Deut. 28:46; Judg. 6:17; 1 Sam. 2:34; 10:7, 9; 14:10; 2 Kings 20:8, 9.

62. Exodus 3:12; Josh. 2:12; 2 Kings 19:29; Jer. 44:29.

63. Deuteronomy 6:8; 11:18.

64. On the etymology of Akkadian *ittu/idatu*, see *CAD/I-J:* 304b, 306b–308a. The two forms are represented by different logograms, Á.MEŠ and GISKIM, respectively; however, GISKIM can be used for both. They also share semantic range. The range is wide and includes "mark, sign, feature," "omen, ominous sign," "password, signal," or "notice, acknowledgement, written proof" (ibid., 304b–310a). The idea of "sign" or "portent" is suggested by the idiom *ittākunu damiqtum[damqātu?]* ("a good sign for you [pl]") in YOS 9 35 i 40, cited in *CAD/I-J:* 306a and by *ittī dunqī šuātina āmurma* ("I saw these favorable signs") in Borger Esarh. 2:23, ibid., 306b.

65. See Michael Fishbane, "On Biblical Omina," *Shnaton Ha-Miqra'*1 (1976): 213–34 (Hebrew); Michael V. Fox, "The Sign of the Covenant: Circumcision in the Light of the Priestly *ʾôt* Etiologies," *RB* 81 (1974): 557–96. Fox identifies three categories of signs in the Bible: "proof signs," "symbol signs," and "cognition signs," the latter of which he further divides into "identity signs" and "mnemonic signs." All

The word *'ôt* is not a memory term in Deuteronomy. The signs referenced by D are part of the history to be remembered, as in the expression "signs and wonders," but they have no mnemonic function of their own.[66] Indeed, D is highly suspicious of signs that claim contemporary significance, and it associates them with outlawed forms of divination and with false prophecy (Deut. 13:2-6). Only in Deut. 6:8 and 11:18 do signs in the present serve a positive, albeit ambiguous, function. Context, however, strongly suggests that the instruction to place the teaching as "a sign on your arm and *ṭôṭāpōt* on your forehead," is likely a metaphor for the continual repetition and transmission of the law and the resulting fulfillment of it.[67]

In the priestly tradition *'ôt* has considerable significance.[68] While every "sign" in priestly literature has a visible component, there are differences among them. One group of "signs" described by the term *'ôt* includes Yahweh's divine demonstrations (as in "signs and wonders") in Egypt, but whereas in Deuteronomy such demonstrations are in the past, in P they take place and are observable in the present. A second category is the one-time sign of the blood on the Israelite houses that protects them from the Destroyer on the exodus night. A third category is the eternal signs: paradigmatically, the bow of Genesis 9, and subsequently circumcision (Genesis 17) and the Sabbath (Exodus 31). A subset of the last category consists of signs that have a secondary designation such as Aaron's rod, which is also called a *mišmeret*, the plating on the altar, also called a *zikkārôn*, and the "sign on your hand" partner to the "*ṭōṭāpōt* between your eyes."

Summary

In the deuteronomic tradition, the mental process of remembering encompasses a variety of aspects and modalities of speech, which is mirrored in the rich collection of verbs describing the act of remembering. What the vocabulary privileges grammatically is also privileged conceptually. Deuteronomic religion understands memory as a dynamic process involving both cognition and action

the "signs" in P, he claims, are cognition signs: "in the priestly *'ôt*–etiologies the *'ôt* is a permanent sign whose purpose is to stir up cognition, with the result that a covenant, a promise, or a commandment is maintained by God or man." Ibid., 570.

66. Deuteronomy 4:34; 6:8, 22; 11:3, 18; 13:2, 3; 26:8, 46; 29:2; 34:11.

67. See Chapter 4.

68. I am excluding Gen. 1:14 and Num. 2:2 from this discussion. In Num. 2:2, *'ôt* refers to the ensign or flag of a given tribe. In Gen. 1:14, it refers to the constellations. It is possible, however, that the association of the constellations with the calendar endows this "sign" with some measure of cultic (and covenantal) significance.

that is prompted and energized by recollection. Both thinking and doing are conceived of in physical terms. D also associates memory with loyalty to the covenantal obligations. Deuteronomic texts consistently combine the commandment to remember with an action that the Israelites must perform, or they invoke memory to reinforce Israel's obligation to God, or to chastise Israel for its faulty memory.

The semantic field of memory in priestly literature similarly reveals the priorities of this tradition. Specifically, it demonstrates that a primary concern is the engagement and maintenance of God's memory, and that the mechanisms needed to achieve it are concrete, sensory triggers. The place of the cult as the source of these triggers is reflected in the special vocabulary to denote commemorative and mnemonic ritual instruments. The priestly tradition also looks to sensory objects and experiences in connection with Israel's memory. The *ʾôt* is not part of Israel's memory-prompting arsenal, but the *zikkārôn* and the *mišmeret* can be used for this purpose.

PART II

Memory at Work in the Lived Covenant

4

"Remember, do not forget": Israel's Covenantal Duty in Deuteronomy

Introduction: Deuteronomic Ritual

Deuteronomy is not usually associated with ritual. Its law code says almost nothing about the practices associated with the shrine such as sacrifices and purification rites other than that they must be performed "only in the place which [Yahweh] has chosen."[1] When it does stipulate specific activities, such as the pilgrimage festivals (Deut. 16:1-17) or sacred donations (Deut. 14:22-29; 15:19-21), it couches them in hortatory reiteration of the religious principles to be gleaned from observance: the sacrificial system becomes an instrument of social welfare;[2] the slavery laws to teach gratitude for God's blessing.[3] Only the ritual for the unsolved murder has no obvious pedagogical feature.[4] The deuteronomic charges that surround the law code exhibit a similar orientation. They are general rather than specific, focusing, for instance, on observance of laws and statutes as a whole (e.g., Deut. 4:1; 7:8; 11:1).[5]

1. Didactic aspects of deuteronomic ritual are generally acknowledged. For example, Bernard Levinson and others observe that Deuteronomy reinforces the policy of centralized worship by relocating locally performed rituals to the central shrine. Bernard M. Levinson, *Deuteronomy and the Hermeneutics of Legal Innovation* (New York: Oxford University Press, 1997), especially chapters 2 and 3. In a similar vein, note Weinfeld's argument that Deuteronomy uses the sacrificial system both as an instrument of social welfare and as a means of inculcating it as a value. Moshe Weinfeld, *Deuteronomy and the Deuteronomic School* (Oxford: Clarendon, 1972; repr., Winona Lake, IN: Eisenbrauns, 1992), 211–13.

2. For example, Deut. 12:18-19; 14:29. See Weinfeld, *Deuteronomy and the Deuteronomic School*, 211–13.

3. Deuteronomy 15:18.

4. Weinfeld, *Deuteronomy and the Deuteronomic School*, 210–12. The phrase "in the land that Yahweh your God is giving you to inherit" in 21:1 may be designed to stress God's gift of the land or may simply define the boundaries within which the law applies.

5. Or the segregation from Canaanite tribes necessary to protect Israel from the lure of idolatry (Deut. 7:1-5).

Although ritual, in the strictest sense of the term, is not a deuteronomic concern, it would be wrong to say that Deuteronomy ignores religious practice altogether. On the contrary, D prescribes a number of mandatory practices that, in their codification, can justly be understood as the deuteronomic equivalent of ritual. Both the presentation of the first fruits during the Festival of Weeks (Deut. 26:1–11) and the triennial payment of tithes (Deut. 26:12–15) involve precisely scripted declarations. The law is to be read before all the people on every seventh celebration of the Festival of Booths (31:9–13). The requirement of domestic instruction is fulfilled through parents' recital of the law and scripted answers to their children's questions (6:7, 20–25). To this must be added the performance of the song of Deuteronomy 32. Although it is not expressly stated, periodic performance of the song seems to be the intent underlying its presentation to the Israelites.[6] Practices such as these are *intellectualized* rituals.[7] They are content-filled rather than symbolic; didactic rather than experiential; and meant to lead the practitioner directly to action rather than to effect transformative change either in the community or the cosmos.

Common to all the religious practice represented in D (excepting the unsolved murder ritual) are the incorporation and exploitation of memory. It is memory that promotes observance of commandments and motivates right treatment of the disadvantaged. For Deuteronomy, memory of slavery, of the exodus, of the wilderness period, of all that Yahweh has done for Israel, provides the cognitive foundation for Israel's covenantal loyalty. If the cause of Adam's transgression was that he "listened to the voice of your woman," as the garden narrative suggests, then the best way to prevent Israel's disobedience is to ensure the people listen to the right voice remembering and reminding them of their obligations to Yahweh. Deuteronomy is keenly aware of the possibility of succumbing to the wrong voice:

> If your brother, the son of your mother, your son or your daughter or the wife of your bosom . . . entices you . . . saying, "Let us go after

6. I am aware that the list conflates rituals that may date from different periods. The pilgrimage festivals, first-fruits ritual, tithes, firstlings, and the ritual for the unsolved murder are prescribed in the deuteronomic law code dated to the late seventh century BCE, while reading of the law in the seventh year and the song are mandated in the narrative material that follows the law code and that probably post-dates it.

7. It is more than mere substitution of speech for action (as, at the instruction of Rabbi Gamliel, one iterates in lieu of offering the elements of the paschal sacrifice in the *Haggadah*), or written codification of ritual actions for teaching and studying purposes (as in the *Mishna*). Speaking *is* the ritual. Its purpose is to keep the people—the party responsible for sustaining the covenant—continually aware of both their obligation vis-à-vis the covenant, and the duties it imposes upon them.

> and serve other gods. . . . Do not listen to him or look softly upon him. . . ." (Deut. 13:4, 9)[8]

Because of the ease with which wayward and deviant behavior can be learned, Deuteronomy twice cautions against such instruction: In Deut. 18:9, Israel is warned against learning "to do the abominations of those nations [in the land of Canaan]," and in Deut. 20:18, the reason apostate Israelite towns within the land must be banned is so that the people as a whole will not be taught to behave as had the rebels.

As Mendenhall observed more than fifty years ago, a validating function analogous to the "historical prologue" in ancient Hittite suzerainty treaties is performed in the reference to God's saving acts that opens the Decalogue (Exod. 20:2; Deut. 5:6). Both rehearsals of the past reference the sovereign's demonstrated power to protect its vassal as the justification for the vassal's exclusive loyalty. The assertion, "I Yahweh am your God who took you out of the land of Egypt, the house of servitude," rationalizes the command: "You shall have no other gods before me." Deuteronomy, however, broadens both the information rationalizing Israel's debt to Yahweh and the occasion for articulating it. God's claim upon the people is substantiated not only through the words spoken directly to the Israelites at Sinai/Horeb. The whole of Moses' instruction does so. Moses' instruction, moreover, does not simply substantiate God's claim; both it and the law associated with it are what must remain eternally present in the minds of God's people if total fidelity is to be ensured.[9] The covenant in Deuteronomy involves cognitive, emotional, and performative elements, all three of which are motivated by memory. As expressed in Deut. 6:5, Israel is required to "love Yahweh your God with the entirety of your heart, the entirety of your selfhood, and the entirety of your power."[10] The "love" that is commanded is total; it involves all of the self, all of the time.[11] Memory

8. In Deuteronomy, the dangers of enticement are always associated with turning to false gods, and by implication, rejecting Yahweh (cf. Deut. 7:3–4).

9. On the role of education in the deuteronomic project, see David M. Carr, *Writing on the Tablet of the Heart: Origins of Scripture and Literature* (Oxford: Oxford University Press, 2005), 134–42.

10. An exact translation of *nepeš* is exceedingly difficult to provide. In a great number of times, the word seems to mean "personality" or "emotive center," i.e., individuality and cognitive-emotional capacity. The word "selfhood" combines those two meanings, both of which are implied by Deut. 6:5.

11. The meaning of *'āhab* in Deuteronomy, and in particular in this verse, has been the subject of considerable scholarly discussion. William L. Moran's seminal article, "The Ancient Near Eastern Background of the Love of God in Deuteronomy," *CBQ* 25 (1963): 77–87, argues that the love commanded in Deuteronomy is essentially fealty. Just as the covenant in Deuteronomy evinces parallels with Assyrian sovereign–vassal treaties, the requirement that Israel love Yahweh should be seen as

provides the epistemological and psychological basis from which to carry out this obligation.[12]

As scholars have observed, Deuteronomy's conceptualization of covenant exhibits ideational affinities both with the northern prophetic tradition represented by the eighth-century BCE prophet Hosea, and with the sapient traditions of the ancient Near East. Like Hosea, for Deuteronomy knowledge of God and love of God are intricately related, and both are necessary ingredients of fidelity to God. The straying wife in Hos. 2:4-15 is ignorant of God's providential acts: "But she does not know (*wᵉhîʾ lōʾ yādᵉʿâ*) that *I* gave her the grain and the new wine and the new oil . . ." (Hos. 2:10). Lacking knowledge of what God has done, she has no knowledge or memory of God. "And *Me* she has forgotten," God declares (Hos. 2:15).[13] The equation of forgetfulness and lack of piety, and its inverse, the identification of memory with faithful observance that is found in Hosea, assumes central importance in deuteronomic literature. Similarly in deuteronomic literature, memory leads to knowledge of

analogous to "the Assyrian practice of demanding an oath of allegiance from their vassals expressed in terms of love" (84). Another analogy is proposed by J. W. McKay, who finds a close connection between the filial love prescribed in the wisdom tradition and the love commanded in Deuteronomy. He writes, "'love' in this context [Deut. 6:5] is not a sentiment of emotion, but *pietas*, the filial love and obedience that the son offers to the *pater familias*, and this is something which can be commanded." McKay, "Man's Love for God in Deuteronomy and the Father/Teacher–Son/Pupil Relationship," *VT* 22 (1972): 432. For additional positions on this topic, see Susan Ackerman, "The Personal Is Political: Covenantal and Affectionate Love (*ʾāhēb, ʾahăbâ*) in the Hebrew Bible," *VT* 52 (2002): 437–58, and Jacqueline E. Lapsley, "Feeling Our Way: Love for God in Deuteronomy," *CBQ* 65 (2003): 350–69. I maintain, however, that the totality of the deuteronomic commandment implies more than either political fealty and allegiance or filial love. Covenantal love requires complete devotion of the mind and body—all the time. Such devotion as construed in Deuteronomy is ceaseless and has an intensity and an obsessive quality like the intensity and obsessive quality of new romantic love, although it itself is not romantic. To love Yahweh, one must continually think about Yahweh, think about one's obligations toward God, and act upon the constant thought bodily through the fulfillment of obligations. It is worth noting that McKay recognizes the resultant action implied by the mental act of loving. "When we turn to the passages in the rest of the Book of Deuteronomy and the D-history where אהב is used of man's love for God, we find that 'love' is always virtually synonymous with obedience" (loc. cit., 433). But even this observation obscures the total concentration and devotion that loving God involves for Deuteronomy. The reciprocity implied by the juxtaposition of the commandment in 6:5 to Deut. 6:4 confirms this: just as Yahweh is indivisible, the loving self must be indivisible. In other words, the entirety of the self is involved.

12. Note Brueggemann's comment to Deuteronomy 6: "The issue of remembering/forgetting pertains both to the *concreteness of command* and to the *narrative lore* that energizes the commands." *Deuteronomy*, AOTC (Nashville: Abingdon, 2001); italics in original.

13. "Knowledge of God" is the final, climactic element in the terms of God's espousal to Israel in Hos. 2:21-22, and its absence provides the ammunition for God's lawsuit against God's people in chapter 4:1-6. For Hosea, without knowledge of God, Israel inevitably strays and turns to the worship of Baal.

God and God's laws, to love of God and to the intentional implementation of God's commands.

Deuteronomy is also associated with ancient Near Eastern wisdom literature.[14] It shares topics and terminology with Egyptian, Akkadian, and Sumerian wisdom texts as well as with the biblical book of Proverbs.[15] The characterization of God's relationship toward the Israelites in the wilderness when God tested and chastised them "as a man disciplines his son" (Deut. 8:5), for example, recalls Proverbs' preoccupation with parental training and disciplining of children (cf. Prov. 12:1; 13:24, etc.). And like Proverbs, Deuteronomy regards generational transmission as the preferred pedagogical model.[16]

But Deuteronomy differs from these literatures in three respects. In Deuteronomy, wisdom is theologized. The law (*tôrâ*) is Israel's wisdom (Deut. 4:6–8) and Israel's particular experience is the curriculum accompanying it. Moreover, learning has one purpose: it is to be harnessed to obedience and service to God. Deuteronomy also evinces a real concern for understanding as well as knowing by rote what is learned. For instance, Deuteronomy does not simply command that when a slave is released, he or she must be provided the material good needed to set up independent life. The text explains, "Do not regard it as difficult when you send him free from you, for your servant has earned double his wages [in] the six years, and Yahweh your God will bless you according to all you do" (Deut. 15:18). And finally, wisdom for Deuteronomy is dynamic. One learns as one teaches and one enacts what one learns. Proverbs, as Michael Carasik observes, offers an essentially passive model for learning content that is not specifically directed to the present generation as a dynamic community charged with performance. He writes:

> In comparison with the Bible generally, Proverbs replaces learning (למד) with receptivity (שמע), and awareness (זכר) with retention (שמר). Both of these changes point to the same conclusion. In Proverbs generally, and with apparent deliberateness in Proverbs

14. See Weinfeld, *Deuteronomy and the Deuteronomic School,* 244–54; and idem, *Deuteronomy 1–11,* AB 5 (New York: Doubleday, 1991), 62–64

15. For instance, rules on weights and measures in "Instruction of Amenemope," xvii 19–20 [*COS* 1:115]; and on wisdom's availability, "Babylonian Theodicy," 26 [*COS* 1:494].

16. The book of Proverbs exemplifies this preference. Despite the highly literary structure of the book, which points to its origin in scribal circles, the conceit of Proverbs is education that takes place in a domestic setting wherein a father teaches his son. I am grateful to David Carr for bringing this observation to my attention.

> 1–9, we find an emphasis not on mental *processes* but on the *contents* of the mind. (Italics in original.)[17]

In contrast, the deuteronomic conceptualization of wisdom emphasizes both the process and the content of learning, because learning that sticks, so to speak, requires continual rehearsal of the lesson and performance of the commandments learned.

Another departure from Proverbs is the particularistic orientation of Deuteronomy. That orientation reflects what H.-P. Müller describes as the

> synthesis . . . in which the earlier wisdom theology, which for the most part had not advanced beyond the stage of implications, was combined with theological schemata based on law and history.[18]

According to deuteronomic thinking, Israel's history, particularly God's work in that history, provides the curriculum for Israelite piety, as the explanation for the public reading of the law illustrates.[19] By recalling and verbalizing that history, the Israelites are instructed and reminded about the proper reverence to maintain before God, the value of discipline and memory to sustain reverence, and the ongoing applicability of the law.

The pedagogic impulse is most evident in the requirement that parents teach their children, but it can be found as well in the scripted recitations that Deuteronomy stipulates.[20] Moreover, the textual representation of these practices and the explanations surrounding them provide, in addition to direction on how they are to be performed, further instruction on points of theology for their audience. Hence, for both the Israelite participant and the hearing or reading audience, religious practice in Deuteronomy is a mechanism for recalling, retaining, and transmitting learned theological lessons.

Instruction: "Teach them to your children" (Deut. 11:19; 6:7)

The command to "repeat (*šinnantām*) [my words] to your children; say them when you are in your home and when you are on your way, when you lie down and when you stand up" (Deut. 6:7; cf. 11:19) refers to the obligatory

17. Carasik, *Theologies of the Mind in Biblical Israel*, Studies in Biblical Literature 85 (New York: Peter Lang, 2006), 157. For the support underlying this assertion see ibid., 150–57.

18. Hans-Peter Müller, חָכַם "*chākham*," *TDOT* 4:381.

19. See the discussion of Deut. 31:9-13 below.

20. The exception, surprisingly, is Passover, for which no liturgical recitation is stipulated. (See the discussion below.) Donation of firstlings also lacks a liturgical component.

exercise of continuous pedagogy. It is the deuteronomic ideal. Somewhat tautologically, it demands that every Israelite, every day, all day recite Deuteronomy itself.

Moses models this pedagogy in his opening speech in Deuteronomy 1–3. As Brueggemann has said, "These introductory chapters in the book of Deuteronomy are a mixture of speech by Moses and *narrative* memory."[21] Moses reviews the history of the Israelites from their departure from Horeb to the very moment where they stand on the cusp of entry into the land. That the history departs in some instances from the accounts found in Exodus and Number matters little. What the narration accomplishes is to present in a more thoroughgoing way the story that is to enter into the collective memory of the people. Again, Brueggemann expresses this well:

> The narrative memory serves as a matrix out of which Moses may address Israel in a compelling and didactic way. From the *context of memory* the voice insists that Israel must ponder its past in order that in the present, it may be more fully, obediently, and responsibly the people of YHWH. The intention of the retrospect is to make cogent and palpable Israel's distinct identity in the present, an identity rooted in loyalty to YHWH. (Italics in original.)[22]

That story reiterates the signal moments within the drama of the forty years that illustrate the doctrinal points identified above: the theological points made in the sermons, in the first-fruit liturgy, and in the song. At the same time, Moses' recitation is a model for the kind of instruction that will keep memory of the past alive and will ensure the transmission of doctrine from generation to generation. What does it mean to teach one's children the lessons of the past? Moses' demonstration is a guide.

More precisely scripted than the daily educational program is the command to answer one's children's questions about the law (Deut. 6:20-25). The instruction reinterprets the explanation for the observances associated with Passover in Exod. 13:14-15. In its earlier incarnation, however, it pertained to the cultic observance of the festival, in particular the dedication of the firstborn (*peṭer reḥem*). Deuteronomy, however, removes it from the cultic context and makes it, like the teaching commanded in 6:7 and 11:19, an ongoing obligation.[23]

21. Brueggemann, *Deuteronomy*, 25 (italics in original).

22. Ibid.

The integration of cognition and action that is so important to Deuteronomy makes Israel's acts of learning, performing, and transmitting knowledge as important as the knowledge itself. This perspective transforms both types of instruction into a form of religious practice. Teaching or learning—that is, speaking the narrative—one keeps the law, the history, and the obligation that both place on Israel as a covenanted people, continually in mind, at the service of loyal obedience.

Creedal Recitations

As Ricoeur contends, the role of formal, ceremonial recitation of canonic material, whether national lore or religious doctrine, can be a vital tool for encoding official traditions.[24] Verbalizing a narrative, the speaker takes ownership of it. Or as Gabrielle Spiegel, commenting on medieval Jewish liturgy, explains:

> In liturgical commemoration, as in poetic oral recitation, the fundamental goal is, precisely, to revivify the past and make it live in the present, to fuse past and present, chanter and hearer, priest and observer, into a single collective entity. The written text, when it represents a transcription of a once-lived recital, commemorates both the past which is sung *about* and the performance itself (italics in original).[25]

In consequence, the official memory and theology encoded in the recitation become integrated into the speaker's memory. The creedal recitations prescribed in Deuteronomy likewise serve to sustain codified versions of the past that in turn inculcate and reinforce authoritative values and doctrine. Articulating formalized creedal histories, the worshiper internalizes the national memory and makes it his or her own.

23. Weinfeld, *Deuteronomy and the Deuteronomic School*, 34–35. See Chapter 7 on the Holiness tradition's reinterpretation of Exod. 13:16.

24. See the discussion above in Chapter 3.

25. Gabrielle M. Spiegel, "Memory and History: Liturgical Time and Historical Time," *History and Theory* 41 (2002): 152. See as well the discussion of "formative" and "normative" text and rites as instruments of collective memory formation and maintenance in Jan Assmann, *Religion and Cultural Memory: Ten Studies*, trans. R. Livingstone (Stanford: Stanford University Press, 2006), 37–41; cf. the discussion above, p. 52. Assmann contends that through "formative" and "normative" rites and texts, "cultural memory disseminates and reproduces a consciousness of unity, particularity, and a sense of belonging among the members of a group" (ibid., 38).

Recitation should be distinguished from prayer, in that it is both codified and collective. Deuteronomy does not address personal or spontaneous prayer. This does not mean it had no place in deuteronomic religion. Surely for individuals removed from the center of cultic activity, prayer would be a meaningful personal act of fidelity, gratitude, or lament. And as Moshe Greenberg has shown in his short book on the topic, biblical narrative, including narrative in the Deuteronomic History, provides examples of personal prayer.[26] Furthermore, the variety of genres represented in Psalms may support the view that individuals made use of formal texts to express personal petitions or statements of praise.[27] Nevertheless, Deuteronomy is not concerned with formalizing this element of religious practice. Its concern lies with individual participation in the collective covenant and the collective religious program that supports it.

The Presentation of First Fruits (Deut. 26:1-11)

The annual[28] declaration made upon presenting the first fruits of the land is one of the clearest examples of liturgy in the Pentateuch.[29] *Bikkûrîm* ("first fruits") is probably a very ancient practice, but in its deuteronomic incarnation, it is the model for all rituals.[30] Both word and action are scripted and choreographed.

26. Moshe Greenberg, *Biblical Prose Prayer as a Window into the Popular Religion of Israel* (Berkeley: University of California Press, 1983), 7–18, 31–37, 51–52.

27. Ibid., 45.

28. Peter C. Craigie maintains that both this ceremony and the declaration made in connection with the third-year tithe are one-time rituals, the former observed upon settlement in the land and the latter two years later. "The view that 26:1-15 deals with two particular ceremonies, each to be held once only on particular occasions, is implied not only by the wording and the locations of the passage at the end of specific stipulations, but also by the fact that the general legislation relating to the normal celebration of both ceremonies has been mentioned earlier in the discourse on the law" (*The Book of Deuteronomy* NICOT [Grand Rapids: Eerdmans, 1976], 319). He also contends that while the first-fruits ceremony takes place at the central shrine, the tithe ceremony is domestic (ibid., 322). Although Craigie bases his argument in the temporal specificity of the language ("When you enter the land . . ." "you take possession of it") (his translations), I believe he misses the point of the ritual as a mechanism for transcending generational experience. By reciting the liturgy, everyone who participates in this ceremony—whenever they do so—internalizes the history and identifies with it.

29. According to Gerhard von Rad, the ceremony has a very ancient provenance as a "cultic occasion for the recital by the individual of this short confessional statement of God's redemptive activity" (*The Problem of the Hexateuch and Other Essays*, trans. E. W. Dicken [Edinburgh and London: Oliver & Boyd, 1965], 5). See also his *Old Testament Theology*, 2 vols. (New York: Harper and Row, 1963), 1:121–28.

30. The preexilic law recorded in Numbers 28 agrees with Deuteronomy 26 in linking *bikkûrîm* and the Festival of Weeks. In contrast, the postexilic Holiness Code version in Lev. 23:9-22 describes them as two occasions, separated by seven weeks. According to Lev. 23:10, one makes a barley offering when the

The ritual takes place at the central shrine to which the worshiper brings a basket containing the earliest of "all the produce of the earth which you bring forth from your land which Yahweh your God is giving you" (Deut. 26:2). The worshiper presents it to the priest with the formal declaration: "I declare today to Yahweh your God that I have come to the land Yahweh promised our ancestors to give to us" (Deut. 26:3), a statement that attests to God's fidelity to God's word (cf. Deut. 6:10) and identifies the worshiper with the first generation to enter the land. The priest waves the presentation as an offering before the altar, and the worshiper continues:

> An Aramean who wandered was my father,[31] and he went down to Egypt and dwelled there for a short time. He became there a great nation, strong and mighty. But the Egyptians dealt badly with us and they afflicted us and they imposed hard labor on us. We cried out to Yahweh the God of our fathers and Yahweh heard our voices. He saw our affliction and our burdensome labor[32] and our oppression. Yahweh took us from Egypt with a strong hand and an outstretched arm and with great sights and with signs and with wonders. He brought us to this place and he gave us this land, a land flowing with milk and honey. Now, behold, I am bringing the first fruits of the land which Yahweh gave to me. (Deut. 26:5–10a)

The heart of the recitation is an abridged version of the national history: the worshiper's ancestors went to Egypt where, in fulfillment of the promise made to them (cf. Gen. 12:2; 15:5), they grew into a mighty people. When enslaved,

grain first appears (*wahăbēʾtem ʾet-ʿōmer rēʾšît qᵉṣîrᵉkem ʾel-hakkōhēn*), presumably during *Nissan* in order to permit nonsacral consumption of new produce. Seven weeks later, one makes a second offering in connection to the pilgrimage Festival of Weeks.

31. There is a considerable variety in the translations of this phrase, which itself has attracted a considerable body of scholarship. Arnold B. Ehrlich prefers "wandering" (*Mikrâ ki-Pheshutô*, 3 vols. [repr., with Prolegomenon by H. M. Orlinsky; New York: Ktav, 1969], 1:360); Anthony Phillips uses "homeless" (*Deuteronomy* [London: Cambridge University Press, 1973], 172); Craigie proposes "ailing" (*The Book of Deuteronomy*, 321); Alan R. Millard suggests "the nuance of 'refugee'" ("A Wandering Aramean," *JNES* 39 [1980]: 155); and J. Gerald Janzen argues for "starving" ("The 'Wandering Aramean' Reconsidered," *VT* 44 [1994]: 374). Akkadian *abātu* B ("to flee" or "to run away") may be a cognate. See *CAD*/A 1:45a–47a.

32. The noun *ʿāmāl* is often translated as "oppression." *HALOT* (2:845) lists "trouble" as its first meaning, and ascribes the meaning to its occurrence in Deut. 26:7. However, in verbal constructions, the root *ʿml* conveys the sense of labor and exertion (ibid.). In the present context, I believe the noun refers to the burden resulting from the hard labor and ill-treatment imposed by the Egyptians.

the people cried out to God, God heard and saw them (cf. Exod. 2:23–25)[33] and, the creed continues in characteristically deuteronomic language, delivered them with "a strong hand and outstretched arm and with great sights, and with signs and with wonders." A gesture of reciprocity closes the recital. God "brought us" (*wayᵉbīʾēnû*) to "this place" and "gave us" (*wayyitten-lānû*) the fertile land; the worshiper now brings (*hēbēʾtî*) the fruit of the land "that God gave me" (*ʾăšer-nātattâ lî*) (Deut. 26:9–10).

The shifting pronouns dramatize the process by which this history is internalized. The speaker at first refers to "my father" with the third person masculine singular: "he went down . . . he became . . . great." Next, he becomes part of the collective people: "the Egyptians dealt badly with us . . . afflicted us . . . imposed hard labor on us . . . we cried out . . . our fathers . . . our voices . . . our affliction and our burdensome labor and our oppression. Yahweh took us . . . brought us . . . gave us . . ." Finally, as he closes the recitation, he moves to the first person singular: "Now, behold, I am bringing . . . ," and the process of internalization is complete.

Furthermore, as J. Gerald Janzen observes, the contrast between the occasion for the declaration (celebrating agricultural success in the land) and the conditions recalled in the history (stateless and precarious "wandering") provides "thematic congruence" to the ritual.[34] This intensifies its didactic power, for it causes the speaker to appreciate how great is the debt to God. At the same time, the act of verbalizing the history of God's providential care militates against the predictable tendency to forget, so often invoked in Deuteronomy. Deuteronomy 8:11–17 in particular warns against willful amnesia that leads not just to ingratitude, but to hubristic satisfaction in one's own achievements:

> Guard yourself lest you forget Yahweh your God . . . lest you eat and are satisfied and you build good homes and dwell [in them] and your cattle and your flock increase, and silver and gold multiply for you, and everything you have increases, and your heart becomes haughty and you forget Yahweh your God who took you from the land of Egypt, from the house of bondage; who led you through the great

33. Deuteronomy both attributes more agency to Israel and more constancy to God than does the priestly version of the start of the exodus story. According to Exod. 2:23–24, the people do not cry out explicitly to God. Rather their undirected cry "went up" to God who then hears it.

34. Janzen finds "thematic congruence" in evidence as well in the covenant reaffirmation ritual of Josh. 24:2–24, where the declaration of loyalty to Yahweh in the present (24:24) contrasts with the idolatrous worship of the ancestors in the distant past (24:2) ("The 'Wandering Aramean' Reconsidered," 374).

> and terrible wilderness . . . and you say to yourself, "My power and the strength of my hand achieved this wealth for me."

The recitation returns the credit for success to God, while prompting the worshiper to "remember Yahweh your God, that [it is] he who gives you the power to achieve wealth in order to keep his covenant that was sworn to your ancestors, as is the case today" (Deut. 8:18).

The absence of Sinai/Horeb from this recital, noted in all the commentaries, is perhaps surprising, but can be understood in light of its central themes of land and gratitude, which serve as the thematic fulcrum for the theological tenets rehearsed in the creed:[35] deliverance from Egypt as the basis for Israel's obligation to God; the land as a gift from God; success in the land as a manifestation of God's beneficence.

Not only does the ritual keep the worshiper mindful of doctrine, its textual presentation, and in particular the use of key words and phrases, also helps to inculcate the text's audience in these tenets. The repeated use of *nātan* ("to give"); *bw'* ("to come") or *hēbî'* ("to bring"); and *'ereṣ* ("land") or *'ădāmâ* ("earth") in the recited liturgical text and the directional material framing it reinforce the central message that the land is a gift from God, and its bestowal a demonstration of God's fidelity to the promise to the ancestors. The verb *nātan* occurs seven times in the pericope (vv. 1, 2, 3, 6, 9, 10, 11), all but one of them (v. 6) describing God's giving the land. In verses 1, 2, 9, and 10, the text repeats the ideas of "coming/bringing to the land," "bringing" to the shrine, "bringing" forth from the earth.

At the end of the pericope, the text echoes the worshiper's description of the land as a land "flowing with milk and honey." The land is part of "all the good" that God has given, and for this the audience, like the worshiper, should rejoice.

The recitation is the central feature of the ritual of the first fruits, but the choreography also supports doctrinal objectives. Its setting reinforces not only

35. The tradition-history explanation for this omission is that this declaration reflects a wilderness tradition originally separate from the Sinai tradition. See Martin Noth, *A History of Pentateuchal Traditions*, trans. B. W. Anderson (Englewood Cliffs, NJ: Prentice-Hall, 1972), 51–54, 59–62, and von Rad, *The Problem of the Hexateuch*, 3–8, 13–20, 54–57. Von Rad calls the ritual a creed and identifies it as one of the earliest passages in Deuteronomy (ibid., 55–56). Weinfeld calls it a prayer of thanksgiving and sees it as a signature example of the deuteronomic "liturgical oration" (*Deuteronomy and the Deuteronomic School*, 33). In fact, excepting Nehemiah 9, the Sinai/Horeb tradition is absent from all the historical recitations found outside the Pentateuch (e.g., Psalms 78, 105, 106, 135, 136). Possibly its absence is due to thematic reasons. The historical recitations emphasize the theme of deliverance, while Sinai/Horeb pertains to the covenant.

the policy of centralization but the theological reason behind it. The ritual begins when the worshiper brings the offering to "the place that Yahweh has chosen . . ." (Deut. 26:2).[36] It concludes with the worshiper celebrating by sharing the bounty "which Yahweh your God has given to you and to your household," with the Levite and the stranger (Deut. 26:11).

The Third-Year Tithe (Deut. 26:12-15)

According to Deut. 14:28 and 26:12-15, every third year, each Israelite is required to donate a tenth of his produce to the Levite, stranger, orphan, and widow, the groups that Deuteronomy recognizes as disenfranchised and dependent.[37] The stipulation in Deuteronomy 14 comes in the context of general instructions for bestowal of the tithes. In years other than the third, the tithe is to be consumed in the premises of the central shrine (14:23). In the third year, it is to be left "in your gates" for the same disenfranchised group to consume there (14:28-29). Deuteronomy 26:13 adds the stipulation that after leaving the third-year tithe at home, one must formally attest to having fulfilled this obligation, "before Yahweh your God," as follows:[38]

> I have removed the consecrated [grain?] from the house, and as well, I have given it to the Levite, the stranger, the orphan and the widow according to all your commandments which you have commanded me. I have not transgressed your commandments, nor have I forgotten [them]. I have not eaten from it while in mourning,[39] and I have not removed it while unclean, nor have I given it to the dead. I have heeded the voice of Yahweh my God; I have done all that you have commanded me. Look down from your

36. Thomas W. Mann attaches importance to the dramatic aspect of the ritual, which he characterizes as a reenactment of the original entry into the land. He writes, "The declaration 'I have come into the land' (26:3) is thus an autobiographical fiction played out within the drama of worship. The ritual is literally a rite of passage that celebrates coming into the promised land. But entrance into the land is only part of Israel's grand central story, and remembering this part alone is necessary, but not sufficient for complete Israelite identity. Therefore, the worshiper is required to recite the entire story, beginning with Jacob. . . ." Mann, *Deuteronomy*, WestBC (Louisville: Westminster John Knox, 1995), 139.

37. Tithing is addressed in three other places as well: Lev. 27:30-33 and Num. 18:21-29, which deal with tithing for the benefit of the Levites, and Deut. 12:17-19, which alludes to the tithing laws of Deuteronomy 14.

38. Craigie, I believe, is mistaken in maintaining that the declaration is not made at the central shrine as is the declaration accompanying the first fruits ceremony. *The Book of Deuteronomy*, 322–23.

39. *B^{e}'ōnî*: On the meaning of this expression, see Theodore J. Lewis, *Cults of the Dead in Ancient Israel and Ugarit*, Harvard Semitic Monographs 39 (Atlanta: Scholars, 1989), 103.

holy dwelling place from the heavens and bless your people, Israel, and the land that you gave us as you swore to our ancestors, a land flowing with milk and honey. (Deut 26:13-15)

There is some debate over the origin of this ritual.[40] The oath in verse 14 with its concern for ritual propriety is widely considered to be pre-deuteronomic. But the material that frames it (vv. 13 and 15) is deuteronomic additions in which the speaker affirms the theological tenets appropriate to the paying of tithes: the gift of land; care for the indigent and powerless who are the beneficiary of the tithes; and especially, the promise of blessing as reward for providing such care.[41]

The allusion to dead ancestors in verse 14 makes the latter affirmation all the more emphatic. As Theodore Lewis has demonstrated, cults of the dead in the ancient Near East were "directed toward the deceased functioning either to placate the dead or to secure favors from them for the present life."[42] Providing dead ancestors with offerings was a central feature of such cults.[43] On the basis of selected prohibitions in Deuteronomy (self-laceration [Deut. 14:1], consulting spirits of the dead [Deut. 18:11]), and narrative passages in deuteronomic literature (the witch of Endor [1 Sam. 28:3-25], David's rites over his dying child [2 Sam. 12:15-24], and Absalom's monument [2 Sam. 18:18]), Lewis suggests that cults of the dead had "a lasting appeal in certain forms of 'popular religion'" in Israel.[44] In contrast, the worshiper in Deut. 26:13-15 piously repudiates any suggestion that he or she would participate in such

40. On the one hand, as Jeffrey Tigay points out, the law of the third-year tithe is found only in Deuteronomy. Tigay, *Deuteronomy*, The JPS Torah Commentary (Philadelphia: Jewish Publication Society, 1996), 242. Yet as Richard Nelson observes, both the concern for "ritual innocence" and "the verbal chain and partitive *min* prepositions" point to a pre-deuteronomic origin. Nelson, *Deuteronomy: A Commentary*, Old Testament Library (Louisville: Westminster John Knox, 2002), 310. Because Leviticus and Numbers do not address when nor how often tithes are to be given, they do not shed much light on the performance of this ritual. Weinfeld seems to accept a pre-deuteronomic ceremony that Deuteronomy has revised, but he is not explicit on this point. Weinfeld, *Deuteronomy and the Deuteronomic School*, 215–16.

41. The doctrine of centralized worship receives reinforcement from this ritual as well. Indeed because the *ritual* element, namely the declaration, must take place at the shrine ("before Yahweh your God"), and the donor must make a separate trip unconnected to the actual donation which is made at home according to Deut. 14:28-29, the central shrine is made all the more important.

42. Lewis, *Cults of the Dead*, 2.

43. Ibid., 38–39, 70, 97.

44. Ibid., 174.

idolatrous practices. Blessings, the worshiper maintains, come not from dead ancestors, but from God alone.

The worshiper may also be affirming the proper use of memory. Another feature of cults of the dead is invocation of the names of dead ancestors.[45] In his discussion of Absalom's monument, built because Absalom has no son to "invoke my name" (*hazkîr šᵉmî*), Lewis adduces a Ugaritic text from the Aqhat epic, known as "The Duties of the Ideal Son," and an Assyrian text (*CAD* E, 400a), which point to the importance of preserving the name of dead ancestors.

> This Ugaritic parallel suggests the possibility that Absalom's actions were in some way tied to a cult of the dead. This is made even more plausible when we look more closely at the duty which Absalom's "non-existent" son was to have performed, namely *hazkîr šĕmî*. . . . Compare . . . the following Assyrian text: *šumka itti eṭemmē azkur šumka itti kispī azkur*, "I have invoked your name with the spirits of the dead (of my family), I have invoked your name with the funerary offerings."[46]

Just as the relocation of the tithing ritual to the central shrine pulls religious practice away from local, kin-centered practices (hospitable to the worship of dead ancestors), the recitation redirects the worshiper's memory from dead ancestors to the God who will bestow blessings on the nation and the land.

One other feature of this ritual deserves attention. As pointed out in Chapter 3, the donor's twofold claim that he has neither transgressed nor forgotten the tithing laws establishes a semantic parallel in his mind that equates the ideas of transgression and forgetfulness, and therefore between obedience and memory. While making the brief declaration, the donor becomes aware of the intimate connection between memory and fidelity to covenantal obligations. On the one hand, the donor declares he that has rightly kept both. At the same time, he reminds himself of the role of memory in keeping him faithful to responsibility. The effect is somewhat circular, but nonetheless supportive of the deuteronomic agenda. Remembering to present the tithe and make the declaration, the speaker reminds himself of the crucial place of memory in his religious life.

45. Ibid., 32–33.
46. Ibid., 119.

Recitation of "This Torah" (Deut. 31:9–13)

Transmission of the law occurs in two ways according to Deuteronomy. The primary and most essential way is through verbalized parental instruction discussed above. A second means of transmitting the law is the septennial reading of the law during the Festival of Booths. According to Deut. 31:9, Moses writes "this torah" (*hattôrâ hazzōʾt*), which he gives to the priests and elders with the instruction that every seven years it be read before the Israelites assembled at the central shrine.

> You shall assemble the people: the men and the women and the little children and your stranger who is within your gates so that they may hear and so that they will learn to revere Yahweh your God and they will be careful to do all the words in this torah. And their children who do not know will hear and will learn to revere Yahweh your God all the days that you live on the land that you are crossing the Jordan to possess. (Deut. 31:12–13)

In the intervening years, "this torah" is kept "alongside the Ark of the Covenant of Yahweh your God" (*miṣṣad ʾărôn bᵉrît-yhwh ʾĕlōhêkem*) (Deut. 31:26), which, according to Deut. 10:5, holds the two tablets of the law. The conjoined presence of the tablets of the law and the torah, which has just been written down, raises questions about the content of the latter. Context suggests the torah contains the text of the Law Code, but it is equally possible that as well it contains the theological doctrine that Moses taught as prologue to the code and, as proposed earlier, is also positioned as revelatory. In light of the thematic content of the recitations discussed thus far, the second solution seems reasonable. Like the recitations, Moses' instructions are a sustained argument for the pedagogical value of the past. Even though, as noted at the start of this chapter, Deuteronomy's presentation of the law is itself an opportunity for instruction, the concentration of asseverations and intellectual imperatives in the sermons makes their content especially memorable. The public reading of both the sermons and the law would provide a powerful instrument for the transmission of deuteronomic theology, the semantic basis for fulfillment of the law.

A particularly noteworthy feature of this commandment is its inclusiveness. Nowhere else in Deuteronomy are women and young children explicitly included in a ritual observance. Normative practice appears to be that one celebrates sharing the sacrificial offerings presented at the central shrine with one's sons, daughters, male and female servants, and the Levite (Deut. 12:12,

18), and one celebrates the pilgrimage festivals with these groups as well as with the stranger, the orphan, and the widow (Deut. 16:11, 14). It is not clear that wives automatically participate in the rituals that require travel to the central shrine, possibly because of the need to remain at home with very young children, as indeed Hannah does in 1 Sam. 1:22.[47] But in the seventh year, even mothers with infants assemble to hear "this torah" read. Familiarity with the law and mindfulness of the ideas and values embedded in it are crucial for the maintenance of the covenant. For the sake of this relationship, no Israelite can be ignorant of what God demands and what God deserves.

It is worth pointing out that reading the torah, albeit only once every seven years, is the only stipulated observance associated with the celebration of the Festival of Booths in Deuteronomy. The instructions concerning the festival in Deut. 16:13–15 say only that one must "rejoice" (*wᵉśāmaḥtā*) with one's sons and daughters, with the Levite and the stranger. It seems, therefore, that from the perspective of Deuteronomy 31, the festival (at least in the seventh year) exists principally as another opportunity to absorb anew the instruction that one is to think about and act upon constantly.

The Problem of Passover (Deut. 16:1–8)

Alone among the three pilgrimage festivals, Passover has no liturgical recitation associated with it, a surprising omission in light of the explicit acknowledgment in Deut. 16:3 of the powerful commemorative and mnemonic function of the festival. Its evocative power was understood as well by Hezekiah and Josiah, each of whom appreciated the propagandistic value of Passover as a basis for solidifying national unity. Most striking of all, earlier Passover traditions include a liturgical element. Exodus 13:8 instructs, "You will tell your son on that day, saying because of this [which] Yahweh did for me when I went out of Egypt," while Exodus 13:14–15 describes a didactic conversation between father and son:

> And when in the future your son asks you saying, "what is this?" you shall say to him, "With a strong arm Yahweh took us from Egypt,

47. The word *ṭap*, "little child," occurs seven times in Deuteronomy (1:39; 2:34; 3:19; 20:14; 29:10; 31:12) and in all but 1:39, in the phrase "women and children" (or "children and women" in 29:10). On the other hand, when Deuteronomy refers to "your sons and/or daughters" (*binkā/bittekā*), "women" do not occur as a category along with them. In other words, *ṭap* appears to denote an infant or very young child still attached to, and in the constant care of, its mother. By including infants in connection with this practice, Deuteronomy emphasizes that even mothers of young children must attend the hearing of the law. (This was suggested to me by Susan Ackerman in private conversation.)

> from the house of bondage. For he made it difficult for Pharaoh to send us out and Yahweh killed all the first-born in the land of Egypt. . . . Therefore I am sacrificing to Yahweh all the first-delivered males of the womb, and all the first-born of my sons, I am redeeming.

The deuteronomic version of Passover calls for no verbal instruction. Instead, it is the act of eating unleavened bread with the Passover offering and in haste that is meant to prompt recollection (*lᵉmaʿan tizkōr*) (16:3) of the exodus from Egypt.[48]

Recourse to symbolic behavior to stimulate memory is hardly typical in deuteronomic literature. In fact it is only here and in the ritual for the unsolved murder that Deuteronomy incorporates symbolic behavior into a ritual. This then raises two questions. Why rely on the act of eating to educate? Why no formal declaration?

Most commentators explain the deuteronomic Passover in terms of the tradition's centralization polemic. Deuteronomy's reworking of Passover merges it completely with the pilgrimage Festival of Unleavened Bread and transforms a formerly domestic rite into a communal festival at the central shrine. The threefold insistence that the festival take place "in the place that Yahweh has chosen to have his name dwell in" (16:2, 6; cf. 7) plus the explicit prohibition *against* sacrificing the Passover offering "in one of your gates" (16:5) is strong evidence that centralization is the main principle to be derived from Passover, and that it is best derived by the actual relocation of the sacrifice to the central shrine. Another possibility is that the authors of Deuteronomy sought to shake the cultic overlay to Passover given to it in Exodus. In Exodus, Passover is intimately linked to two cultic practices. The original Passover of Exodus 12 involves the apotropaic smearing of blood on the doorposts while the Passover of Exodus 13 includes dedication of the *peṭer reḥem* ("first issue"), a priestly term

48. In Brueggemann's opinion this is enough: "The purpose of the bread—eaten *without rising, in haste, at night*—is to replicate the ominous moment of escape from Egypt and the glorious emancipation that resulted on that night that is like no other night. As much as is imaginable in Israel, the purpose of the festival is to replicate the experience and the emotional intensity of the original Exodus emancipation" (Brueggemann, *Deuteronomy*, 174; italics in original). I differ on two counts. First, Deuteronomy does not seek to replicate the night of the exodus. Instead of mandating that unleavened bread be eaten "*without rising, in haste, at night*," the direction is to eat it "for seven days" along with the Passover sacrifice. The ritual that replicates the exodus is the one prescribed in Exod. 12:11. The deuteronomic version makes a clumsy association with the experience of the exodus by conflating two different features of the bread. It is "bread of affliction," eaten "because in haste you went out. . . ." Second, if Brueggemann is correct, Passover would represent the only deuteronomic ritual that attempts to replicate experience and emotion. Everywhere else, ritual appeals to the thinking mind.

for the firstborn whether animal or human. The practice is mentioned as well in Num. 18:15-17. The liturgy found in the Exodus versions of Passover is, therefore, a cultic liturgy. Although the brief statement prescribed in Exod. 13:8 is innocuous enough (it is not even clear what is meant by the deictic "this" [*hazze*]), the lengthier response to the child's question in 13:14-15 is entirely about *peṭer reḥem*. The first issue must be dedicated to God in repayment for having been spared when God killed the firstborn of Egypt.[49] Deuteronomy knows of dedication of first-issue to God (Deut. 15:19-23), but it in no way attaches the practice to the terrifying aspects of the exodus story, nor would it. Such a story is foreign to Deuteronomy's picture of deliverance from the affliction of servitude in Egypt (hence "bread of affliction" eaten "in haste") by an all-powerful, transcendent deity.

Milgrom's explanation of the requirement to return home on the morning after the sacrifice at the central shrine has been made (Deut. 16:7) suggests another solution. Milgrom proposes that this requirement reflects the exigencies of an agricultural calendar wherein labor cannot be spared from the fields. The farmer was required to leave his fields to make a pilgrimage for the day of the sacrifice, but the rest of his household would remain at home to work, and he, too, would return home as soon as possible. If this scenario is correct, it would mean that most of the household would not be in a position to recite or hear recited whatever canonical liturgy would have been prescribed. The absence of an occasion for communal recitation would then necessitate Deuteronomy's anomalous recourse to the symbolic act of eating unleavened bread in haste as the means of prompting memory.[50]

It is interesting to note that in connection with Passover, Deuteronomy does not use the "remember . . . therefore" formula it typically employs to assert the logical relationship between memory and a commanded act and hence, the power of memory to spur fulfillment of the commandment.[51] In the case of

49. Exodus 13:8 is a Holiness text (see Chapter 7) and antedates D. Exodus 13:14-15 (and 16) is P.

50. Milgrom, *Leviticus*, 3 vols., AB 3–3B (New York: Doubleday, 1991–2001), 3:1980–81. Bernard Levinson, however, explains the requirement to return home in terms of the authors' strategy in transforming the locally observed Passover into a pilgrimage. Having transformed, in Deut. 16:2, the locally observed rite of the slaughtered animal into a *zebaḥ*, i.e., consecrated meat or a "sacrifice" (*tizbaḥ ʾet-happesaḥ*) performed at the central shrine, the authors of Deuteronomy transformed the Festival into a "neutered local observance. . . . So forcibly does the new Passover usurp that original identity of Unleavened Bread that the pilgrim who paradoxically *goes to the Temple for the Passover offering* must immediately make a pilgrimage *away* from the sanctuary in order to return home to celebrate Unleavened Bread." Levinson, *Deuteronomy and the Hermeneutics of Legal Innovation*, 75, 89 (italics in original).

51. See Chapter 3, p. 60.

Passover, the movement between memory and action is reversed. The Israelites are instructed to eat the Passover sacrifice as required, with unleavened bread so that they will remember their departure from Egypt:

> For seven days eat unleavened bread with it—bread of affliction—for in haste you went out of the land of Egypt, so that you remember the day of your going out of the land of Egypt all the days of your life. (Deut. 16:3)

The ritual act may be meant to trigger memory, but the relationship between the act and what is to be recalled is crudely contrived. The Israelites are to remember the hasty departure from Egypt; the action to stimulate memory is to eat unleavened bread. How are these two related? One would expect Deuteronomy to cite the exegetical link provided in Exod. 12:39: "because they were driven from Egypt and they could not linger and as well, they had not made any food provisions. . . ." Instead it juxtaposes two indifferently related explanations. One eats *maṣṣôt* because unleavened bread is "bread of affliction"; one eats it because the Israelites were "in haste." The justification of the ritual seems almost gratuitous.[52] The practice itself cannot be ignored, but the author of Deuteronomy 16 does not believe that mere reenactment of an element of the flight from Egypt can transmit understanding of its theological and covenantal implications. Indeed, at the end of the passage on Passover laws, the text falls back on the tried-and-true justification for commandments: "Remember you were slaves in Egypt. Be careful to observe these laws" (Deut. 16:12).

Moses' Song (Deut. 31:19—32:47)

Nowhere does Deuteronomy assert the didactic role of memory in ritual as intensively as in 31:19-21, in the command to Moses to write down the words of a song and teach it to the Israelites. Deuteronomy 31 reports that Moses is instructed to write out the text of the song, "teach it to the Israelites and place it in their mouths" (v. 19b) so that in the future, when they experience "great evils and troubles," the song will remind them why they deserve their condition: "And when they encounter great evils and troubles, this song will answer them [and be] a witness before them" (31:21). "Do not forget!" God interjects midway though this instruction as if to acknowledge the certainty that the Israelites *will* forget their past. When they do, the song will dredge up past experiences and force the people to remember the deliverance and care

52. Compare Lev. 23:43 and the explanation for living in booths during Sukkoth.

they received from God's hands, the covenantal obligations they accepted in the plains of Moab, and their own wayward nature that undermines the endurance of the covenant.

The provenance of Deuteronomy 32 is uncertain, but it most certainly had a *Sitz im Leben* outside of Deuteronomy. In a seminal article on the subject, Ernest Wright classified Deuteronomy 32 as a classic prophetic *rîb* or lawsuit, similar to Isaiah 1 (with which it shares several features, including the appeal to heaven and earth at the song's start).[53] Matthew Thiessen offers a convincing critique of Wright, out of which he concludes that Deuteronomy 32 is best understood as "a hymn with an embedded *rîb*."[54] Thiessen identifies three features in the song that evince a liturgical function: the multiple shifts in person; changes in speaker; and the frequent use of imperatives. Together, he maintains, these imply that the song was to be performed.[55] With the *rîb* contained within it, the song replicates the prophetic message, substituting a single fixed example in place of live, spontaneous prophetic speech. But even as it resembles the prophetic genre, ultimately in its deuteronomic context, the primary function of the song is pedagogic.[56] The song is meant to testify to God's fidelity and Israel's waywardness at such time in the future when, inevitably, Israel will have failed in its covenantal obligations and will face God's righteous and punitive anger. It is a "witness," but a witness that Israel itself will produce because the song is to be placed in their mouths. Memorizing a canonic version of the prophetic rebuke, the Israelites will internalize its message by performing it. They will have embedded knowledge of their covenantal obligations and will not be able to excuse themselves on the basis of forgetfulness. In fact the song has multiple functions. It will prove the legitimacy of whatever punishment God sends to Israel, and it will keep alive in the minds of the people all that Moses has taught, warned, and exhorted in his lengthy valedictory addresses.[57] Further, as I will demonstrate, the first half of the song (vv. 1-26) rehearses, in nearly the same sequence, the major themes in

53. G. Ernest Wright, "The Lawsuit of God: A Form-Critical Study of Deuteronomy 32," in *Israel's Prophetic Heritage: Essays in Honor of James Muilenburg*, ed. B. W. Anderson and W. Harrelson (New York: Harper & Brothers, 1962), 26–67.

54. Matthew Thiessen, "The Form and Function of the Song of Moses (Deuteronomy 32:1-43)," *JBL* 123 (2004): 407.

55. Ibid., 407–10.

56. Wright, as Theissen acknowledges, recognized the pedagogical function of the song. "This conclusion is not altogether different from Wright's own argument. The difference is one primarily of emphasis. Wright, and those who base their work on his essay, stress the idea of the *rîb*. Wright's statement that this lawsuit is merely an 'instructional device,' rightly points in another direction—to the subversion of this form to the purposes of hymnic form." Thiessen, "Form and Function," 421.

the Mosaic addresses: the singularity of God; the original and ongoing grounds for the covenant; the wilderness journey as a period of covenantal education; the propensity of the people to ignore or forget their obligations; and the consequences of disobedience. It provides a ritualized medium through which to retain and transmit Deuteronomy's doctrinal messages.

Numerous studies attest to the power of song to aid the retention of information.[58] A signature model is the Hindu *Vedas*, which were transmitted accurately orally for three millennia or more.[59] Albert Bates Lord's important work on the transmission of oral tradition also demonstrates that certain features of poetry (and song) facilitate their being remembered. In particular meter, rhythm, and syntax combine to impress the lyrics of song on the mind:[60]

> If one looks in detail, as I have done . . . one finds that something other than conscious memorization has been taking place. An analysis of the syntactic, acoustic, and metric, or rhythmic structures of the individual groups of lines, couplets, triplets, and so forth, shows that they are easily remembered. They are memorable, and they are frequently repeated. Singers have not memorized them; they have remembered them.[61]

Even though the torah deposited next to the Ark of the Covenant is to be read every seven years, and even though like the song it is called a "witness," the

57. Mark Leuchter, "Why Is the Song of Moses in the Book of Deuteronomy?" *VT* 57 (2007): 295–317.

58. See, for instance, M. D. Schulkind, "Is Memory for Music Special?" *Annals of the New York Academy of Sciences* 1169 (2009): 216–24; Timothy Powhida, "Classroom Songs: Aiding in the Retention and Recall of Test Material with Fourth Grade Students" (Masters' Thesis, SUNY, Potsdam, 2008; http://hdl.handle.net/1951/43066); Sidney Mayfield Hahn, "The Effect of Music in the Learning and Retention of Lexical Items in German" (http://eric.ed.gov/PDFS/ED119455.pdf); and Suzanne L. Medina, "The Effects of Music upon Second Languages Vocabulary Acquisition" (School of Education, California State University; Educational Resources Information Center database; ERIC Document #ED, 352–834).

59. See William Albert Graham, *Beyond the Written Word: Oral Aspects of Scripture in the History of Religion* (Cambridge: Cambridge University Press, 1993), 69–75.

60. I have not attempted to provide a thoroughgoing poetic analysis of the song in this work. For the present purposes I maintain only that Deuteronomy, by introducing a *song* as a vehicle for communicating doctrine, exploits the pedagogical and retention-aiding properties of song and poetry to impress ideas on the mind. How the particular elements of meter, assonance, and other poetic qualities might factor into this process must be the subject of a separate study.

61. Albert Bates Lord, *Epic Singers and Oral Tradition* (Ithaca, NY: Cornell University Press, 1991), 237.

two are not redundant.[62] The song appeals to different cognitive faculties than does the public reading of the law. Its poetic format makes the song especially effective in inscribing its content on the minds of the people where it remains remembered.

As most commentators observe, the song, for all its lack of true historical particularity, seems to provide "a kind of condensed history of Israel."[63] But more than that, it restates the history as understood in the hortatory frame with which Deuteronomy surrounds the law code, with the same emphases and the same consequences. Specifically, it rehearses themes found in the Mosaic sermons in Deuteronomy 4, 6, 8, 9, and 11 as well as the curses of Deut. 28:15-68 set forth to warn the people of the consequences of disloyalty, and it makes use of language and metaphors particularly evocative of those prose passages.

Not every theological idea in the song corresponds to deuteronomic theology. For instance, the graphic birth imagery in verse 18 and the reference to the "demi-gods" in verse 8 (if 4QDeut[j] and the LXX versions are accepted as primary) are foreign to Deuteronomy.[64] In addition, the provision for reconciliation with God in the second half of the song (i.e., 32:27-43) has no parallel in Deuteronomy except for Deuteronomy 30, which is an exilic addition.[65]

62. A source-critical explanation for the two mnemonic "witnesses" would attribute Deut. 31:19-23 and 32:24-26 to separate sources. While that may be correct, because the written (and publicly read) law and the written (and continually sung) song appeal to different cognitive faculties, the presence of both can be justified in terms of Deuteronomy's objective of ensuring the retention of its doctrine.

63. Harold Fisch, *Poetry with a Purpose: Biblical Poetics and Interpretation*, Indiana Studies in Biblical Literature (Bloomington: Indiana University Press, 1988), 56. "It will . . . act as a mnemonic, an aid to memory, because during the intervening period it will have lived unforgotten in the mouth of the reader or hearer, ready to come to mind when the troubles arrive. Poetry is thus a kind of time bomb; it awaits the hour and then springs forward into harsh remembrance. . . . It will live in their minds and mouths, bringing them back whether they like it or not, to the harsh memory of the desert sojourn. Once learned it will not be easily forgotten. The words will stick, they will be importunate, they will not let us alone." Ibid., 51.

64. Most scholars agree that the MT appears to have revised an earlier version preserved in 4QDeut[j]. The LXX and 4QDeut[j] have ἀγγέλων θεοῦ ("angels of God") and *bny 'lhm* ("divine beings") respectively for *b[e]nê 'ādām*. On the possible MT revision, see, for example, Michael S. Heiser, "Deuteronomy 32:8 and the Sons of God," *BSac* 158 (2001): 52–74; Patrick W. Skehan, "A Fragment of the 'Song of Moses' (Deut. 32) from Qumran," *BASOR* 136 (1954): 12; and Tigay, *Deuteronomy*, 513–15. On the other hand, the Samaritan Pentateuch, Aquila, Symmachus, Theodotion, Vulgate, *Tg. Onq.*, *Tg. Neof.*, and *Tg. Ps.-J.* agree with the MT. See *BHQ*, *Deuteronomy*, ad loc.

65. In some respects, the theology expressed in the second half of the song is more reminiscent of First and Second Isaiah than Deuteronomy. The plan to punish the hubris of Israel's enemies in order to

The hymnic prologue (vv. 1-3) introduces three ideas central to deuteronomic theology: the conceptualization of God in terms of God's Name; the contrast between God's constancy and Israel's predisposition to stray; and the importance of verbalized instruction. Much like the start of Moses' perorations in Deut. 4:1a, 5:1b, and 6:4, the song begins with a summons to attention: "Give ear O heavens that I may speak; Listen O earth to the words of my mouth" (32:1). The song addresses heaven and the earth, presenting itself as a testament before these witnesses. Nevertheless, the line that immediately follows positions the song as a source of sagacious teaching *for Israel*:

> Let my teaching drip like rain; my words trickle like dew. Like rain on new grass; and like spring rain on grasses. (32:2)

Instruction, rather than testimony, is now shown to be the song's object. The jussive appeal, "let my teaching . . . my words," revises the sense of the imperatives "give ear" and "listen," and directs them to Israel who is summoned to attend to the words of the song. It is for Israel that the teaching will be a source of wisdom as long as Israel remembers and heeds its lessons, just as Moses instructs in Deut. 4:1b. In the same way that rains keep the grasses alive, the lessons taught by the song will sustain Israel in the land of its inheritance. The thematic parallels can be observed below:

Deuteronomy 32	Deuteronomy
32:1 Give ear O heavens that I may speak; Listen O earth to the words of my mouth.	**4:1a** And now Israel, listen to the laws and the statutes which I am teaching you to do them . . .
	5:1b Hear O Israel the laws and statutes which I am speaking to your ears this day . . .
	6:4 Hear O Israel . . .

vindicate God's reputation in Deut. 32:27-35 recalls God's response to Assyria in Isaiah 10. The emphatic monotheistic claims in Deut. 32:39-43 are remarkably like similar claims in Isa. 44:6 and 45:5-8.

Deuteronomy 32	Deuteronomy
32:2 Let my teaching drip like rain; my words trickle like dew. Like rain on new grass; and like spring rain on grasses	**4:1b** So that you will live and come into and inherit the land that Yahweh the God of your ancestors is giving you.
	4:6 For [the laws and statutes] are your wisdom and your intelligence . . .

Because it will be internalized through repeated performance, the song will also testify that the Israelites are aware of the obligations imposed upon them by the covenant. The allusion to rain and spring rain is a clear reference to the covenant. As Geller points out and as Deuteronomy 11 makes explicit, "Rain is . . . the special gauge of Israel's obedience or disloyalty to covenant."[66]

The exhortation to praise "Yahweh's Name" at the end of the prologue is also reminiscent of deuteronomic thought. The song states: "For I declare Yahweh's Name; Let us exalt our God" (32:3). References to God's "name" saturate Deuteronomy, usually in connection with the central shrine where the name "dwells" (12:5, 11, 21; 14:23, 24; 16:2, 6, 11; 26:2) but also as a way to proclaim and exalt God (28:10a). In fact, although the context of Deut. 28:10a (the pronouncement of God's name as a sign of blessing) differs from that of 32:2 (praise from within the chosen community), the wording is almost exactly the same.

Elaborating on the theme of praise, the song employs the deuteronomic metaphor of God's law as a "way" or "path" (*derek*). To live according to God's law in Deuteronomy is to walk in God's way (5:33; 8:2, 6; 9:12; 10:12; 11:22, 28; 13:6; 19:9; 26:17; 28:9; 30:16; 31:29). The song declares: "Perfect are his deeds and all his ways (*dᵉrākâyw*) are just" (32:4). Israel, in contrast, is crooked and deals "corruptly" (*šiḥēt*) with him; they are "children unworthy of him. That crooked, perverse generation—their baseness has played him false"(*šiḥēt lô lōʾ bānâyw mûmām dôr ʿiqqēš ûpᵉtaltōl*)[67] (Deut. 32:5). In the Pentateuch, outside of Gen. 6:11-13 and Exod. 32:7, only Deuteronomy uses the word *šiḥēt* to signify moral corruption as almost a technical term for breaking the covenant[68]

66. Stephen A. Geller, "God, Humanity, and Nature in the Pentateuch," in *Gazing on the Deep: Ancient Near Eastern and Other Studies in Honor of Tzvi Abusch*, ed. J. Stackert, B. N. Porter, and D. P. Wright (Bethesda, MD: CDL, 2010), 445.

67. *Lô lōʾ* is probably the result of dittography. In any case the verse is exceedingly difficult to translate. I have used NJPS. JPS has, "Is corruption His? No; His children's is the blemish; A generation crooked and perverse." See the discussion in Tigay, *Deuteronomy*, 301.

or violating a law of nature. In Deut. 4:16 and 25 *šiḥēt* is associated with idolatry ("Be very careful . . . lest you act corruptly (*pen-tašḥitûn*) and make for yourselves a graven image . . .") (4:15–16); in Deut. 31:29, it is tied to turning from the "way" God has commanded. Even without reference to "corruption," Deuteronomy makes frequent reference to the theme of Israel's rebelliousness. In Deut. 9:24, Moses exclaims, "Rebels you have been against Yahweh as long as I have known you." Similar statements occur in Deut. 6:16 and 9:7. The song corroborates the charge.

Following the introduction, the song attests to God's many acts of kindness and to Israel's unique state as a "treasured" people. Here too thematic parallels with the deuteronomic sermons abound. Yahweh chose Israel as his own special treasure and assigned them a position unique among all the nations:

Deuteronomy 32	Deuteronomy
32:9 For his own people are Yahweh's portion; Jacob: his allotted territory.	**7:6** For you are a consecrated people to Yahweh your God. You, Yahweh your God chose to be his treasured people . . .

The song dwells especially on the wilderness period:

> [God] found them in a desert wilderness. In a vast emptiness, a howling wasteland, he surrounded them protectively, cared for them constantly. He guarded them like the pupil of his eye. (32:10)

Deuteronomy 8:2–4 relates that God fed and clothed the Israelites in the wilderness. It was there that Israel learned to recognize its total dependence on God and that the price for God's vigilant care is total obedience and loyalty to God. The song also recounts God's provisions of "honey from a rock" and "oil from a flinty rock," of milk and meat from lambs, rams, and goats, of fine wheat and "blood grape" for wine (32:13–14). God "suckled" (*wayyēniqēhû*) Israel like a mother (32:13), a metaphor that recalls Moses' description in Deut. 1:31 of God carrying the people in the wilderness "as a man carries his son" and God instructing them "as a man disciplines his son" (8:5).

Nevertheless, Israel failed to remain grateful:

68. In Genesis 6, *šiḥēt* implies breaking laws of nature. The usage in Exod. 32:7, in connection to the idolatrous worship of the golden calf, approximates Deuteronomy's usage.

> "But Yeshurun grew fat and kicked. You became fat, thick, coarse, and you ignored the God [who] made you; you spurned the Rock that saved you." (32:15)

The people's self-satisfied rejection of God beginning in Deut. 32:15 fulfills the prediction made by Moses in Deut. 8:11–17. There, as observed earlier, Moses warns of the danger of arrogance and hubris in the face of plenty.

> Guard yourself lest you forget . . . lest you eat and are satisfied and you build good homes and dwell [in them] and your cattle and flock increase, and silver and gold multiply for you, and everything you have increases, and your heart becomes haughty and you forget Yahweh your God who took you from the land of Egypt, from the house of bondage . . . and you say to yourself, "My power and the strength of my hand achieved this wealth for me."

Exactly as Moses warns, the Israelites of the song misbehave. The two visions are virtually identical. Well fed, well situated, the people lose sight of their dependence on God, ignore their obligation to God, and instead "sacrifice to demons [and] no-god, gods they never knew" (32:17).

The song provides a deuteronomic diagnosis for the moral perversity of the people. They are "a stupid people without wisdom" (32:6b). They have forgotten God: "You forgot the Rock which bore you and you forgot the God who labored you forth" (*ṣûr yᵉlādᵉkā tešî watiškaḥ ʾēl mᵉḥōlᵉlekā*) (32:18).[69] The judgment is deuteronomic, but the birthing metaphor is unusually graphic and anthropomorphic for Deuteronomy, and therefore intensely memorable. Significantly, the startling image is attached to the song's most pungent accusation. Forgetting is among the most serious lapses of all acts of rebellion recounted in the song, and Deut. 32:18 emphasizes its egregiousness by using two distinct verbs to denote forgetting. The contrast between the uncharacteristic imagery and the profoundly characteristic rebuke serves to shock the singer and listener into attention. For Deuteronomy, as this work has demonstrated, just as to remember God is necessary for the covenant's maintenance, forgetting God is tantamount to abrogating the covenant with God. But as the song reports in Deut. 32:17, not only does Israel forget God, it turns to "gods they did not know" (*ʾĕlōhîm lōʾ yᵉdāʿûm*). This expression, and its variant, "gods you do not know" occurs in Deut. 11:28, 13:3, 13:7, 13:14, and

69. Numbers 11:12 uses similar birth imagery when Moses complains to God: "Did I conceive all these people? Did I give birth to them?"

29:25 to denote the false deities that Israel foolishly worships and that, in God's eyes, are ("abominations" (*tôʿēbōt*).[70]

To express Israel's betrayal of God even more pungently, the song mimics the reciprocity of the covenantal relationship in Deuteronomy. The ideal version of this is expressed rhetorically in Deut. 26:17-18. There God and Israel declare their attachment to each other in parallel statements: "you have verbally affirmed Yahweh . . . and Yahweh has verbally affirmed you" (*ʾet-yhwh heʾĕmartâ . . . wayhwh heʾĕmîrᵉkā*). In 32:21, however, the song describes the *quid pro quo* in decidedly negative terms. Because Israel "provokes" by worshiping false gods, God will respond in kind:

> They made me jealous (*qinʾûnî*)[71] with their no-gods, they provoked me (*kiʿăsûnî*) with their vanities. I will make them jealous (*ʾaqnîʾēm*) with no-people, with a stupid nation I will provoke them (*ʾakʿîsēm*). (32:21)

The song invokes the same bulwarks against apostasy as does Deuteronomy. Pointing to the twin pillars of memory on the one hand and learned lessons of the past on the other as the means through which to maintain fidelity to God and covenant, the song commands:

> Remember (*zᵉkōr*) the days of old; consider (*bînû*) the years of the generations. Ask (*šᵉʾal*) your father and he will tell you (*wᵉyaggēdᵉkā*); your elders and they will speak [of it] to you. (32:7)

Both the song and Deuteronomy properly enumerate the consequences of rebellion. Deuteronomy 27:15-26 lists the curses that will fall upon those who break the covenant, while Deut. 28:15-68 details the horrors that ensue once the covenant has been abrogated. The song contains an abbreviated, but no less terrifying, prospect. God promises to destroy the people with plague and famine (32:24), to let loose sword and terror (32:25), and to "strike them down and remove their memory from among men" (32:26). The function of the curses in the Law Code is to threaten and to warn the people as they stand ready to enter formally into the covenant with God. In the song, however, the pedagogical

70. Deuteronomy 32:16.

71. *Qinʾûnî*. Or "enraged me." *Qnʾ* has many senses. It can mean "to be zealous" as in 1 Kings 19:10, 14; "to be jealous," "to arouse jealousy," "to be filled with rage," or even "torment" or "annoy." See *HALOT* 3:1109b–10a and Michael Fishbane, "Accusations of Adultery: A Study of Law and Scribal Practice in Numbers 5:11-31," *HUCA* 45 (1974): 35–36.

function is primary. By forcing the people to articulate the certain consequences of disloyalty and disobedience, the song teaches and reminds them to stay true to their obligations.

The song recapitulates, in capsulated form and with poetic structure to impress its message on the mind, Deuteronomy's primary themes: Yahweh, who is known by and in terms of the name, Yahweh, is just and constant. Israel, though chosen, is predisposed, especially when well off, to forget its obligation to God. Memory and instruction are the most important means of keeping true to the covenant and maintaining a devotional attitude toward God. The song, which will "answer [you] . . . through the mouth of your offspring" (31:21), therefore serves as a condensed liturgical catechism that each generation is required to "put in your hearts" (32:46), to verbalize and remember.

Conclusion

Deuteronomy seeks to promulgate a particular understanding of the covenant between Yahweh and Israel. It is a covenant that requires of every Israelite total allegiance and total loyalty to Yahweh, incessant mindfulness of Yahweh's commandments, obedience, and wholehearted fulfillment of the commandments. Because of its concern for Israel's mental attitude and for *understanding* that which it is required to do, Deuteronomy is regarded by some scholars as more akin to the wisdom tradition than to a theology concerned with holiness and sacredness. Yet deuteronomic religion introduces something beyond the appeal to wisdom. It proposes an integrated notion of peoplehood and selfhood that demands the participation of the totality of the individual in the obligation of the people. By recapitulating the national story and the national experience, each individual internalizes and becomes united with the entirety of the people. It is the unity of self with peoplehood that makes every individual in every generation as authentically part of the redeemed and covenanted people, as was the generation that left Egypt and stood at Horeb/Sinai.

Verbalized, intellectualized rituals are the instrument of this integration, which leads to a different kind of actualization than that proposed by von Rad and Childs. The integrated self for whom the Israelite experience is actualized through memory (including through rituals) must then fulfill that which is required of Israel. The incessant mindfulness demanded by Deuteronomy obtains to every aspect of life. For von Rad and others, this represented a program of "secularization," resulting from the centralization of worship,[72] but it might be more correctly understood as a program of ultra-sacredness, that is, the investiture of every aspect of quotidian life with covenantal significance. Because the covenant is maintained in the execution of ordinary activities, Moses' teaching and the law itself must be continually borne in mind. This *is* religious practice for Deuteronomy. The Israelites must "remember you were slaves in the land of Egypt," so that the people will recognize their obligation to care for the poor, the widow, the orphan, the Levite, and the stranger, and will remain aware of their obligation to the God who delivered them from slavery.

Memory is a verbal exercise for Deuteronomy, as its vocabulary for memory demonstrates. It is also a content-oriented exercise, a mechanism for retaining information in semantic form. The Israelites are charged to plant memories by narrating a history or reciting doctrine, and they will remember the same way. Remembering is a dynamic act whereby the content of memory is retained and sustained rather than stored and retrieved. Because the content of memory is information, the very act of remembering is implicated in the mindfulness so essential to covenantal behavior. When Israel is commanded to remember, the act is not simply a prompt to subsequent fulfillment of duties or obligations. It is part of the fulfillment, for in remembering its history or the law, Israel is drawn to think on Yahweh and all that is due to their God.

The centrality of memory to deuteronomic literature frees the religion it imagines from constraints of time and place. The Israelites' "memory" of hearing God at Horeb is as genuine as was the experience of the exodus generation actually at Horeb. The farmer presenting first fruits is as keenly aware of how God brought him or her to the land as were the Israelites who first entered the land under Joshua. What is true for Moses' audience is true for the exiles from Judah and for the audience of the book, including present-day readers. All parties are brought into the covenant and made responsible for its maintenance through the exercise of memory.

72. Von Rad, *Old Testament Theology*, 1:80: ". . . [F]or by the centralisation of the cult, Deuteronomy in a most drastic fashion secularised Israel's realm of existence—a great part of what it seeks to do in its *paraeneses* serves the purpose of giving the people a guiding hand for their life out in the exposedness of the secular world."

5

The Priestly Solution: Sensory Stimuli for God

Introduction

According to the priestly tradition, the revelation at Sinai consists of the plans, practices, and laws associated with Israel's cult. Moses receives directions for the construction of the tabernacle and its furnishings and vessels, and for making the priestly vestments. He also receives commands concerning the ordination of the priesthood and the consecration of the tabernacle, and descriptions of the sacrifices, purification processes, and dietary laws that form the ongoing practices in Israel's worship. Yahweh introduces the whole with the promise: "Make for me a sanctified place and I will dwell among you" (Exod. 25:8). As these words imply, given a suitable sanctified environment, Yahweh can be a proximate presence, and laws associated with the cult delineate the means by which that environment is established and maintained.

One might imagine that the priestly desire to keep God's mind and attention firmly and continually on Israel would be satisfied by Yahweh's promise; however, embedded within it are the grounds for some insecurity. If Yahweh can dwell among the Israelites, Yahweh can, by the same token, be elsewhere. Indeed, as Benjamin Sommer's work on divine embodiment suggests, priestly religion faced this very theological problem. As Sommer maintains, numerous passages in the biblical text, as well as found examples of ancient Israelite material culture, testify to the belief on the part of some Israelites that Yahweh could exist simultaneously in several bodies or locales, a belief they shared with their northwest Semitic and Mesopotamian neighbors. Sommer names the concept underlying this notion "fluidity of divine embodiment," and he ascribes the notion to the authors behind the JE narratives in the Pentateuch.[1] However, the priestly traditions, Sommer claims, like the deuteronomic writers, reject this view.[2] The rejection of multiple, simultaneous embodiments of God comports fully with the deuteronomic tradition's belief in an utterly transcendent deity whose name (*šēm*) was only a "sign of divine presence, not a manifestation of God Himself."[3] But for the priestly tradition, God exists as an immanent presence, a presence that P expresses with the term *kābôd*.[4] God may be manifested in the fire consuming sacrifices (cf. Lev. 9:24), or even embodied in such appearances as the cloud hovering over the Israelite camp. Such embodiment is in evidence at the end of Exodus 40 when the tabernacle is erected. God's *kābôd* fills the structure to such extent that Moses cannot enter the structure. Sommer explains that "in priestly literature the *kabod* resides in one place only."[5] If this is so, God can fill the tabernacle, but God can also leave it; and if God leaves it, then God is not present among the Israelites.[6] A central purpose of the cult, therefore, is to ensure that God remains immanently present for Israel and mindful of the covenant with Israel. The importance of keeping God present and attentive is not merely a national concern. Because Israel's covenant replicates the covenant of re-creation in Genesis 9, God's memory and maintenance of it are of cosmic significance.

The sensory panoply of the cult can be readily inferred from the vivid detail with which God instructs Moses about the tabernacle and its furnishings, the vessels and the priestly garments, and it is reinforced in the repetition of those details when the text narrates their fabrication. Among the many elements housed within the tabernacle, several are explicitly designated as reminders for God: *zikkārôn*, *ʾazkārâ*, or *ʾôt*. Of these the *ʾôt* or "sign" is of particular

1. Benjamin D. Sommer, *The Bodies of God and the World of Ancient Israel* (New York: Cambridge University Press, 2009), 38–57. Sommer describes this attitude as reflecting a "fluidity model" of the divine, of which, he argues, the tradition describing God's presence "descending" onto the tent of meeting (which is also located outside the camp) rather than dwelling within the tabernacle, namely E, is an example. In this model God's presence is not fixed but can be located in different places at different times.

2. Ibid., 58.

3. Ibid., 62.

4. In place of providing an English translation, I chose to use the transliterated form of the Hebrew. In English, *kābôd* is usually translated as "glory," a term that does not adequately express the idea conveyed by the Hebrew original. The consonantal root *kbd* implies both the physical sense of weightiness and the abstract sense of honor. Sommers gives a good explanation: "We have seen that the term *kabod* in biblical Hebrew can refer to a body and that this term is also associated with conflagrations, intense light, smoke, and clouds associated with God's manifestation. Priestly literature's use of the term recalls (or perhaps underlies) all these uses, for in it, *kabod* refers to God's body and hence to God's very self." Ibid., 68.

5. Ibid., 75.

6. Ibid., 80. "It follows that if God has a body, then at any moment some place enjoys a privilege that other places lack."

importance, yet differs conceptually from the other two. For this reason, I delay discussion of it to Chapter 8.

Zikkārôn

1. *The High Priest's Vestments*

While the cult as a whole contributes to the program of keeping God mindful, it is the high priest and the rites appropriate to him that play the central role. Exodus 28 concerns the fabrication of the vestments for the high priest. Eight garments are specified, four of which are unique to him and four of which are worn by both the high priest and ordinary priests. In the latter group are the tunic, sash, headpiece, and breeches.[7] The garments worn only by the high priest "to consecrate him as my priest" (*l*ᵉ*qadd*ᵉ*šô l*ᵉ*kahănô-lî*) are "sacred garments" (*bigdê-qōdeš*) (Exod. 28:3-4). These are the ephod (*'ēpôd*),[8] breastpiece (*ḥōšen*),[9] robe (*m*ᵉ*'îl*), and the diadem attached to his headdress (*ṣîṣ*). The high priest wears the sacred garments when carrying out the rites specific to the outer sanctum of the tabernacle (the area in front of the curtain of the holy of holies), which are his exclusive responsibility: the daily lighting of the lamps (*nēr tāmîd*) (Exod. 27:20-21; Lev. 24:2-4), weekly provision of the bread of the presence (*leḥem pānîm*) (Exod. 25:30; 39:36; Lev. 24:5-9), and the incense offering (*q*ᵉ*ṭōret*) (Exod. 30:1-9).[10]

7. The high priest's tunic is more ornate than that worn by regular priests. The latter is simply designated a *kŭttōnet* ("tunic") (cf. Exod. 28:40), whereas the high priest's tunic is described as *k*ᵉ*tōnet tašbēṣ* (Exod. 28:4). *Tašbēṣ* is a *hapax legomenon.* The LXX translates it as κοσυμβωτόν ("fringed"); *Tg. Onq.* as *mrmṣn* ("woven in a checkered pattern"). Different terminology also distinguishes between the respective headdresses of Aaron and of his sons. The high priest's headdress is called *miṣnepet,* "turban-like headband" (28:4); that of the ordinary priests is called by a different term, *migbā'â* ("headband") (cf. 28:40), and in *Tg. Onq. qwb'* ("helmet, turban"). The LXX makes no distinction between the two headdresses, calling both κίδαριν/κιδάρεις.

8. *HALOT* 1:77a–b. The term is virtually untranslatable. It appears to be cognate to Old Assyrian *epattu* ("precious garment") and Ugaritic *ipd* ("garment"). Mishnaic Hebrew, Jewish Aramaic, and Syriac cognates (*'āpūdā* and *pedtā* = "priest's garments") are likely based on the biblical meaning. The verb *'āpad* ("to bind or fit closely") is a denominative of *'ēpōd* and therefore offers no additional information.

9. *HALOT* 1:362b. Like "ephod," the term is obscure. *HALOT* suggests it may be related to Arabic, *ḥasuna* ("to be beautiful") or *jaušab* ("bodice, for battle"). There do not appear to be Akkadian or Ugaritic cognates.

10. Menahem Haran, *Temples and Temple Service in Ancient Israel: An Inquiry into Biblical Cult Phenomena and the Historical Setting of the Priestly School* (Oxford: Clarendon, 1978; repr., Winona Lake, IN: Eisenbrauns, 1985), 205–15. To the high priest alone also belongs the responsibility for the Day of

The ephod (Exod. 28:6–12) is made of "gold, purple-blue, purple and crimson cloth, and twisted linen worked in a rich design." Haran describes this as a "sort of apron encircling the body from the loins downward."[11] Two shoulder pieces secure the upper part of the ephod. The *ḥēšeb*[12] of the ephod, which may be a cloth barrier between the ephod and the breastpiece, is worn over the ephod or, possibly, is part of the garment covering the chest.[13] The ephod is fancy; the gold ornamentation and colorful fabric combine to produce a flashy garment that can catch God's eye. Beyond its vibrant and rich appearance, however, the most important element of the ephod, occupying two-thirds of the directions concerning it, is the pair of engraved stones that are inset on the shoulder-pieces.

> You will take two carnelian stones (*ʾabnê šōham*[14]) and engrave upon them the names of the Israelites. Six of their names on the first stone and the names of the remaining six on the second stone, according to their birth order. Finely cut stones[15] like the engraving of a seal you shall engrave the two stones with the names of the Israelites. Surrounded with gold plating you shall make them. And you shall place the two stones on the shoulder of the ephod. Stones of remembrance (*ʾabnê zikkārōn*) for the Israelites. And Aaron shall carry their names before Yahweh on his two shoulders, as a remembrance (*lᵉzikkārōn*). (Exod. 28:9–12)

The emphatic repetition that characterizes this instruction further underscores the centrality of the stones to the ephod's importance. Following the initial command (v. 9) to engrave them is the belabored explanation, "Finely cut stones like the engraving of a seal you shall engrave the two stones" (*maʿăśê ḥāraš ʾeben pittûḥê ḥōtām tᵉpattaḥ ʾet-šᵉtê hāʾăbānîm*) (Exod. 28:11). Reference to the engraved "names" occurs five times within the four verses. Milgrom maintains the names on the stones are a reflection of the responsibility for all Israel that the high priest assumes.[16] The text, however, indicates that it is God's memory the stones

Atonement rites in the inner sanctum, but for these he wears special garments exclusive to that day and its rites.

11. Ibid., 166.

12. *HALOT* 1:360b suggests "decorated" or "skillfully woven" band. See the discussion in Haran, *Temples and Temple Service*, 160–61.

13. Haran, *Temples and Temple Service*, 167 n. 39.

14. In some translations, "onyx" (NRSV, JPS) or "lazuli stones" (NJPS).

15. In some translations "the work of a lapidary" (NJPS), "as a gem-cutter engraves signets" (NRSV).

address. Because they serve "as a remembrance . . . before Yahweh" (*lipnê yhwh*) whenever the high priest officiates in the tabernacle, they draw God's attention to the Israelites on whose behalf the rites are performed.[17]

Like the ephod, the breastpiece of judgment is a fancy, flashy item, made of finely worked linen, gold, purple-blue, purple, and crimson cloth. Functionally, its purpose is to hold the *Urim* and *Thummim* (Exod. 28:30), presumably in a pouch or some kind of pocket. The breastpiece is a square piece, the size of a doubled *zeret*[18] attached to the ephod at the shoulders with gold rings. The whole is decorated with twelve different precious stones arranged in four columns of three stones apiece. Engraved on each stone is the seal of a tribal family ("engraved seals of each man, according to his name") (Exod. 28:21) so that "Aaron will carry the names of the Israelites on the breastpiece of judgment on his heart when he comes into the sanctuary as a remembrance before Yahweh eternally (*lᵉzikkārōn lipnê yhwh tāmîd*)" (Exod. 28:29).

The next item described, the robe of the ephod (*mᵉʿîl hāʾēpôd*), is made entirely of purple-blue cloth (Exod. 28:31-35). Gold bells and cloth appliqué pomegranates of purple-blue, purple, and crimson alternate around its hem. The pomegranates are certainly ornamental, but the sound made by the bells is more purposeful:

> Whenever Aaron is obligated to officiate, their sound will be heard (*wᵉnišmaʿ qôlô*), when he comes into the sanctuary before Yahweh and when he leaves so he will not die. (28:35)

Ronald Hendel suggests that the bells collaborate in a "form of sacred etiquette," necessary because of the "essential difference between the high priest and the God whom he serves":

> This rule is a form of sacred etiquette, a formal announcement of the human servitor's presence when entering Yahweh's dwelling. It affords metaphysical protection from the danger of Yahweh's

16. Milgrom, *Leviticus*, 3 vols., AB 3–3B (New York: Doubleday, 1991–2001), 1:54.

17. In this, the stones of remembrance resemble inscriptions on ossuaries from the Second Temple period on which the petition: *zkyr lṭb* . . . or *zkwr lṭwbh* . . . ("remember for good . . .") is written, presumably on behalf of a donor. The point of such inscriptions is to keep the donor's contribution and therefore the donor him/herself present in God's mind. See Joseph Naveh, *On Stone and Mosaic: Aramaic and Hebrew Inscriptions from the Period of the Second Temple, the Mishna and the Talmud* (Jerusalem: Magnes, 1992), 126–43 (in Hebrew).

18. A measure equal to ½ cubit or one hand.

> presence. . . . [W]hen the high priest enters into the presence of the Divine King, he must be announced. And in the absence of a butler, the pure golden bells on the high priest's robe must suffice. But this is not a matter of mere announcement of a servitor—the sound of the bells wards off God's deadly wrath. The musical noise protects the high priest from automatic death, and reminds God not to kill his guest.[19]

The allusion to death in the instruction about the bells implies that the sanctuary is a place of extreme danger, even when approached in a legitimate fashion. That God's power can wreak destruction is implied by both the flood story and the account of the exodus night. In the one, God provided a sign to keep God true to the promise to stay destruction; in the other, God told the Israelites to alert God with a sign for the same purpose. Yet in addition to warding off, rather automatically, the power of the numen, the bells may be directed to God's aural perception for positive reasons. When they are heard, God will be forewarned of Aaron's entry and departure from the sanctuary, and disposed to attend to the rites he performs.

The final garment unique to Aaron is his headdress or turban (*miṣnepet*), the central feature of which is the gold diadem (*ṣîṣ*), probably floral in design (Exod. 28:36-38).[20] Set on or suspended from a cord of "twisted purple-blue cloth" (*p*ᵉ*tîl t*ᵉ*kēlet*) and placed on the front of the headdress, the diadem is engraved with a seal bearing the words, "consecrated to Yahweh" (Exod. 28:36). Like the ephod and breastpiece, the headdress both identifies and calls attention to the high priest and his role. Possibly it has an expiatory function, as Milgrom suggests, expunging "any imperfection inadvertently offered by the people,"[21] for as the text explains,

> Aaron will bear the guilt of the consecrated things (*w*ᵉ*nāśā' 'ahărōn 'et-'ăwōn haqqodāšîm*) which the Israelites consecrate through their sacred offerings. It will be on his forehead eternally that they may be acceptable before Yahweh. (Exod. 28:38)

19. Ronald Hendel, "Purity and Danger in the Temple Cult," forthcoming.

20. While *ṣîṣ* may be a technical term for the medallion (NJPS: "frontlet") on the turban, its primary meaning is "flowers or blossoms," as in Num. 17:23: "flowers burst [from Aaron's rod] and blossoms bloomed and it bore ripe almonds" (*wayyōṣē' peraḥ wayyāṣēṣ ṣîṣ*). A connection between the two verses is hardly accidental, as I will consider in Chapter 8.

21. Milgrom, *Leviticus*, 1:55. See also the discussion on *nāśā' 'ăwōn* in Roy Gane, *Cult and Character: Purification Offerings, Day of Atonement and Theodicy* (Winona Lake, IN: Eisenbrauns, 2005), 100–105.

Yet an expiatory purpose seems odd in that the laity does not participate in the rites of the outer sanctum, and hence have no opportunity to sully the ritual materials. More convincingly, Haran maintains that the relationship between the rituals of the outer sanctum and the garments worn by the priest when performing them is hardly casual, but rather crucial. He argues that the vestments are

> conceived as ritual appurtenances in their own right, on a par with the altar, the lampstand, and the table inside the tabernacle. In other words, the wearing of these garments inside the tabernacle becomes an act of ritual significance, in the course of which Aaron performs several genuine rites additional and complementary to the first three [tending the lamps, providing the bread of the presence, offering the incense].[22]

The three rites themselves involve sensory appeals to God's attention. God will see the lights, smell the incense, and (metaphorically) taste the bread. The vestments compound and direct the communicative power of the three rites by explicitly invoking the Israelites whom the high priest represents. Although only the ephod and the breastpiece are specifically termed a "remembrance," taken together, this is the function of all the sacred garments of the high priest. As Haran summarizes, they "arouse divine remembrance" in God and "evoke divine *grace*" for God's people, Israel.[23]

2. *"TO MAKE ATONEMENT FOR YOUR LIVES . . ."*

In addition to the materials required to construct the tabernacle and its appurtenances, the Israelites are required to make contributions to the tabernacle that shall be a "reminder" (*zikkārôn*) "to make atonement for your lives." The first is the half-shekel payment to be collected in connection with census-taking (Exod. 30:12-16); the second is the booty from the battle with the Midianites (Num. 31:50-54). The contexts for these two contributions differ: the first is mandated as a regular element of Israel's cultic-life, while the second is associated with the grotesque apostasy at Baal Peor (Numbers 25). The context for the booty contribution may explain the atoning properties of this *zikkārôn*. Not only does the Israelites' impiety lie behind them, they also failed to execute the battle properly by sparing the females, "the very ones who in the matter of Balaam led the Israelites away from Yahweh" (Num. 31:16).[24] Housed

22. Haran, *Temples and Temple Service*, 212.

23. Ibid., 215 (italics in original).

in the tabernacle, the booty reminds Yahweh that the Israelites have paid their debt. It may also, prophylactically, remind Yahweh not to inflict plague or other expressions of wrath against Israel in the future. As Baruch Levine explains:

> [T]he designation *lezikkārôn* seem[s] to refer to an act of cultic devotion that brings the Israelites to the attention of their God, not because it is displayed or noticed, in the usual sense, but because God knows that it has been given. . . . Because of the cultic devotion of the people and its commanders, Israel will be remembered for good by their God.[25]

The purpose of the half-shekel contribution is less obvious. According to Exod. 30:12, this contribution is required in connection with every census taken of the Israelite people:

> When you take a count of all the Israelites, each man shall give a ransom (*kōper napšô*) for himself to Yahweh, when they are counted, so no affliction will come to them (*w*ᵉ*lōʾyihyeh bāhem negep*) when they are counted. This is what they shall give when they are entered into the census: a half-shekel . . . as an offering to Yahweh. (Exod. 30:12-13)

The half-shekel is explained further as "a reminder before Yahweh as atonement for your lives" (*l*ᵉ*zikkārôn lipnê yhwh l*ᵉ*kappēr ʿal napšōtêkem*) (Exod 30:16). What is the connection between the census and the possibility of "affliction"? Although taking a census can be regarded as impious when God does not request it, here is it divinely sanctioned, even mandated.[26]

The protective power of the half-shekel recalls the apotropaic power of the blood on houses that saved the Israelites from the Destroyer on the night of the exodus (Exod. 12:13). Indeed, with the language—*w*ᵉ*lōʾ yihyeh negep bāhem*—virtually identical in both cases, the association of the half-shekel with

24. Baruch Levine suggests that the donation is required because the "salutary results [of the census taken after the battle] reported to the effect that not a single person was missing. God has spared the lives of the combatants, who now owed God their lives." In this reading, the donation of booty as a *zikkārôn* is like a receipt that proves to God that God has been adequately compensated. Levine, *Numbers*, 2 vols., AB 4A–B (New York: Doubleday, 1993–2000), 2:463.

25. Levine, *Numbers*, 2:463.

26. (Cf. 2 Samuel 24). Nahum Sarna, *Exodus*, JPS (Philadelphia: Jewish Publication Society, 1991), 195.

the blood is inescapable. What is more, the silver from the half-shekel tax appears to be used in the construction of the Tabernacle, furthering the analogy with the blood on the Israelite houses.[27] The contribution, it can now be understood, is the permanent equivalent of the one-time sign of the blood.

3. "YOU SHALL BLAST THE TRUMPETS . . ."

The third "reminder" for God is the blast of the silver trumpets sounded by the priests in times of war and in tandem with the presentation of selected sacrifices. Yahweh assures Israel that the sound of their blasts will cause Yahweh to remember his people.

> When you go to war in your land against your enemies who attack you, you shall sound a war-cry with the trumpets and you will be remembered (*w^enizkartem*) before Yahweh your God and you will be delivered from your enemies. And on your days of rejoicing and on your fixed times and on your New Months, you will blow on the trumpets, for your burnt offerings and for your sacrifices of well-being. They will be for you a reminder before your God (*l^ezikkārôn lipnê yhwh ʾĕlōhêkem*). I am Yahweh your God. (Num. 10:9–10)

We know from Amos 5:22, Isa. 1:13, and Jer. 14:12 that Yahweh's receptivity to Israel's sacrifices cannot be assumed. Yahweh may reject them, even those associated with set times (Isa. 1:13), and Yahweh's rejection of sacrifice is tantamount to the rejection of his people.[28] The trumpet blasts militate against this possibility by directing Yahweh's attention to the Israelites' offerings and ensuring Yahweh's receptivity to them. God's attention is also mightily needed in times of war, for it is God who leads Israel's armies (Num. 10:35) and delivers Israel before all its enemies (Deut. 20:4).[29] Nevertheless, Yahweh's attention

27. Exodus 30:16a instructs: "and give it [over to] the work on [or service in?] the Tent of Meeting" (*w^enātattā ʾōtô ʿal-ʿăbōdat ʾōhel môʿēd*). According to Exod. 38:24–28, the silver is used for the sockets of the tabernacle and the curtain. See Ibn Ezra's comment to Exod. 38:24 and Sarna on Exod. 30:16 in Sarna, *Exodus*, 196. Levine briefly discusses the use of the silver in "The Descriptive Tabernacle Texts of the Pentateuch," *JAOS* 85 (1965): 310.

28. Cf. Lev. 7:18 and 19:7. For Yahweh's acceptance of sacrifices as evidence of his acceptance of the cult as a whole, see Lev. 9:24 and Ezek. 43:27.

29. Deuteronomy provides the most thoroughgoing theology of warfare in which the waging of [legitimate] war has a sacred dimension and therefore is carried out with God's imprimatur and assistance. This theology finds its way into virtually all biblical passages concerning warfare, whether or not deuteronomic (e.g., Exod. 17:8–13; Numbers 31; Joshua 6). See also Levine, *Numbers*, 2:452, 467–70.

must first be roused if he is to save his people, as is attested in Ps. 44:24, 27 ("Wake up! Why do you sleep, Yahweh? . . . Advance and assist us! Take note of us for the sake of your loving fidelity") and elsewhere.[30]

The Rêaḥ Nîḥōaḥ and the ʾAzkārâ

1. "Pleasing Fragrance to Yahweh"

Of the rituals prescribed by the priestly tradition, sacrifices must rank among the most significant. Leviticus 1–7 is devoted entirely to the choreography and disposition of burnt offerings (*ʿōlâ*), sacrifices of well-being (*šᵉlāmîm*), and sacrifices of purgation (*ḥaṭṭāʾt*) and guilt (*ʾāšām*),[31] and Numbers 28–29 enumerates what is to be offered daily, on the Sabbath and new moon, and for each festival. A good deal of scholarship exists on the sacrificial system, and important work has been done on such areas as the phenomenology of priestly sacrifice and its component elements, the function of individual categories of sacrifice, especially of the *ḥaṭṭāʾt* and *ʾāšām*, and on the terminology associated with priestly sacrifice.[32] Less attention has been paid to God's response to sacrifice even though offerings are made or presented to God, presumably with the intention that "it [the donor's offering] be accepted before Yahweh" (*lirṣōnô lipnê yhwh*) (Lev. 1:3).[33] That eliciting a response from God is an object of at least some categories of sacrifice is clear from the expression "a pleasing fragrance to Yahweh" (*ʾiššê rêaḥ nîḥōaḥ layhwh*) or (in Lev. 3:11) "a burned food offering to Yahweh" (*leḥem ʾiššê layhwh*) in the description of particular sacrifices. The burnt offering, the fat (and kidneys) of the well-being and guilt offerings, and the "token portion" (*ʾazkārâ*) of grain offerings (*minḥâ*) are turned to smoke on the altar to make "a pleasing fragrance to Yahweh."[34] Moreover, the entirety of the fragrance belongs to God, for no part of what burns is

30. See Isa. 51:9-10 and Ps. 7:7.

31. These sacrifices are dealt with again in an abbreviated and somewhat altered form in Num. 15:1-31. Levine believes that the Numbers passage is based on Leviticus 4–5 with evidence of innovation. *Numbers*, 1:385–86, 295–98.

32. The literature is extensive. See, for example, Milgrom, *Leviticus*, in particular, 1:253–92 on the *ḥaṭṭāʾt* and 1:339–78 on the *ʾāšām*; Gane, *Cult and Character*, especially chapter 6; and Ithamar Gruenwald, *Rituals and Ritual Theory in Ancient Israel* (Leiden: Brill, 2003), chapter 5.

33. Exceptionally, Levine and Haran allude to God's response to sacrifice, but even they do not make it a primary concern. See Haran's discussion in *Temples and Temple Service*, 207-10, 216-17. In the introduction to his Leviticus commentary, Levine merely observes that "[v]iewing the cult from the perspective of the God of Israel, the divine recipient of sacrificial offerings, might help us arrive at an imaginative method of deepening our understanding of religious phenomenology" (*Leviticus*, xxxviii).

consumed by either priest or lay donor. Presumably, fragrance draws God's attention to these offerings just as it did when Noah offered his sacrifice at the end of the flood.

The power of olfactory memory has been demonstrated in a number of scientific studies. Both behavioral results and brain-imaging data have shown that odor-cued memories are more vivid than those evoked by corresponding words, and that they "produce a stronger feeling of being brought back in time" than do memories triggered by verbal and even visual cues. Some studies even suggest that memories cued by olfactory stimuli are more emotionally arousing than those triggered by other media.[35] The link between smell and memory may help explain the meaning of the *ʾazkārâ* since providing a fragrance seems to be its principal function. Analysis of this technical term may also offer insight into the role of sacrifice for God's memory more generally.

Except when taken from a *ḥaṭṭāʾt*,[36] incense is the central ingredient of the *ʾazkārâ*, and can be presumed to be integral to its function. The *ʾazkārâ* of the grain offering contains all the incense included in that offering. In connection to the bread of the presence, *ʾazkārâ* refers exclusively to the incense laid next to the bread. Hence smell, and specifically the aroma of incense, is the distinguishing feature of this particular offering.

Incense is also the only thing offered in the outer sanctum, the most important part of the tabernacle in the daily life of the community. The outer sanctum is where the high priest carries out his *tāmîd* responsibilities—lighting the lamps, offering incense, and (weekly) laying out the bread of the presence. Because he carries them out in the special garments designed to draw God's attention to his service, the rites of the outer sanctum serve to bridge the divide between Yahweh and the community and keeping Yahweh mindful of the community. Since incense associates the *ʾazkārâ* with the rites of the outer sanctum and the various activators of God's memory employed there, the function of the *ʾazkārâ* itself may be to produce an effect similar to those rites,

34. According to Lev. 4:31, the priest burns all the fat of the purgation offering made on behalf of an individual for a "pleasing fragrance. . . ." While the expression *rêaḥ nîḥōaḥ* occurs nowhere else in the pericope on the *ḥaṭṭāʾt* (Leviticus 4), it is reasonable to suppose that it applies as well when the fat from the *ḥaṭṭāʾt* is offered for sins committed by the high priest (Lev. 4:3-12), the whole community (Lev. 4:13-21), or a *nāśî* ("prince") (Lev. 4:22-26).

35. See, for example, Yaara Yeshurun, Hadas Lapid, Yadin Dudai, and Noam Sobel, "The Privileged Brain Representation of First Olfactory Associations," *Current Biology* 19 (2009): 1869–74; Johan Willander and Maria Larsson, "Smell Your Way Back to Childhood: Autobiographical Odor Memory," *Psychonomic Bulletin and Review* 13 (2006): 240–44.

36. Cf. Lev. 5:11-12.

but in the less sacred courtyard region. Of the three regions of holiness in the tabernacle, the courtyard involves no exclusive role for the high priest. Perhaps the *ʾazkārâ*, which is burned in the courtyard, serves to invest the rituals of the courtyard with a suggestion of the status accorded those of the two areas for which the high priest is responsible. It is an offering meant to evoke those responsibilities and the effect they have on God and God's memory.

The situation with the bread of the presence offers another explanation of the term. According to Lev. 24:5-9, the twelve loaves of display are placed on a table in the inner sanctuary, and pure frankincense (*l*^{e}*bōnâ zakkâ*) is added on top, making the loaves "bread to cause remembrance, a fire offering to Yahweh" (*l*^{e}*bōnâ zakkâ w*^{e}*hây*^{e}*tâ lalleḥem l*^{e}*ʾazkārâ ʾiššê layhwh*) (Lev. 24:7). The bread recalls the need for food as the vessels evoke drink, and both serve as symbols or "reminders" of food and drink offerings.[37] In ancient non-Israelite religions, it was common to provide the deity with food and drink several times a day.[38] While limiting the presentation of the bread of the presence to once a week dissociates Israelite rites from the concept of actual provision of godly sustenance, the display of the bread of the presence seems to allude to the idea of propitiatory offerings of food. This idea, moreover, has reflexes in the account of Noah's sacrifice after the flood in Gen. 8:20-21. There, it will be recalled, the smell from the sacrifice induces God to promise never again to destroy the world with a flood. Genesis 8:20-21 is attributed to J while the material on the bread of the presence is generally attributed to P.[39] Nevertheless, the possibility that the bread of the presence stands for a propitiatory offering can be entertained. In this case, its designation as an *ʾazkārâ* may be understood as "commemoration" or "symbol" that inspires awareness or memory. Alternatively, the twelve loaves of bread are meant to be a visual reminder for God, like stones on the breastplate of the high priest (also proper to the inner sanctuary), of the tribes of Israel. Its symbolic value as a

37. Haran, *Temples and Temple Service*, 216–17. Geller has suggested that the bread of the presence is reinterpreted in Exodus 16 as "bread given by the Presence, i.e. God, the provider of manna, and not, as earlier, as bread provided to be eaten by the gods" ("Sabbath and Creation: A Literary-Theological Analysis," *Interpretation* [forthcoming]). Moreover, as he explains, because it has been reinterpreted as "bread given by the Presence," the cultic bread is "symbolic of God as sustainer and nourisher in the desert and ever after" ("Manna and Sabbath: A Literary-Theological Reading of Exodus 16," *Interpretation* 59 [2005]: 12).

38. Israel Knohl, *The Sanctuary of Silence: The Priestly Torah and the Holiness School* (Minneapolis: Augsburg Fortress Press, 1995; repr., Winona Lake, IN: Eisenbrauns, 2007), 132.

39. Knohl, however, differs from the majority opinion and attributes it to H.

substitute for food would heighten in mnemonic power as it would continually recall the sacrifices with their "sweet savor" that are presented daily to God.

2. *Excursus: The Trial of the Suspected Adulteress (Num. 5:11–31)*

The trial of the suspected adulteress is one of the very few rituals in the Pentateuch for which the procedures are described in detail.[40] (The other one is the ritual of the heifer for unsolved murder in Deut. 21:1–9.) As Tikva Frymer-Kensky points out, the situations necessitating these two rituals are analogous. In one instance (the heifer), there is a certain crime but no suspect; in the other there is a suspect but no certainty of a crime.[41] The two crimes in question, moreover, are capital crimes. I focus on the trial of the suspected wife not only because the lack of witness obviates capital punishment and leaves both judgment and punishment in God's hands,[42] but also because the ritual itself involves two kinds of reminders.

The first step in the ritual of the accused woman has her husband bring an offering of barley unadorned by either oil or frankincense to the tabernacle on her behalf. Described as a "meal offering of jealousy, a remembrance grain-offering, that which recalls iniquity" (*minḥât qᵉnāʾōt minḥât zikkārôn mazkeret ʿāwōn*), in its contents, the offering resembles the purgation offering when it is made of grain (cf. Lev. 5:11).[43] With the thrice-named offering in hand, the

40. On the ritual for the accused woman, see Michael Fishbane, "Accusations of Adultery: A Study of Law and Scribal Practice in Numbers 5:11-31," *HUCA* 45 (1974): 25–45; Tikva Frymer-Kensky, "The Strange Case of the Suspected Sotah (Numbers V 11-31)," *VT* 34 (1984): 11–26; Jacob Milgrom, "Encroaching on the Sacred: Purity and Polity in Numbers 1-10," *Interpretation* 51 (1997): 241–53; and Prina Galpaz-Feller, "Private Lives and Public Censure: Adultery in Ancient Egypt and Biblical Israel," *Near Eastern Archaeology* 67 (2004): 152–61.

41. Frymer-Kensky, "The Strange Case of the Suspected Sotah," 11.

42. Ibid., 24. See also Milgrom, "Encroaching on the Sacred," 245–46. In fact, the trial of the suspected adulteress addresses two possible cases: one in which there are no witnesses to a real act of adultery and the woman is defiled (*wᵉhîʾ niṭmāʾâ*) (Num. 5:13), and one in which there was no adultery and she is not defiled (*wᵉhî[w]ʾ lōʾ niṭmāʾâ*) (Num. 5:14).

43. The LXX translation is θυσία ζηλοτυπίας θυσία μνημοσύνου ἀναμιμνήσκουσα ἁμαρτίαν, "a sacrifice of angry jealousy, a memorial sacrifice, to remind of sin." The latter part of the name given to the offering—*minḥat zikkārôn mazkeret ʿāwōn*—occurs only in this context, and its meaning is not certain (Num. 5:15). In modern commentaries, it is variously translated as "grain offering of record, which calls attention to wrongdoing" (Levine, *Numbers* 1:183); "memorial offering causing remembrance of guilt" (Rolf P. Knierim and George W. Coats, *Numbers*, FOTL 4 [Grand Rapids: Eerdmans, 2005], 80); "meal offering of remembrance which recalls the wrongdoing" (Milgrom, *Numbers*, 38–39); "grain-gift of reminding that reminds of iniquity" (Everett Fox, *The Five Books of Moses* [New York: Schocken, 1995]); and "meal offering of suspicion, an evocatory offering" (Timothy R. Ashley, *The Book of Numbers* [Grand

priest stands the accused woman "before Yahweh," and places in her hands "the grain offering of remembrance and the grain offering of jealousy" (Num. 5:18). He pronounces the curse that will ensue if the woman is guilty, writes it down, and dissolves the text in water mixed with dirt. Then the priest presents the jealousy offering on the altar and dissolves the writing in water and takes "from the meal offering the *ʾazkārâ*" and offers it on the altar. The trial concludes with the accused woman drinking the bitter water prepared by the priest.

Among the peculiarities of the ritual, four features stand out: the apparent redundancy of three names for the offering; the incorporation of the root *zkr* in two of them; the designations given to the offering at different points in the trial; and the *ʾazkārâ*. An explanation for all four may be found in the correspondence between the threefold name and the three distinct concerns of the parties present at the ordeal: the accusing husband, the suspected woman, and the high priest. The suspected woman undergoes the trial and suffers its humiliations, but all three parties present are deeply invested in its outcome. I begin with the husband.

The first of the three names given to the offering is "grain offering of jealousy," and this is its designation when presented on the altar. It was noted above that the offering replicates the purgation offering (*ḥaṭṭāʾt*); the procedure followed for its presentation is also nearly identical to that of the *ḥaṭṭāʾt* when made with grain, differing only in that the former is waved before God.

> The priest shall take from the woman's hand the grain offering of jealousy, wave the grain offering before Yahweh, and bring it to the altar. The priest shall take from the grain offering the *ʾazkārâ* and turn it to smoke on the altar. (Num. 5:25-26)

Identified both with jealousy and the necessity of purgation, the grain offering reflects the state of the accusing husband and, if his wife proves to be innocent, his offense. If she is innocent, then the husband's unsubstantiated and libelous accusation remains an unsettled debt. The text alludes to that possibility in the postscript to the trial, where once again the two situations necessitating the ordeal are identified, but in different terms than at the outset. Numbers 5:14 and 5:30 both describe the situation wherein the woman is innocent. But whereas in 5:14, her innocence is described in terms of defilement ("and she is not defiled"), that is, with reference to the husband's concern, the description in Num. 5:30 hints at the offense felt by his wife, the husband's jealousy, jealousy that forced

Rapids: Eerdmans, 1993], 127). Leveen translates it the same way as Milgrom (*Memory and Tradition in the Book of Numbers* [New York: Cambridge University Press, 2008], 74).

her to endure a humiliating trial: "Or a man over whom comes a spirit of jealousy and is jealous concerning his wife." From this perspective, the man's jealousy is a "sin" that must be purged and that requires the propitiating aroma provided by the *ʾazkārâ*.

Minḥât zikkārôn is the second name the offering is called, and in this capacity it reflects the needs of the accused wife. On trial literally before God, she is at risk of horrible bodily punishment if found guilty and is entirely dependent on God's judgment. In analogy to the half-shekel remembrance and the Midianite booty remembrance, the "grain offering of remembrance" may serve a placating function on her behalf, staving off God's anger at a time that it could be unleashed. Alternatively, the designation *zikkārôn* may associate the offering with the stones of remembrance on the high priest's ephod. As such, they would draw God's attention to the accused woman's case at a time when she needs God to be favorably disposed toward her.

The third and most opaque name given to the offering is the one that does not occur again in the explanation of the ritual: *mazkeret ʿāwōn*, roughly translated as "a reminder of wrongdoing."[44] *Mazkeret* is a *hapax legomenon* and an ambiguous grammatical from, but its meaning may be illuminated by resonance between the expression *mazkeret ʿāwōn* and *nāśâ. . .ʾet-ʿăwōn* ("carry . . . the wrongdoing") which, as noted above in the discussion of the high priest's vestments, is the high priest's role when officiating in the outer sanctum as a way of eliciting divine remembrance. In the present case, the offering as a *mazkeret ʿāwōn* provides a way for the high priest to effect atonement for the whole community.

In the prophecies of Hosea (1–2), Jeremiah (2, 3), and Ezekiel (16, 23), adultery is both a metaphor for the "disruption" of the covenant between God and Israel, and an actual violation of the covenant.[45] Moses' response to the apostasy at Sinai further testifies to the intimate conceptual association of the crimes of adultery and apostasy. In a variation of the ritual mandated for the suspected adulteress, Moses mixes the ground-up residue from the incinerated golden calf with water and forces the people to drink the mixture (Exod. 32:20).

44. It can be taken as a substantive derived from the *qal* meaning "memento" or "token," or as a variant of the *hipʿil* participle, a classification that still admits a range of causative meanings, including "reminding of," "referring to" (from the idea of "mentioning"), "pronouncing," "indicting," and so on. On the ambiguity surrounding this form and on the *maqtil* form, see Jan Retsö, *Diathesis in the Semitic Languages: A Comparative Morphological Study* (Leiden: Brill, 1989), 67–70.

45. Galpaz-Feller, "Private Lives and Public Censure," 158. As Fishbane explains, "In the divine or prophetic accusations of covenantal infidelity, Israel is caught *in flagrante delicto*, so to speak; divine suspicion, or zeal, is not without foundation" ("Accusations of Adultery," 40).

If the woman in question in Numbers 5 is guilty of adultery, her defilement spreads to the whole community, which then requires an atonement that only the high priest can make. The quick action undertaken at Baal Peor in Numbers 25 (about which, see Chapter 6 below) dramatizes the power of the high priest to assuage God's righteous anger over Israel's infidelity.[46] Even if she is innocent, the charge of adultery, which brings the equally serious crime of idolatry into the mind of the community, leaves alive an association too terrible to ignore. The mere suggestion or reference to the sin must be expunged. The priest's "reminder of wrongdoing" serves a preventive purpose, that of atoning lest a wrong had been committed.

Conclusion

The panoply of sights, sounds, and smells that make up the activity of the cult produce a lively and continuous signal to God of the people and of their commitment to God. The tabernacle is hardly a "sanctuary of silence," as described by Knohl. It is a sensory symphony and a dazzling display. The multicolored, flashy vestments of the high priest in particular provide a cultic reinterpretation of the "[rain]bow."[47] But so too does sacrifice, which, when

46. Fishbane, "Accusations of Adultery," 40. At the same time, as Prina Galpaz-Feller argues, the communal implications of the violation explain the requirement that the community as a whole participate in punishing adulterers: "The biblical laws view the involvement of the public in punishing the adulteress as a reinforcement of the covenant between the people and their God" (Galpaz-Feller, "Private Lives and Public Censure," 158). She bases this interpretation on deuteronomic law (Deut. 22:22-24) and in particular the explanation for the sentence of death, "You will remove the evil from Israel" (v. 22). In the Holiness Code, adultery is included among the totality of forbidden sexual relations "with the concomitant implication that adultery is regarded as a sin against God, the consequences of which apply to both the man and to the woman who committed the act." Ibid.

47. The association of the high priest's vestments with the iridescence of a rainbow is suggested in a number of medieval piyyutim composed for the *Avodah* service of the Day of Atonement, based in turn on Ben Sira 50:6-12 [5-10 in LXX], especially verse 8[7]: "Like the sun shining in the temple of the King; like a rainbow (*qšt*) seen in the cloud[s]." As Cecil Roth explains in an article on Sephardic and Ashkenazic examples of these piyyutim, "All . . . took as their basis the relevant portions of the Mishnah-tractate *Yoma*, in which the proceedings of the day are graphically described. . . . The oldest text of the sort as yet known is that beginning שבעה ימים קודם ליום הכפורים, two passages of which are quoted in the Talmud (*T. B. Yoma* 56b) as having been recited in the presence of the Babylonian scholar Rava (c. 280–352)." "Ecclesiasticus in the Synagogue Service," *JBL* 71 (1952): 171. An example he brings from an Ashkenazic rite is especially striking: In *truth how glorious was the High Priest as he came forth from the Holy of Holies in Perfect peace*/As the brightness of the vaulted canopy of heaven [was the countenance of the Priest]/As lightning flashing from the splendour of the *Chayoth.*/As the celestial blue in the thread of the fringes./As the iridescence of the rainbow in the storm-clouds./As the glory wherewith the Rock has clothed his pious servants./As a rose planted in the midst of a pleasant garden./As a diadem set on the

Noah offered it, reconciled God to the reality of the re-created world. The relationship between the cult and creation is suggested by these elements. The full realization of that relationship comes into view with the signs that Israel's cult provides God.

brow of a king./As the mirror of love in the face of a bridegroom./As a halo of purity shining forth from the mitre of holiness. Ibid., 172–73.

6

Israel's Memory in the Priestly Tradition

While the deuteronomic tradition prescribes relatively few ritual practices, in the priestly tradition ritual is a central concern. The attention to the mechanics of ritual is what leads some readers to identify Leviticus (plus portions of Exodus 25–40 and Numbers 1–8) as a manual for the priesthood. Admittedly, there is something doctrinal, not in the sense of theological creed but in terms of orthopraxy, about the priestly attention to the procedures and mechanics of ritual. The specificity with which the materials of the cult, the sacrifices, the observance of each festival, and the management of impurity are detailed evinces an intense preoccupation with correct cultic performance.[1]

But the attention to the minutiae of ritual is not only a function of such utilitarian objectives. It is part of a broader conceptual orientation that privileges sensory, particularly visual, perception and experience as epistemological tools. The priestly tradition associates memory with sensation, and it relies on sensation to induce Israel's memory as well as God's. There is a difference between divine and human memory. When God's memory is triggered or awakened, the effect is the restoration or renewal of God's awareness and commitment. Israel's memory is also activated by the senses, but what is to be remembered is singular experience or specific duty. The point of memory is not to teach the details of law nor to provide explanations for practices. Instead, memory motivates or constrains behavior in the moment.[2]

1. On orthopraxy and Leviticus, see Gilbert Lewis, "Religious Doctrine or Experience: A Matter of Seeing, Learning, or Doing," in *Ritual and Memory: Toward a Comparative Anthropology of Religion*, ed. H. Whitehouse and J. Laidlaw (Walnut Creek, CA: AltaMira, 2004), 155-72.

2. As Lewis points out, this is obviously not the case for the Levites and priests themselves. As a manual for religious practitioners, the instructions for constructing the tabernacle and its appurtenances, and the laws of sacrifice, purity and impurity, and the dietary laws form a body of doctrine that this class must learn and remember. See "Religious Doctrine or Experience," 157–61. Nevertheless, although semantic

The preexilic priestly writers have a decidedly negative opinion of Israel's unchecked memory, as shown by the one instance they narrate. The only time Israel's *act* of memory is reported in P, the behavior is both false and impious. In Num. 11:5, a full year after the exodus from Egypt, the hungry and culinarily bored Israelites look with distorted nostalgia back to Egypt:

> The assembled throng that was in their [the Israelites'] midst felt a great craving. They sat and wept and said, "If only we had meat to eat! We remember (*zākarnû*) the fish we ate freely in Egypt, the cucumbers, and the melons, the leeks, the onions and the garlic!" (Num. 11:4-5)

Hardly comporting with the picture of servitude in Exodus 1–5, the Israelites' memory is not merely delusional. It is tantamount to rejection of the unique nourishment provided directly by God. Alone among all people, the Israelites were fed *manna* from God. Yet they imagine fine food from the hands of their Egyptian taskmasters. Tellingly, the false memory rouses the people into rebellion against Moses with horrific consequences. God becomes enraged. To punish them, God responds to their request with a nauseating superabundance of meat meant to underscore the baseness of their complaint, and then smites the people with a plague (Num. 11:33). As Adriane Leveen observes, this passage appears to dispute "the wisdom of relying on memory at all."[3] Certainly, it implies that, unregulated, Israel's memory is unreliable. Yet, if the Israelites can be brought to remember falsely by the sensation of hunger and the sharpness of their craving, authorized visual cues may also bring them to remember appropriately. Hence, the preexilic priestly writers look to commemorative objects to remind the community of the priests' authority.

Regulating Memory: Commemorative Objects

Israel's false memory in Numbers 11 is part and parcel of the people's recurring acts of rebellion against Moses, Aaron, and God. In fact, it launches the wayward behavior that characterizes the Israelites in the center of the book (Numbers 11–25). In her book on Numbers, Leveen casts these chapters as the centerpiece of a historiographic triptych. The first ten chapters of Numbers,

content is important as far as the clerical audience is concerned, the priestly writers do not exhibit the concern for explanation and exegesis that characterizes Deuteronomy and the recitations and verbal instruction it demands of Israel.

3. Adriane Leveen, *Memory and Tradition in the Book of Numbers* (New York: Cambridge University Press, 2008), 21.

she demonstrates, outline the organization of the community as envisioned by the priesthood; the middle section offers a "collective memory" of disastrous events in the wilderness to justify priestly authority; and the final section describes the reorganization of the people chastened by the consequences of their rebellions. Overall, this analysis shows convincingly that Numbers is deliberately structured to impress the need for priestly governance upon those who will return to Judah. Leveen's discussion of the three mnemonics for Israel introduced in Numbers—the fringes (Numbers 15), the plating on the altar (Numbers 17), and Aaron's rod (Numbers 17)—interprets them in that context.[4] Their conceptual significance, however, requires further exploration, as does the relationship between these mnemonics and priestly notions of memory and of covenant. Because the fringes are a Holiness innovation, I take them up in the next chapter. Here, I turn to the plating and the rod, both of which come from P.

1. ". . . A ZIKKĀRÔN FOR THE ISRAELITES": THE PLATING

Two traditions of wilderness rebellion come together in Numbers 16–17: a priestly account of a Levitical challenge to the Aaronide priesthood led by Koraḥ, and a JE tradition of the subversive challenge to Moses' authority represented by the Reubenites, Datan, and Abiram.[5] Koraḥ's grievance is against the hierarchy that places Aaron's branch of the tribe of Levi above all the others, but he voices his complaint in more democratic terms:

> You make yourselves too great, for the whole congregation—all of them—are holy and Yahweh is among them all. Why are you elevated above the community of Yahweh? (Num. 16:3)

Moses responds to Koraḥ by proposing a test to determine "who is consecrated to him and may approach him and whom he has chosen to offer to him." He instructs Koraḥ and his followers to put fire and incense in their firepans and present them before God, who will, by accepting one, identify "the man

4. Ibid., 97–139.

5. In the redacted version of this event, the two rebellions have been conflated, and it is not easy to identify the elements proper to each story. For a breakdown of the two strands present in this narrative, see Israel Knohl, *The Sanctuary of Silence: The Priestly Torah and the Holiness School* (Minneapolis: Augsburg Fortress Press, 1995; repr., Winona Lake, IN: Eisenbrauns, 2007), 73–85, and Baruch Levine, *Numbers*, 2 vols., AB 4A–B (New York: Doubleday, 1993–2000), 1:405–6. Milgrom's commentary in *Numbers*, JPS (Philadelphia: Jewish Publication Society, 1990), 129–42, provides a helpful guide to the sequence of events in this episode. See also Leveen, *Memory and Tradition*, 114–33. Leveen specifically addresses the commemorative firepans on pp. 128–33.

whom Yahweh has chosen" (Num. 16:5–7). The test is hardly capricious, as the twice-daily incense offering is the exclusive responsibility of the high priest. It is presented not on the bronze altar in the courtyard where animal offerings are burned, but on the gold altar in the outer sanctuary where the priest wears his sacred garments (*bigdê-qodeš*) and which is immediately in front of the "holy of holies" where the ark resides. The law is explicit in Exod. 30:1–8:

> Aaron shall offer (*hiqṭîr*) fragrant incense upon it every morning when he attends to the lamps, and when Aaron goes up to [light] the lamps in the evening, he shall offer incense, continually before Yahweh, through all your generations.

The test presumably takes place, but the text is silent as to its outcome. Instead, the narrative shifts to the suppression of the second rebellion, the one against Moses (Num. 16:28–34), and only then returns to the firepan test: "A fire went out from Yahweh and it consumed the 250 men who were offering incense" (Num. 16:34). Then, as instructed, Eliezar the son of Aaron hammers the firepans into plating for the altar[6] as

> a reminder (*zikkārôn*) to the Israelites so that no unauthorized person (*'îš zār*),[7] [anyone] not of the seed of Aaron, will offer incense (*lᵉhaqṭîr qᵉṭoret*) before Yahweh and will not become like [i.e. meet the fate of] Koraḥ and like his cohort, as Yahweh said through Moses. (Num. 17:4–5)

Forged from the now consecrated firepans, the plating evokes Koraḥ's rebellion. But because of the conflation of storylines, it becomes a "reminder" of both rebellions. And because the plating covers the bronze altar in the tabernacle courtyard, it is visible to Levites and Israelites alike, reminding both of priestly authority.

6. The firepans must be taken out of common use because they were rendered "holy" as soon as they were presented and dedicated in the course of preparing for the test (Num. 17:2). See Menahem Haran, *Temples and Temple Service in Ancient Israel: An Inquiry into Biblical Cult Phenomena and the Historical Setting of the Priestly School* (Oxford: Clarendon, 1978; repr., Winona Lake, IN: Eisenbrauns, 1985), 176–77; Levine, *Numbers*, 1:418–19.

7. The word *zār* generally means "foreigner" (Isa. 1:7), "strange" (Prov. 7:5), or "unknown" (Isa. 43:12). Here, the meaning "unauthorized" is the same as found in Lev. 10:1 regarding the offering of Nadab and Abihu—*'ēš zārâh 'ăšer lo' ṣiwwāh 'otām*—"strange fire, which [Yahweh] had not commanded them [to bring]," and in Exod. 30:9 concerning the incense altar: *lō'-ta'ălû 'ālâyw qᵉṭoret zārâ* ("do not put any unauthorized incense upon it").

2. ". . . A SAFEGUARD": AARON'S ROD

Evidently that reminder is not sufficient, for a third uprising of "the whole Israelite congregation against Moses and Aaron" comes the next day (Num. 17:6-7). Their complaint—"You are causing Yahweh's people to die!"—is not about hierarchy, but again proof is required to confirm authority and leadership. God's initial response is to send a plague that kills 14,700 people before it is checked by Aaron's expiatory incense offering (Num. 17:9-14).[8] God then commands a second test, this one definitive. The head of each tribe is to bring his rod, inscribed with the tribal name, to the Tent of Meeting. Yahweh declares "the one whom I choose, his staff will sprout flowers and I will be relieved of the complaints of the Israelites which they complain against you" (Num. 17:20).[9] Aaron wins the contest when his rod spouts blossoms and almonds: "flowers burst [from Aaron's rod] and blossoms bloomed (*wayyāṣēṣ ṣîṣ*) and it bore ripe almonds" (Num. 17:23). Like the plating, the result of this test is to be commemorated eternally:

> Yahweh said to Moses: "Return the rod of Aaron before the [ark of] the testimony as a safeguard (*mišmeret*) and a sign (*'ôt*) for the rebels that their complaints against me cease so they do not die." (Num. 17:25)

Clearly the rod, like the plating, is meant to stand as a reminder of Aaron's unique role, but the designation of the latter as a "safeguard" associates it with the only other permanent "safeguard," the jar of reserved *manna* (Exod. 16:32-33). The *manna* as we shall see shortly is related to the Sabbath, which in turn is related to creation (cf. Exod. 20:8-11; 31:16-17). A creation aspect attaches to the flowering rod[10] as well, making both "safeguards" cultic emblems of creation. Both may also be emblems of the priestly covenant idea through associations: for the rod, with the "covenant of priesthood," that God makes with Pinchas; and for the *manna*, with the Bread of the Presence, which according to Lev. 24:8 is an "eternal covenant."[11] *Mišmeret*, it now appears, has a broader commemorative function than that of a *zikkārôn*. The difference in this case is not absolute because both the plating *zikkārôn* and the rod *mišmeret*

8. See the discussion of the narration of the rebellion below.

9. *"Relieved"* from *škk*. See Levine, *Numbers* 1:422.

10. See the discussion in Chapter 8.

11. Stephen Geller proposes that the reserved *manna* (Exod. 25:30; Lev. 24:5-9) is also called an "eternal covenant." See "Manna and Sabbath: A Literary-Theological Reading of Exodus 16," *Interpretation* 59 (2005): 7, 12.

are also "signs." Nevertheless, as a *safeguard,* the rod is more than a warning of the consequences of rebellion, and more than a reminder that God has chosen Aaron. The "safeguard" rod visually commemorates and recalls the complete convergence of the cult and [re-]creation, and the maintenance of both by the priests.

Religious Life and Experience

I now turn to the postmonarchical priestly writers, and their literary representation of Israel's religious life and experience. Because the religious program of the priestly tradition does not offer many examples of lay participation, one might expect the topic to be rather thin. The Israelites are largely observers of, rather than participants in, cultic pageantry. They provide the raw materials with which Bezalel and Hur build the tabernacle and make the furnishings, vessels, and other materials necessary for the cult's functioning and then, for the most part, step aside and let the priests minister to the tabernacle service. They provide the offerings that the priests then sacrifice in connection with purification rites, and they have the opportunity to bring offerings of thanksgiving, but here too, the lay Israelite's role is to present the offering to the priest who then carries out the sacrifice.

The priestly tradition also pays little attention to the life-cycle rituals found in most cultures, such as marriage rites and adolescent initiation rites.[12] The biblical treatment of the one life-cycle ritual enjoined upon the Israelites, circumcision of males on the eighth day after birth, is neither a rite of passage nor an initiation.[13] Although there is biblical evidence of circumcision functioning in rite-of-passage contexts (for instance, Ishmael's circumcision at age thirteen [Gen. 17:25], the circumcision of the men of Shechem [Gen.

12. Of course, life-cycle rites were likely part of Israelite religious life. A growing body of scholarship looks at ritual practices that may be gleaned from biblical narratives (e.g., rites associated with giving birth [Leviticus 12] and weaning infants [1 Sam. 1:24–28], female adolescent coming-of-age rituals [Judg. 11:37–40], and mourning rites [e.g., Deut. 21:12–13; 2 Sam. 1:11–12]). See, for instance, Saul M. Olyan, "What Do Shaving Rites Accomplish and What Do They Signal in Biblical Ritual Contexts?" *JBL* 117 (1998): 611–22; Peggy L. Day, "From the Child Is Born the Woman: The Story of Jephthah's Daughter," in *Gender and Difference in Ancient Israel*, ed. P. L. Day (Minneapolis: Fortress Press, 1989), 58–74; Susan Ackerman, "Coming-of-Age Rituals in Ancient Israel" (paper presented at the annual meeting of the Society of Biblical Literature, Atlanta, November 21, 2010); and Ackerman, "Women's Rites of Passage in Ancient Israel: Three Case Studies (Birth, Coming of Age, and Death)," in *Family and Household Religion: Toward a Synthesis of Old Testament Studies, Archaeology, Epigraphy, and Cultural Studies*, ed. R. Albertz, B. Alpert-Nakhai, S. M. Olyan, and R. Schmitt (Winona Lake, IN: Eisenbrauns, forthcoming).

13. It is a sign of the covenant, not the procedure for entry into it.

34:14–17, 22, 24], and possibly the circumcision of Israelite males upon entering the land [Josh. 5:2–5]),[14] the salience of circumcision lies not in marking the transition of the male from uncircumcised to circumcised, but in the signatory function of the circumcised penis, which is a "sign" of the covenant that God makes with Abraham and his descendants.[15]

The Representation of Religious Experience

As a nation, however, Israel experiences events that exhibit ritual features and can be analyzed in terms of ritual theory. Whitehouse's divergent modes theory, referenced earlier in this work, is a useful heuristic model for this analysis. Whitehouse maintains that communities that privilege sensory-induced memory also tend to have religious systems that emphasize singular experiences, particularly initiation rites, as the means of revelation, and they codify revelation in an analogical and iconic fashion. They make use of visual symbols whose meaning derives largely from the perceived "resemblance between the inherent characteristics of the symbols and their referents," but which are also multi-vocalic and ambiguous.[16] We have already observed the priestly use of commemorative objects to represent both the consequences of rebellion and the authority of the priesthood. Now I look at the literary representation of Israel's revelatory experience.

Transformation of a People

As a nation, Israel goes through two significant transformative events in contexts replete with cultic and ritual overtones. Their representation in P offers the opportunity to consider the priestly tradition's concept of religious activity for the laity. The night of the exodus marks the transition of the Israelites from slaves to free people. The events at Mount Sinai mark a second transition as the people enter into their status as a "kingdom of priests" (*mamleket kōhănîm*) and as God's treasured nation.[17] Both Passover and Sinai, therefore, have an

14. Ackerman, "Coming-of-Age Rituals in Ancient Israel."

15. The timing of male circumcision on the eighth day after birth may have been related to the point at which the infant's viability and survival prognosis seemed assured; however, this function of the rite is nowhere referenced in the text.

16. Harvey Whitehouse, *Arguments and Icons: Divergent Modes of Religiosity* (Oxford: Oxford University Press, 2000), 64.

17. Ilana Pardes has also interpreted the Sinai event as an initiation in *The Biography of Ancient Israel: National Narratives in the Bible* (Berkeley: University of California Press, 2000), 65–99. In her reading, the initiation process continues through the episodes of the golden calf and the tabernacle building as well as the events of Exodus 19–20.

initiatory function, and the cultic features of the two events provide a basis for investigating them as ritual moments in Israel's life.

Initiation rites vary from society to society and it is difficult to make general statements about this particular rite of passage. Some discussions of initiation rites emphasize the sensation of separation from one's original identity followed by transition to, and incorporation of, a new identity;[18] the use of bodily fluids, especially blood, in the course of the initiation ritual;[19] or the experience of what di Nola and Pelton call "unveiling the *sacra*."[20] Whitehouse finds that the initiation rites of communities that privilege episodic memory are characterized by intense, often painful or terrifying, sensory experiences that produce awareness of the mysterious forces supporting community life. The initiate gains a degree of insight, yet on an explicit level the semantic content of revelation remains enigmatic.[21] All these elements are present in the Passover and Sinai events to a degree sufficient to consider them in terms of the initiation experience.

1. Passover (Exodus 12)

The first Passover, during which the Israelites leave Egypt and slavery, takes place under fraught conditions that heighten the drama of the experience. In the course of it they are changed forever. Their slave identity ends and a new identity as a nation under the special protection of God begins. There are symbolic actions to be performed, new information and practices to be mastered. The night involves smearing blood on walls, huddling inside protected homes while a deadly Destroyer goes through the land. Terror and dread join with awe and the excitement of escape.

The account opens with preparatory instructions for the last days in Egypt:

> On the tenth day of this month they shall take for themselves, every man, a lamb for his father's household. A lamb for each household. If the household is too small for a lamb, he and his neighbor who is close to his home shall take it for the household; according to

18. Arnold van Gennep, *The Rites of Passage* (Chicago: University of Chicago Press, 1960; repr., London: Routledge, 2004), 67.

19. Mircea Eliade, "Australian Religions. Part III: Initiation Rites and Secret Cults," *History of Religions* 7 (1967): 67–68, 72, 74–75, 77.

20. Alfonso M. di Nola and Robert D. Pelton, "Demythicization in Certain Primitive Cultures: Cultural Fact and Socioreligious Integration," *History of Religions* 12 (1972): 2.

21. See also Eliade, "Australian Religions," 69, 71–72. One feature Eliade identifies in most of the rituals he describes is that of unintelligibility from the novices' perspective.

> the number of people in it, according to what he eats, you shall apportion the lamb. (Exod. 12:3b–4)

The lamb is to be kept for four days and on the fourteenth of the month, slaughtered and roasted.

> And this is how you shall eat it: Your hips girded and your sandals on your feet and your staff in your hand. And you shall eat it in haste. It is a *pesaḥ* offering to Yahweh. (12:11)

To this is added something more startling. The Israelites are instructed to paint some blood from the slaughtered lamb on their homes so that they will be exempt from the destruction awaiting the Egyptians.

> They shall take some of the blood and put it on the two doorposts and on the lintel, on the houses in which they will be eating [the lamb] . . . the blood will be for you a sign on the houses which you are in. And I will see the blood and I will rescue[22] you, so that you will not be afflicted by the Destroyer when I smite the land of Egypt. (12:7, 13)

The provision for apotropaic blood markings on the houses adds the element of danger to the evening, while the instructions themselves impart a ritual character to the exodus night and the first Passover. What confirms the *initiatory* function of the practices performed, however, is the declaration that opens the pericope: "This month will be for you the first of months, the first [month] it is for you, of the months in the year" (*haḥōdeš hazzeh lākem rōʾš ḥŏdāšîm riʾšôn hūʾ lākem lᵉḥodšê haššānâ*) (Exod. 12:2). We have already observed that the date associated with Israel's national beginning has cosmic and cultic resonances. In terms of the Israelites' experience, the calendar reference is an emphatic pronouncement of the transitional significance of the activities they will perform. The Hebrew word for month, *ḥōdeš*, also means "new." Together with *rōʾš* ("beginning") and *riʾšôn* ("first"), the words allude to "newness" five

22. *Pāsaḥtî.* The meaning of "protect" is demonstrated through the parallelism in Isa. 31:5, "Like winged birds, thus Yahweh of Hosts will be a shield over Jerusalem: shield and save (*gānôn wᵉhiṣṣîl*), protect and provide refuge (*pāsōḥ wᵉhimlîṭ*)." It is possible, though by no means certain, that the expression *lêl šimmūrîm* ("night of guarding" or "night of watching over") in Exod. 12:42 may be a gloss on the more obscure term. The erroneous translation, "pass over," likely derives from a secondary meaning for *psḥ*, "lame" (cf. 2 Sam. 9:13; 19:27).

times in the single verse. The new month is also the first month. It is on this *initial* month of the year that the Israelites will be initiated into a new and singular state of being. Not only will they be transformed from slaves to free people, the events of the Passover night will also distinguish them from their Egyptian neighbors. With words expressing "newness" five times in Exod. 12:2, the descriptive statement of time becomes a predictive statement of transformed ontology. For the Israelites, the exodus is a new beginning. It is literally the first day of the rest of their lives.

The initiatory character of the exodus night is intensified by the element of terror that accompanies it. Nighttime, when the first Passover takes place, is a liminal time between full consciousness and simulated death. Under normal circumstances, danger abounds; all the more so on this night when a "Destroyer" threatens. All that protects the Israelites from the fate of the Egyptian firstborn is the blood marking their doors. Like the blood of circumcision, this blood is a sign identifying the Israelite homes. It protects them by alerting God to the identity of each house's occupants. Thus the exodus experience also initiates the Israelites into the nature of their relationship with God. They are a special people, whose uniqueness is identified through rites involving blood.

Further evidence of the initiatory function of the exodus night is its singularity. The Passover in Egypt is a one-time event, as rabbinic tradition makes clear through the designation "Egyptian Passover" (*pesaḥ miṣrāyîm*). All subsequent celebrations are "Passover of the generations" (*pesaḥ dōrôt*). This particular Passover differs from the ongoing commemoration both in its location (home) and in the practices performed. Only on this Passover do the Israelites eat dressed in special journey clothing and participate in the rite of smearing blood on their houses. These practices form part of the ritual of transformation that makes the Israelites into a nation.

The Israelites' status as a people bound by boundaries and law comes upon them in connection with the first Passover, and this contributes yet further to the initiatory function of the event. During the night of the first Passover, a group of laws are revealed: not just any laws, but laws intimately tied to this foundational event in their history. The laws concerning the ongoing observance of the Festival of Unleavened Bread (Exod. 12:15-20; 13:6-7), *pesaḥ* (12:43-49), and dedication of the firstborn (13:2, 11-15) explicitly relate these practices to the exodus, and in particular the night of the first Passover.

The laws of circumcision may also be revealed to Israel at this time, specifically in the stipulation in Exod. 12:44-48.[23] The episode at the inn in Exod. 4:24-26 suggests that Moses (Genesis 17 and 34 notwithstanding) was not yet acquainted with this commandment. Moreover, textual evidence suggests a conceptual link between the law of circumcision and Passover. The blood from circumcision that saves Moses at the inn foreshadows the blood on the doorposts that will save the Israelites. Making that connection even more pronounced, the text juxtaposes the account at the inn with a clear allusion to the night of the exodus when the last plague will be executed. God tells Moses,

> Say to Pharaoh, "Thus says Yahweh: 'Israel is my firstborn.' And say to him 'Send my son out that he may serve me. But if you refuse to send him out, behold, I will kill your firstborn.'" (Exod. 4:22-23)[24]

The law given in Exod. 12:44-48 explicitly relates Passover and circumcision: only if one is circumcised may he eat the *pesaḥ* offering.

The exodus comes to authorize the laws introduced, as is shown by the answers given to the child who asks for explanation in Exod. 12:27: "You shall say, 'It is the Passover sacrifice (*zebaḥ pesaḥ*) to Yahweh who rescued (*pāsaḥ*) the households of the Israelites in Egypt when he afflicted the Egyptians and their households.'" Moreover, the dramatic nature of the exodus event intensifies the didactic power of its memory as a mechanism for promoting proper fulfillment of the new laws.

It is unusual for the priestly tradition to situate law within a historical context; to do so falls outside the normative priestly view of cultic law derived from a creation model.[25] Yet, the appeal to history as an authority for law, especially for the laws of *pesaḥ* and *maṣṣōt*, makes sense in terms of the lay experience of religious life. As we shall see in the discussion of the revelation at Sinai, the Israelites are not initiated into the mysteries of the cult, nor do they learn of the eternal covenant that the cult represents. They need the memory of a historical experience to motivate their adherence to the ritual laws enjoined upon them. The secondary theology, according to which authority derives from God's revelation of law, serves to commit the people in a way that the

23. The priestly tradition locates the origin of circumcision in God's command to Abraham in Genesis 17. Nevertheless, it is possible to read Exod. 12:48 as the point at which it is introduced to the people as a whole.

24. In addition to textual allusions and juxtapositions linking circumcision to Passover in Exodus, Joshua 5 makes an explicit connection. Immediately before they celebrate the first Passover in the land (Josh. 5:10), all the Israelite males are circumcised (Josh. 5:2-9). This event may be explained as the reenactment of Israel's original initiatory experience, but it is also possible that the ritualized entry into the land is, itself, a kind of initiation rite.

25. The explanation for the Festival of Booths in Lev. 23:43 (attributed to H) is similarly unusual for its recourse to history.

dominant creation-derived theology cannot. The creation-centered theology is not abandoned—the reference to the function of the sign in Exod. 12:13 comports with the creation-centered model[26]—but overall, the exodus event is an Israelite experience that serves to solidify the people's investment in the law as a consequence of their initiation into a new identity as not-slaves, and as people cared for by their God.

2. *Sinai (Exodus 19; 20:18-21; 24:3-8)*

Like the Passover night, the revelation at Sinai is a fraught experience. And like Passover, Sinai is an event through which the people acquire the unique identity as the "most treasured [by God] of all people" (Exod. 19:5) and a "kingdom of priests and a holy nation" (19:6). The Israelites' initiation into this state is both carefully prepared and carefully orchestrated. To begin, the people must become ritually pure. They are sanctified and they wash their clothing (19:14; cf. v. 10). Upon becoming sanctified, they must maintain that state for three days (19:15; cf. v. 11). The Israelites are arrayed around the base of the mountain. They are told, "Be careful not to ascend the mountain or to touch even its extreme parts. Everyone who touches the mountain will surely die" (Exod. 19:12). The regulation applies even (anachronistically) to the priests (19:22), for the mountain is designated sacred ground.[27]

The people so arranged, the theophany begins with smoke, fire, thunder, lightning, and trembling earth, accompanied by the sound of the *shofar* (ram's horn), the strong and sustained blast of which announces Yahweh's presence:

> On the third day, in the morning there was noise [thunder?] and lightning and a heavy cloud on the mountain, and the sound of the ram's horn was very strong, and the people in the camp trembled (*wayyeḥĕrad*). . . . All of Mount Sinai was smoke when Yahweh descended on it in fire. Its smoke rose up like the smoke of a kiln and the entire mountain shook greatly (*wayyeḥĕrad*). The sound of the ram's horn went on and on and was very strong. Moses spoke and God answered him in a voice. (19:16, 18-19)

26. See Chapter 8.

27. According to Eliade, preparation of sacred ground is another feature of initiation into sacred mysteries ("Australian Religions," 62). The warning against encroachment on the sacredness of the mountain recalls the warning given to Moses in Exod. 3:5 to respect the boundaries of sacred ground (*'admat-qōdeš*).

The event is so terrifying that the mountain trembles as much as the people do. From the Israelites' perspective, all the senses are involved, but sight is primary. Not only does the theophany take place before all their eyes, sight is the primary sensation that the people register. "All the people saw the sounds (*rōʾîm ʾet-haqqôlōt*) and the lightning and the sound of the ram's horn, and the mountain that was smoking" (20:18).

The cloud they see on the mountain is the manifestation of God's *kābôd*, God's divine immanence. In Exod. 40:34, the cloud fills the tent of meeting as soon as it is erected and it is the presence that guides the Israelites through the wilderness (Num. 9:17–22). The fire on the mountain is another manifestation of God's presence that reappears when God consumes the sacrifices on the newly consecrated altar in Lev. 9:24, at night over the tabernacle or tent of meeting (Exod. 40:38; Num. 9:15–16) and as a destructive force (Num. 11:2–3; 16:35).[28]

In contrast to the deuteronomic account of the revelation at Horeb, in priestly religion the awe-inspiring and terrifying aspects of God's presence are best perceived through sight. God's *kābôd* appears to Moses or in view of the Israelites (cf. Exod. 24:17). When the Israelites see (*w*^{e}*rāʾâ kol hāʿām*) the cloud standing at the opening of the tent of meeting (Exod. 33:10) or they see (*wayyarʾ*) the fire going out to consume the sacrifices (Lev. 9:24), they know Yahweh is present, and they fall on their faces or shout acclaim. After the revelation of the Decalogue, sight is again presented as the epistemological tool of choice. God tells Moses to remind the people that "You saw (*r*^{e}*ʾîtem*) that from the heavens [God] spoke to you" (Exod. 20:22) and for that reason, they are enjoined from making silver or gold idols.[29]

Yet even sight perception affords limited access to the divine. God tells Moses, "you cannot see my face, for no man can see me and live" (Exod. 33:20). The Israelites clearly recognize this danger. Immediately following the conclusion of God's direct speech to them, they ask Moses to stand in their place while they retreat to a distance.

> The people saw the sounds and the lightning and the sound of the *shofar* and the smoking mountain. The people saw and they trembled and they stood at a distance [from the mountain]. They said to

28. And, of course, in the burning bush (Exod. 3:2).

29. This commandment had already been given at the start of the Decalogue (Exod. 20:4). Clearly, the force of the statement in 20:22 is that it is because they have *seen* God's presence, that the Israelites must not make idols.

> Moses: "*You* speak to us and we will listen, but let not God speak to us lest we die!" (Exod. 20:18–19)

Strikingly, only in this instance do the Israelites use the impersonal name "God" (*'ĕlōhîm*) rather than "Yahweh" when they ask Moses to be their intermediary.[30] Not only do they stand at a distance from the event, they create verbal distance between themselves and God. The desire for distance turns out to mean that the semantic content of the revelation heard by the Israelites is abbreviated. God will make known the primary revelation, namely the details of the cult, only to Moses; it will be kept hidden from the people.[31]

It is true that virtually no scholars attribute Exodus 19–20 (other than Exod. 19:1-2a) to P. Nevertheless, as one of the two dominant traditions in the Pentateuch, the priestly tradition clearly makes use of an account not its own to serve its purposes. Specifically, it incorporates Exodus 19 and 20:18–21 to introduce God's revelation of the cult to Moses (Exodus 25ff.). It does so, moreover, in order to distinguish between the two kinds of revelation. Israel's revelatory event is experiential rather than semantic. At Sinai, the Israelites encounter God's *presence*—the "*sacra*." Prior to Sinai, the Israelites have witnessed the "signs and wonders" performed in Egypt, and they have been guided by the pillars of fire and cloud during their journey to Sinai. But at the mountain, God is undeniably in their midst.[32] Communication of law is not the object of this event. Instead, the theophany serves to establish the divine authority of the subsequent revelation concerning the cult that is given to Moses alone. The revelation of presence establishes the divine imprimatur for the cult while simultaneously demonstrating the necessity for exclusive responsibility for its administration.

Revelation Codified

The Sinai event revealed the paradoxical implications of God's presence to the Israelites. On the one hand, Israel's special status invests their religious activity

30. In contrast, the Israelites (or subsets thereof) refer to God as "Yahweh" nineteen times (Exod. 16:3; 19:8; 24:3; 24:7; Num. 9:7; 14:3; 14:40; 16:3[2×]; 17:6; 20:3; 20:4; 21:7[2×]; 27:3; 32:31; 32:32; 36:2[2×]). In addition, Aaron and Miriam refer to God as "Yahweh" in Num. 12:2.

31. Di Nola and Pelton, "Demythicization in Certain Primitive Cultures," 2. The element of mystery is absent of course for the reading and listening audience of Exodus, which is privy to the revelation given to Moses in Exodus 25ff.

32. In contrast to the account in Deuteronomy where God remains in the heavens, in Exodus, God "descends" (19:20) onto the mountain. See Victor Hurowitz, "From Storm God to Abstract Being: How the Deity Became More Distant from Exodus to Deuteronomy," *BR* 14 (1998): 44.

with heightened significance, but on the other, the immanent presence of the deity intensifies the danger associated with the sacred tabernacle precincts, and this means the performance of religious duties and sacred rites must be strictly regulated. The priestly tradition makes use of crucial events in Israelite history to ensure the proper behavior of the Israelite laity. The deaths of Nadab and Abihu, the rebellions of Koraḥ, Datan, Abiram, and their followers, and the terrible plague at Baal Peor create memories searing enough to serve as continual brakes on improper behavior. In a similar fashion, the tradition codifies Israel's positive obligations in the context of dramatic events. The memory of the exodus night, as shown above, motivates fulfillment of practices incumbent on the laity: eating unleavened bread, abstaining from leaven, sacrificing the *pesaḥ* offering, and quite possibly, circumcision of males. The other signal practice enjoined on every Israelite is Sabbath observance, and this duty is codified through the medium of the *manna* that the Israelites encounter and eat throughout the wilderness period.

1. Proper Performance of the Cult: Nadab and Abihu (Lev. 10:1-4)

Leviticus 9 closes with the culmination of the ceremonies for the priests' ordination and the inauguration of the cult. Aaron offers the first sacrifices on the altar and a fire from God consumes them. It is a suspenseful moment because Yahweh's acceptance of the sacrifices is what confirms the acceptability of the cult as a whole. When the divine presence appears and a fire consumes the sacrifices on the altar, the cult is thereby pronounced acceptable and the people rejoice and fall prostrate.

> Moses and Aaron went into the tent of meeting, they came out and they blessed the people, and the *kəbôd* of Yahweh appeared to all the people. A fire went forth from Yahweh onto the altar and consumed the burnt offering and the fat. All the people saw, they cried aloud and they fell on their faces. (Lev. 9:23-24)

However, the ceremony goes shockingly awry. Nadab and Abihu make an improper incense offering of "strange fire which [Yahweh] had not commanded them [to bring]" (Lev. 10:1) and ignite an instantaneous holocaust.[33] Their bodies are consumed in an instant by a second fire that

33. The description of the fire as "strange" recalls the prohibition in Exod. 30:8-9 regarding the daily incense offering (*qᵉṭōret tāmîd*) that the high priest presents on the golden altar in the outer sanctum: "Do not put strange incense (*qᵉṭōret zārâ*) on it, nor a burned offering, a meal offering, and as for libations, do not pour out libations upon it."

"came out before Yahweh" (Lev. 10:2). The event shocks Aaron their father into silence and even leads him to neglect his obligation to eat the sanctified food (Lev. 10:3, 19). The assembled throng receives only minimal explanation of the tragedy, and the explanation given is ambiguous in the extreme.[34] Moses says to Aaron: "This is what Yahweh said, saying, 'Through those close to me I am sanctified and before all the people I am glorified'"(Lev. 10:3). Nevertheless, for the Israelite witnesses to the traumatic episode, the meaning cannot be forgotten. The cult is beneficent; it makes possible the numinous presence of God among the people. But it is also dangerous, for it brings into proximity what Rudolf Otto has defined as the *mysterium tremendum*, the "otherness" of the divine that inspires both awe and fear, terror and bewilderment.[35] Hence, no unauthorized person may approach the altar.[36] God will annihilate anyone who does. God codifies the requirement of proper ministry to the shrine, and the consequences of unsanctioned acts.

2. Koraḥ and Affirmation of the Aaronide Priesthood

The objects commemorating the rebellion against Aaronide authority in Numbers 16–17 were discussed earlier. Now I look at how the narrative report of the events confirms the lessons to be derived from the rebellions and their aftermath.

In response to the attack on his leadership by Datan and Abiram, Moses proposes a test of his authority separate from either the tests of the firepan or the tribal rod. This test is public and involves the entire community. Moses declares that if the ground opens up beneath the feet of the rebels and swallows them alive, God has confirmed Moses as God's messenger. If not, the rebels are vindicated. The results are immediate:

> Just as [Moses] finished saying these things [to the rebels] the ground that was beneath them burst open. The earth opened its mouth

34. As noted above, such ambiguity is a critical feature of "imagistic" religions according to Whitehouse, and directly tied to this modality's reliance on sensual memory cues. Harvey Whitehouse, *Modes of Religiosity: A Cognitive Theory of Religious Transmission* (Walnut Creek, CA: AltaMira, 2004), 420, and *Arguments and Icons*, 63.

35. Rudolf Otto, *The Idea of the Holy: An Inquiry into the Non-rational Factor in the Idea of the Divine and Its Relation to the Rational*, 2nd ed., trans. J. W. Harvey (London: Oxford University Press, 1950), chapters 4 and 5.

36. The midrashic tradition suggests that the event was meant to teach that no intoxicated person may approach the altar. While this explanation is suggested by the juxtaposition of the deaths of Nadab and Abihu with the prohibition in Lev. 10:9 on entering the sanctuary when intoxicated, it does not account for the powerful juxtaposition of Lev. 9:22-24 with the events of Leviticus 10.

> and swallowed them and their households and all the people that were with Koraḥ and all their possessions. They and everything they had sunk alive into Sheol. Then the earth covered them and they vanished from the midst of the congregation. All Israel that surrounded them raised their voices and they cried, "Let not the earth swallow us!" (Num. 16:31-34)

Further proof that God chose Moses comes in the form of a "fire [that] went forth from Yahweh" and consumes the rebels (Num. 16:35) and a plague that ravages the camp when the rebellion resumes the next day (Num. 17:11).

All three acts of devastation come to support Moses' claim, but it is Aaron's actions that restore peace and safety to the congregation. As instructed by Moses, Aaron quickly presents an incense offering, makes atonement, and stands "between the dead and the living, and the plague was checked" (Num. 17:13). Not only do Aaron's actions stop the plague at that particular time, they demonstrate for all time the crucial mediating role of the high priest. The incense offering that stays the murderous plague is the sole purview of the high priest. No one else can make atonement or propitiate God in the same way. The episode thus dramatizes the continually essential role of the high priest in the context of a community graced by God's presence.

3. *Baal Peor*

An almost identical message emerges from the disaster at Baal Peor in Numbers 25. At the end of the forty years of wandering, the people betray God once again by joining with the Midianites (or Moabites) in a bacchanalian orgy (Num. 25:1-3), the most egregious part of which occurs when "a man from among the Israelites came and he brought forward to his kinsmen a Midianite woman, in the very sight of Moses and in the sight of the community of Israel. And they were weeping at the entrance of the tent of meeting" (Num. 25:6). Just what precisely the couple sought to do remains unstated, but without any doubt to stay his actions, Pinchas, the son of Aaron's son Eleazar, reacts by impaling both the man and the woman on his spear—and a plague (heretofore unannounced) is abated. Once again, the actions of a priest save the day. Pinchas, heir to the high priesthood, delivers the community from death. And again, the particular act proves a general rule when God gives Pinchas "my covenant of friendship" (*b^eritî šālôm*) (Num. 25:12), and with his descendants makes an "eternal covenant of the priesthood" (*b^erît k^ehunnat ʿôlām*) (Num. 25:13).[37] God's response confirms that the priesthood is the sole institution for all time that can mediate between the people and the immanent God who dwells among them. Significantly, the events of Numbers 25 concern the second generation, which was supposed to be free of the guilt associated with the episode of the spies in Numbers 14 that had tainted the exodus generation. Yet because the priestly view of humanity is a function of ontology,[38] this generation—like all generations—also needs priestly mediation. Humans err and fail and so by their very nature are incompatible with the divine. For the two to meet requires carefully delineated spaces and procedures that, for Israel, are maintained by the priesthood. To have God in the presence of the community is a profound desideratum, and God's presence ensures providential care. At the same time, God's presence and attention can prove lethal if the setting for God's residence is not prepared and sustained through proper execution of cultic laws of purity, and if the cult itself is violated by improper execution of its rites.

4. The Manna and Sabbath (Exodus 16)

While the priestly tradition uses narrative to reinforce strictures regarding the cult and its rites, when it comes to teaching and reinforcing the positive practices enjoined upon the Israelites, it relies mainly on enumerations and catalogs of law. Yet there is one exception. To codify the law of Sabbath observance, the tradition turns to imaginative experience produced through vivid narrative.[39]

The Sabbath is revealed to the Israelites at Sinai, but it is introduced immediately after the Israelites cross the Sea of Reeds. The introduction also provides an enduring foundation for the people's positive responsibilities concerning the Sabbath.

Once across the sea, the Israelites quickly begin complaining about the lack of food. As it is still early in their relationship with God, the complaints are not held against them. Instead, Yahweh "rains bread from the heavens" for them, producing the miraculous food, *manna*. The provision of *manna* is extraordinary

37. Certainly no irony is intended either in God's bestowal of a covenant or in the use of the word *šālôm* (literally, well-being). The violence, however horrifying to modern sensibilities, is clearly condoned by the text. See John J. Collins, "The Zeal of Phinehas and the Legitimization of Violence," *JBL* 122 (2003): 3–21.

38. Cf. the statement in Gen. 8:21: "the inclinations of man's heart are evil from his youth." As argued in Chapter 3, the priestly authors incorporate this nonpriestly passage, along with the accounts of Noah's sacrifice, God's response, and God's promise that the earth will endure, as the prologue to God's bestowal of the first (and paradigmatic) eternal covenant in Gen. 9:9-17.

39. The law of Sabbath observance itself is laid out in Exod. 20:8-10; 23:12; 31:13-16; 34:21; 35:2-3; Lev. 19:3; 19:30; and 23:3. In addition, Leviticus 24 contains instructions for the weekly arrangement of the bread of the presence on the Sabbath, and Numbers 28 details the offerings to be made on the Sabbath. These laws, however, concern the priests, not the laity.

in itself, and an extraordinary demonstration of God's unique relationship with the Israelites. But when, on the sixth day of gathering *manna*, the Israelites find double the expected amount (Exod. 16:22), its meaning becomes compounded. Moses explains: "Tomorrow is a special Sabbath, a holy Sabbath to Yahweh. What you need to bake, bake, and what you need to cook, cook, and all the rest, reserve it as a set-aside portion until morning" (Exod. 16:23). The next day Moses explains further: "Eat [the *manna*] today, for today is a Sabbath to Yahweh. Today, you will not find it in the field. Six days you shall gather it, but on the seventh day—a Sabbath—there will be none there" (Exod. 16:25-26). When notwithstanding this instruction one Israelite tries to find and gather *manna* (Exod. 16:27), God adds the explicit rule that "no one shall leave his place on the seventh day" (Exod. 16:29). God goes further and mandates a commemorative portion of *manna* be reserved as a *mišmeret* to serve as an ongoing visual reminder of Israel's responsibility for keeping the Sabbath (Exod. 16:32-34). The visual commemoration will ensure that the memory formed by the dramatic demonstration of the Sabbath can be retrieved and revived.

A second memorable event further underscores the law of the Sabbath. This is the story of the Sabbath violator:

> It happened when the Israelites were in the wilderness, they found a man gathering wood on the Sabbath. They brought him, the man who was gathering wood, to Moses and to Aaron and to the whole congregation. They placed him in custody, for it was not decided what to do about him. Yahweh said to Moses, "The man shall die. The entire congregation shall stone him with stones outside the camp." The whole congregation took him outside the camp and they stoned him with stones and he died as Yahweh commanded Moses. (Num. 15:32-35)

In his article on this passage, Simeon Chavel points out that it provides no new information about the Sabbath. All of the prohibitions alluded to in it are implied in other Sabbath texts: "gathering" in Exodus 16, "fire" in Exod. 35:2-3, and the punishment in Exodus 31.[40] What the story does provide is dramatization. With its terse account of the Sabbath violator, Num. 15:32-35 provides an "imagined experience" to illustrate the information given elsewhere. The story graphically reinforces the Sabbath prohibitions while

40. Simeon Chavel, "Numbers 15:32-36—A Microcosm of the Living Priesthood and Its Literary Production," in *The Strata of the Priestly Writing: Contemporary Debate and Future Directions*, ed. S. Shectman and J. S. Baden, ATANT 95 (Zürich: Theologischer, 2009), 49.

providing a vivid enactment of the sentences mandated in Exod. 31:14 ("The one who violates [the Sabbath], will surely die, for whoever does work on it, that person will be cut off from his people") (cf. 31:15; 35:2).

One might wonder why, of all the practices incumbent on the Israelites, Sabbath observance must be reinforced through the medium of experience. The answer lies, I believe, in the designation of the Sabbath as a "sign" (Exod. 31:17) and specifically a sign of the eternal covenant (*bᵉrît ʿôlām*) between God and Israel (Exod. 31:16). The signatory significance of the Sabbath is further reinforced in the law concerning the bread of the presence, which is set out each week on the Sabbath and which also apparently reflects the eternal covenant between God and Israel (Lev. 24:8).[41] But the Israelites have a role to play as well. To ensure they play it properly, the priestly tradition invokes memories derived from vivid experiences and awakened by visual stimuli to reinforce Israel's responsibility for the Sabbath, the sign for God of God's covenant.[42]

The Presentation of Experience

The accounts of the many rebellions of the wilderness period and their cataclysmic consequences are particularly compelling for the audience of the text. Much as theater strives to provoke in the spectator the sense of "being there," the vivid narration of the events creates a sense of immediacy that enables the audience to imagine itself as being actually present when the community faces disasters and is saved only by prompt priestly action.

The literary structure of the rebellion narratives further helps secure their lessons in the audience's mind. Both accounts of rebellion, in Numbers 16–17 and in Numbers 25, follow a similar pattern. A state of relative stability is disrupted and a crisis ensues, righted only by a particular act performed by a priest. In the case of the Koraḥ story, pre-rebellion stability is represented by the regiving of sacrifice laws in Numbers 15. Prior to Baal Peor it is reflected in God's mastery of the prophet Balaam, who is compelled to bless the people. In both cases, the stability of the community is shaken when the people rise up against Moses and Aaron or against the law, and the community is turned upside down when God becomes enraged, punishes the community, and kills many of the offenders. God's rage and the destruction it unleashes are stayed

41. See the discussion of Aaron's rod above.

42. Possibly the exodus night also performs this codifying function with respect to the other Israelite practice called a "sign," namely circumcision. As suggested above, a complex of textual and symbolic associations link the exodus night to the law of circumcision. The trauma of the exodus night may have been meant to create a memory vivid enough to ensure fulfillment of the law of circumcision as well as of the laws associated with Passover.

only by the decisive actions of Aaron and Pinchas, which ultimately restore the stability of community.

These rhetorical features support the codifying function of the narratives with respect to the reading and listening audiences of the text. Made vivid and immediate, the powerfully told stories become etched in the audience's memory, and when recalled, they can instill the fear that prompts proper deferral to the priesthood in all things connected with worship as effectively for the audience as they do for the Israelite witnesses to the events.

The stability–crisis–restoration typology described above also obtains with respect to the narrative presentation of the rites for the Day of Atonement in Leviticus 16. For the audience, the reference to the deaths of Nadab and Abihu that opens the passage situates the purification rites of the day in the context of a crisis. With their "strange fire" offering, Nadab and Abihu transformed the inauguration of cult into a manifestation of chaos. Leviticus 16 describes the procedure for repairing this upset. The message conveyed by the allusion to the two sons is that the purification rites carried out by the high priest can contain and control the chaos represented by Numbers 10 and restore the community to its pristine condition at the cult's inception.[43] At the same time, the death of the two sons was a dramatic demonstration of the power and danger associated with God's presence and the necessity of approaching it with extreme care. By evoking the deaths, the text underscores the crucial importance of proper apprehension of, and engagement with, the completely "other" holiness of God and all that pertains to God.

Two ritual elements unique to the Day of Atonement—the purification rite for the inner sanctum and the ritual of the scapegoat—contribute to the stability–crisis–restoration pattern. As Jenson observes, these two rites reflect "two poles of the spatial dimension of the Holiness Spectrum." In one extreme is the holiest place within the entire tabernacle, which even the high priest may enter only once a year. In the other extreme is the wilderness to which the scapegoat is sent after the community's sins have been confessed over it.[44] There is also another way to characterize these two poles: in terms of creation and chaos. The inner sanctum is the holiest place within the tabernacle because it is the place where the divine presence dwells (Exod. 40:34-35), where it descends

43. The phenomenology of the rites of the Day of Atonement is treated by many scholars, and I will not attempt to duplicate that work here. See for instance Jacob Milgrom, *Leviticus*, 3 vols., AB 3–3B (New York: Doubleday, 1991–2001), 1:1011–67, and Roy Gane, *Cult and Character: Purification Offerings, Day of Atonement and Theodicy* (Winona Lake, IN: Eisenbrauns, 2005), 217–84.

44. Philip Peter Jenson, *Graded Holiness: A Key to the Priestly Conception of the World*, JSOTSup 106 (Sheffield: Sheffield Academic, 1992), 201–2.

onto the ark to instruct Moses (Exod. 25:22; Num 7:89), and where on the Day of Atonement it appears before the high priest (Lev. 16:2). As numerous scholars have shown, the deity's taking up residence in the temple as an indication of the completion of creation is a staple feature in ancient Near Eastern literature.[45] In the priestly Pentateuch, too, the inner sanctum is a sign of creation within the model that is the tabernacle as a whole. On the other hand, the wilderness, as has also been amply demonstrated, is a place of chaos (cf. Deut. 32:10), and it is to this place of chaos that the scapegoat takes the people's sins. For an audience hearing or reading Leviticus 16, the Day of Atonement describes the juxtaposition of chaos and creation and the ultimate restoration of the latter through the mediation of the high priest.

Conclusion

The religious life of lay Israelites may not be an obvious concern of the priestly tradition. Yet it has a role to play both in the maintenance of the overall cultic system and as a complement to the cult. The revelatory experiences that accompany the initiatory events of the first Passover and Sinai demonstrate God's power and the dangers associated with it and, hence, they instill in the people the fear and awe necessary to keep them respectful of the distance from the sacred that must be maintained by all but the Aaronide priests. At the same time, they underscore the Israelites' unique status as God's treasured people and kingdom of priests and therefore provide motivation to observe the practices that come with those identities.

Subsequent revelations in the context of dramatic events codify these principles. With respect to the operations of the cult, the message conveyed to the people is limited. They are not initiated into the details of the tabernacle ritual, and may only observe as the sacred rites are performed, but they are made palpably aware of its importance in sustaining their relationship with God. Dramatic events also codify the positive obligations for which the Israelite people are responsible, foremost among them, the Sabbath through the *manna*, but circumcision in the context of Passover as well.

The importance given to the element of emotional arousal in ritual in the imagistic mode also helps illuminate priestly religion as experienced by the laity. The high level of pageantry implied by the detailed descriptions of the operations of the cult has a parallel in the dramatic and traumatic revelatory

45. Stephen A. Geller, "Sabbath and Creation: A Literary-Theological Analysis," *Interpretation* (forthcoming). Christophe Nihan, *From Priestly Torah to Pentateuch: A Study in the Composition of the Book of Leviticus*, FAT 2:25 (Tübingen: Mohr Siebeck, 2007), 54–55.

events experienced by the laity. An effect of such sensually stimulating experiences is that they form enduring memories in the minds of those who participate. As Leveen argues, one function of such memories and the fear and awe that they revive seems to be to control the behavior of the Israelites and uphold priestly leadership.[46] But when considered in terms of the totality of priestly literature including its religious modality, subtler explanations emerge. Priestly religion is, in a sense, what William Warburton (1698–1779) termed "mystery religion."[47] The Israelites must maintain a position of awe and fear toward the cult because what is at stake—God's presence and attention, and Israel's participation in divine time and space, modeling creation—is simply too crucial to permit easy or casual access to the cult. As Assmann says of ancient Egyptian religion,

> [there is] a very close interdependence between cult and nature, and social and individual prosperity! *The nonobservance of ritual interrupts the maintenance of cosmic and social order.* (Italics mine.)[48]

The interdependence of cult and cosmos and of awe and mystery drives the priestly concept of memory. Of paramount importance is God's memory, which must be continually roused and engaged, for God's memory is what ensures the stable cycles of both sacred and natural time. The role of Israel's memory, therefore, is either to prompt the proper and timely ritual practices that keep God engaged or to restrain improper practices that might jeopardize God's engagement.

46. Leveen, *Memory and Tradition*, 3.

47. See Jan Assmann, *Moses the Egyptian: The Memory of Egypt in Western Monotheism* (Cambridge, MA: Harvard University Press, 1997), 101. In his opus, *The Divine Legation of Moses Demonstrated*, William Warburton, Bishop of Gloucester, attempted to describe the civic underpinnings of religion. He maintained that religions operate on two levels, a "public, open" level (the "lesser mysteries") encompassing accessible ritual and observance, and a "secret" level (the "greater mysteries"), associated with esoteric religious knowledge. He further argued that states utilize (and to a degree, fabricate) the "secret" level in order to arouse "curiosity" and awe on the part of the laity. "[T]he secret in the *lesser* Mysteries was principally contained in some hidden *rites and shews* [*sic*] to be kept from open view of the people, only to invite their curiosity: And the secret in the *greater*, some hidden *doctrines* to be kept from the people's knowledge, for the very contrary purpose. For the *shews* [*sic*] common to both the *greater* and *lesser mysteries*, were only designed to engage the attention, and raise their devotion." *The Divine Legislation of Moses Demonstrated: to which is prefixed, a discourse by way of general preface: containing some account of, the life, writings and character of the author. By Richard Hurd* (London: Millar & Tonson, 1788; 10th ed., London: Thomas Tegg, 1846), 201–2 (italics in original). It should be noted that Warburton's intention is to expose the social and political uses of religion rather than to explain its phenomenology.

48. Assmann, *Moses the Egyptian*, 25.

Priestly religion also provides a level of emotional arousal that binds the people together, intensifies their sense of singularity vis-à-vis other nations, and motivates them to fulfill their obligations even as they respect the boundaries of the cult. The knowledge that they have become God's treasured people, revealed through the extraordinary experiences of Passover and Sinai, provides positive encouragement to the Israelites to remain loyal and obedient participants in the community and the cult, while specific memories of the Passover night and the provision of *manna* prompt them to fulfill properly the observances enjoined upon them. For those who survive the rebellions of the wilderness period, the sense of unique status is intensified. Hence the character of Israel's religious experience in the priestly tradition establishes the groundwork for Israel's right relationship to the rites of the tabernacle, to the sacred environment of the camp surrounding it, and to the God who dwells in their midst.

7

Memory and the Transformation of Priestly Terms into Lay Concepts

The loss of the temple and its rituals left a chasm in the religious experience of the Israelites living in exile. That disaster could well have been understood as God's utter rejection of God's people and the end of the covenant with Israel. With no way to enact the relationship through the rituals of the temple or to keep God present and aware by means of those rituals, the priesthood must have imagined all to be lost forever.

Yet all was not lost. The authors behind the Holiness tradition, who shared many of the concerns of the priesthood, incorporated two particular deuteronomic notions, divine transcendence and an emphasis on the community's role in maintaining the unique relationship between God and Israel. Both concepts were well suited to exile. With those two ideas wedded to a priestly sensibility, the Holiness school translated elements of Israel's cultic life into concepts and practices that could be performed *ex ecclesia*, facilitate the connection between older and new practices, and elevate the covenantal significance of two such practices in particular: circumcision and the Sabbath. It accomplished these transformations primarily through the reinterpretation of priestly memory terminology.

Keeping Institutions

In the main, in priestly literature, "keeping" (*šmr*) conveys a sense of preservation. One keeps or preserves something that is already in existence like "the Ark of Yahweh" (1 Sam. 7:1) or the institution of the priesthood (Num. 3:10; 18:7). When applied to the Israelites, keeping takes on a punctual quality, such as when the Israelites are commanded concerning specific, time-based practices, and in this sense it involves memory. For instance, in Exod. 13:10, they are enjoined to "keep this law [observance of Passover] yearly in its proper time," and in Num. 28:2, they are to "be careful to offer [the sacrifice appropriate to each festival] to me in its proper time." In both passages, it is not only the commanded act but also the sacred time in which it is to be performed that is to be kept. Keeping is often conservative and boundary enforcing, two concepts of some import to the priesthood.[1] The nuances associated with "keeping" endure in Holiness literature, particularly when the Israelites are told to keep the institutions of circumcision and the Sabbath, both of which, most scholars agree, were either exilic religious innovations or were elevated in importance in the exilic period.[2] Both were subsequently taken up by postmonarchical priestly tradition and invested with exceptional significance as signs of the covenant. Because both circumcision and the Sabbath are signs, I defer a full discussion until the next chapter. A few comments, however, may be made in the present context.

1. Circumcision

Even within the context of biblical narrative, circumcision does not appear to be an ongoing religious obligation. Exodus 4 indicates that Moses failed to circumcise his sons, and as observed earlier, Exodus 12 seems to imply the practice was introduced to Israel in connection with Passover. That connection appears to be confirmed in Josh. 5:2-12 when the Israelite males are circumcised immediately prior to making *pesaḥ* offering. It is not until 1 Samuel that circumcision is assumed for Israelite males, and even here the assumption is only implied by references to the Philistines as "uncircumcised" (1 Sam. 14:6; 17:26).

In the context of exile, circumcision as a practice for Israel to "keep" serves two functions. It provides the exiles a way to distinguish themselves from their Babylonian neighbors, a desirable objective in light of the very probable penchant for assimilation.[3] As (or more) importantly, circumcision is an exclusively lay practice that requires no temple and is done without a priest.

1. On the priestly concern for boundaries and its theological and structural implications, see Mary Douglas, *Purity and Danger: An Analysis of the Concept of Pollution and Taboo* (London: Routledge, 1966) and Milgrom, *Leviticus,* 3 vols., AB 3–3B (New York: Doubleday, 1991–2001), 1:718–36. On priestly attention to spatial boundaries, see Hanna Liss, "The Imaginary Sanctuary: The Priestly Code as an Example of Fictional Literature in the Hebrew Bible," in *Judah and the Judeans in the Persian Period*, ed. O. Lipschits and M. Oeming (Winona Lake, IN: Eisenbrauns, 2006), 663–89. Liss argues (p. 680) that the priestly tradition attempts to define a very limited spatial framework for the interaction of the divine and human realms so that "[t]he meeting been Israel and Yahweh can take place only by means of priestly mediation in the cult, its place being the אהל מועד."

2. See the discussion in Rainer Albertz, *Israel in Exile: The History and Literature of the Sixth Century B.C.E.* (Atlanta: SBL, 2003), 133–38.

3. See Albertz, *Israel in Exile.* Note also the polemics against intermarriage in Ezra 9 and Neh. 13.

One might imagine that the association with *pesaḥ* and the exodus would be enough to elevate the importance of circumcision. Nevertheless, the covenantal significance of circumcision is anachronistically established in the patriarchal period when in Gen. 17:9–10 Abraham is instructed to "keep [God's] covenant," the sign of which is circumcision: "This is my covenant that you will keep (*zōʾt bᵉrîtî ʾăšer tišmᵉrû*) between me and you and your descendants after you: circumcise every male" (17:10). The association with Abraham detaches circumcision from *pesaḥ*, which Exodus 12 codifies as a law given to Moses and Aaron. Circumcision instead becomes a practice for which the Israelites are responsible. It is theirs to "keep."

2. *The Sabbath*

Like circumcision, observance of the Sabbath does not occur in narrative portions of the biblical text.[4] And as with circumcision, the suggestion has been made that the practice arose in exile.[5] If that is the case, Knohl's explanation of the Sabbath as conceptualized in H can help explain why it too is a practice for

4. In his detailed study of Genesis 1, Mark Smith develops the already widely held opinion that the Sabbath mandated in the Pentateuch is a priestly innovation that dates from the sixth century BCE. Observing that eighth- and seventh-century references to *šabbāt* occur in connection to festival and new moon observance, Smith suggests that the priestly Sabbath derived from the older seven-day ritual system to which it gave cosmic significance. The new idea of a set Sabbath day was given authority as part of God's creation through the numbering of days leading to the seventh. See Smith, *The Priestly Vision of Genesis 1* (Minneapolis: Fortress Press, 2010), 104–6. Alan Cooper and Bernard Goldstein also posit an earlier sense of *šabbāt* deriving from a Full Moon festival occurring in the Canaanite calendar: "The backbone of [the Canaanite] calendar is the lunar month (*yeraḥ* = Ugaritic *yrh*) that begins with the first visibility of the moon in the evening. The month thus determined reckons New Month (*ḥōdeš* = Ugaritic *ym ḥdt*) and Full Moon (*šabbāt* = Babylonian *šab/puttu*), days 1 and 15 respectively as key dates" ("The Festivals of Israel and Judah and the Literary History of the Pentateuch," *JAOS* 110 [1990]: 20). As well, see Cooper and Goldstein, "The Development of the Priestly Calendar (I): The Daily Sacrifice and the Sabbath," *HUCA* 74 (2003): 12. Cooper and Goldstein do not, however, justify bringing a Babylonian cognate in support of a Canaanite (i.e., Northwest Semitic) ritual, nor do they account for the single /*b(p)*/ and double /*t*/ in the cognate where the Hebrew has a doubled /*b*/ and single /*t*/. Without the priestly explanation, the requirement to rest every seventh day is explained in terms of the Israelites' experience with slavery, and although the commandment in Deuteronomy 5 requires community-wide observance, the underlying explanation does not *necessarily* imply a set day observed by the entire community. That this is the case may be seen from Exod. 21:2 and 22:10–12, both of which incorporate cycles of seven days (or years). The year of a slave's release is clearly determined in this code by when his servitude began. The year in which one's land lies fallow may similarly be determined on a case-by-case basis or may follow a common schedule, as is explicitly the case in Leviticus 25. If both these cycles are determined on an individual, rather than a collective, basis, it seems possible that the obligation to allow one's household to rest every seventh day might also be fulfilled according to individual schedules.

Israel to "keep." It should be noted that Knohl dismisses an exilic provenance for the Sabbath. He maintains that

> HS sought not only to restore honor to the Sabbath, which was neglected in PT,[6] but also to call attention to the qualitative similarity between the Sabbath and the Temple. . . . According to HS, the Sabbath is a sign of the holiness of Israel (Exod 31:13), and Israelites who keep the Sabbath are like priests serving in the Temple.[7]

In Exodus 31, God declares that Israel shall "keep" the Sabbath because it is a "sign between me and you for all generations" (31:13; cf. 31:16) and because it is "sanctified for you" (31:14). I turn to the second of these characterizations here. Even before the Israelites receive this instruction, the "sanctity" of the Sabbath is established in the Decalogue: "Remember the Sabbath to keep it sanctified … for in six days Yahweh made the earth and the sea and everything in them, but he rested on the seventh day" (Exod. 20:8, 11). With its origins in creation, the Sabbath is an institution that can and must be "kept" in the physical world. Because the Sabbath is sanctified time, it is also a practice that can continue without a temple, even though the priestly tradition assigns sacrifices to the seventh day. It also represents a way for every Israelite "to live in accordance with God's primordial design for the universe."[8]

Ṣîṣ and *Ṣîṣit*: The Fringes

In contrast to the somewhat suspicious attitude toward Israel's exercise of memory observed in the previous chapter, the Holiness tradition appears to believe that Israel can be led to remember properly and productively if given an effective nudge. Numbers 15:37-40 introduces such a nudge: the fringes to be attached to the corners of one's garment.

5. See L. C. Jonker, "Religious Polemics in Exile: The Creator God of Genesis 1," in *Religious Polemics in Context: Papers Presented to the Second International Conference of the Leiden Institute for the Studies of Religions (LISOR) held at Leiden, 27–28, April 2000*, ed. T. L. Hettema and A. van der Kooij (Assen: Van Gorcum, 2004), 235–54.

6. HS and PT are Knohl's designations for the "Holiness School" and "Priestly Tradition," respectively.

7. Israel Knohl, *The Sanctuary of Silence: The Priestly Torah and the Holiness School* (Minneapolis: Augsburg Fortress Press, 1995; repr., Winona Lake, IN: Eisenbrauns, 2007), 196. I differ with Knohl's attribution of the *signatory* significance of the Sabbath to H.

8. Samuel E. Balentine, *The Torah's Vision of Worship* (Minneapolis: Fortress Press, 1999), 14. Here Balentine is summarizing Walter Harrelson's *From Fertility to Cult* (New York: Doubleday, 1969).

> Yahweh said to Moses: "Speak to the Israelites and say to them, they shall make for themselves fringes (*ṣîṣit*) on the corners of their garments for all generations. And they shall attach the fringes to the corner with twisted purple-blue linen (*p*^{e}*tîl t*^{e}*kēlet*). You will have the fringes and [when] you see them, you will remember (*zākartem*) all of Yahweh's commandments and do them and not wander after [the desires of] your hearts and after [the desires of] your eyes such that you would whore after them. So that you will remember and do (*tizk*^{e}*rû wa'ăśîtem*) all of my commandments and be holy to your God." (Num. 15:37-40)

The fringes demonstrate that H shares the priestly tradition's reliance on sensation for awakening memory, for with their bright purple-blue of the *t*^{e}*kēlet*, the fringes are visually striking.[9] But unlike priestly commemorations with their retrospective orientation, the fringes have a prospective function. Like continuous recitation in Deuteronomy, their purpose is to keep the people from inadvertent transgression, not to memorialize a past event. The charge associated with the fringes, so "you will remember all my commandments," has ongoing force. In this sense it departs from the tendency in P to define Israel's ritual observance in terms of punctual commandments, such as the celebration of festivals at their proper time, and instead is a durative instruction. Still, the reliance on the fringes shows the Holiness approach to Israel differs markedly from that of Deuteronomy. The Holiness direction does not itemize Israel's ongoing obligations, as Deuteronomy so emphatically does. Nor, notwithstanding the reference to the exodus at the close of the section on the fringes, does it provide a rationale for compliance.[10] The semantic content of memory recedes before the more important connection established between looking at the fringes and obeying the commandments. What matters is to adhere to God's commands, to abjure apostasy, and thereby to be holy.

Because every Israelite must wear them, the fringes do not belong to the cultic setting. Nevertheless, the name given them (*ṣîṣit*) echoes that of the

9. According to Levine, it is the "striking color" of the *t*^{e}*kēlet* that stirs the attention and prompts Israel to remember the commandments. Levine, *Numbers*, 2 vols., AB 4A–B (New York: Doubleday, 1993–2000), *1*:401. In contrast, the deuteronomic version of this law in Deut. 22:12 includes no requirement for visual prominence. Indeed, the *g*^{e}*dīlîm* in Deuteronomy are not implicated in memory at all.

10. Numbers 15:41. The reference to the exodus is part of God's self-presentation, as in Lev. 25:38, 25:55, 26:13. It represents one version of the formula found in H to introduce or conclude laws and assert their divine basis.

diadem (*ṣîṣ*) placed on the high priest's headdress and attached with twisted purple-blue linen (*pᵉtîl tᵉkēlet*).[11] The diadem, it will be recalled, is part of the memory-inducing clothing that the high priest wears to get God's attention. The Holiness tradition transforms it into a garment for all Israel to wear, and it reverses the direction of the mnemonic. Instead of directing God's attention to Israel, the *ṣîṣit* prompt Israel's memory and direct it toward fulfillment of God's commands.

Reimagining Old Practices: The *Zikkārôn* in Holiness Literature

The priestly reminder for Israel (i.e., the plating), as we saw in Chapter 6, is concrete and visible. All but one of those reminders designated for God are likewise concrete objects meant to be seen by God. In Holiness literature, "reminder" assumes a metaphorical property. In two of the three passages where it occurs, Exod. 12:14 and Lev. 23:24, the term *zikkārôn* is associated with a no-longer practical or relevant practice that is given new significance by being understood commemoratively. In both cases, moreover, the *zikkārôn* is a day. In Exod. 12:14 it is the day on which Israel is to celebrate "a festival to Yahweh" and in Lev. 23:24 it is the New Year.

1. *"This Day Will Be for You a Reminder . . ."* Exod. *12:14*

Many scholars have recognized the composite nature of Exodus 12, both with respect to the underlying sources represented in the chapter and to the subject matter contained within.[12] Exodus 12 combines narrative about the departure

11. The LXX roughly follows the MT in its translation of *pᵉtîl tᵉkēlet* in both places that the phrase occurs. In Exod. 28:37, LXX reads ὑακίνθου κεκλωσμένης (literally, "twisted [fabric in the color of] hyacinthus"). In Num. 15:38, it has κλῶσμα ὑακίνθινον. The meaning of the first word is unknown, but the second keeps the idea of "twisted" cloth. The LXX does not, however, capture the allusiveness of the Hebrew *ṣîṣ/ṣîṣit*. In Exodus 28, the LXX reads πέταλον [χρυσοῦν καθαρόν] "flower/leaf [of pure gold]," but Numbers 15 has πτερυγίων ("fringes").

12. Noth attributes 12:1-20, 12:28, and 12:40-51 to P; 12:21-23 and 12:29-30 to J; and 12:24-27 to Dtr. Noth, *Exodus: A Commentary*, OTL (Philadelphia: Westminster, 1962), 95–100. Propp offers a complicated and contradictory analysis that finds P principally responsible for 12:1–13:16 (Propp, *Exodus 1-18*, AB 2–2A [New York: Doubleday, 1999–2006], 373–77) or 12:1-20, 43-49 (ibid., 448). He also attributes Exod. 12:14 to R. Childs finds no evidence of P in the chapter. Instead, he attributes Exod. 12:2-23, 27b, 29-34, and 37-39 to J, and 12:24-27a to D. Brevard S. Childs, *The Book of Exodus: A Critical, Theological Commentary*, OTL (Louisville: Westminster John Knox, 1974). Knohl attributes most of the chapter (vv. 1-30 and 43-49) to H in two stages of composition. Baruch Schwartz assigns 12:1-28 to P, excepting *lᵉmašḥît* in verse 13, *[yi]ttēn hammašḥît* in verses 23 and 12:21a. Baruch Schwartz,

from Egypt, detailed ritual instructions for the exodus evening, and rules for the ongoing commemoration of the exodus when the Israelites are settled in their land. The chapter also addresses the two springtime rituals: *pesaḥ* (the Passover sacrifice) and *maṣṣōt* (the pilgrimage Festival of Unleavened Bread). In the priestly calendar the two observances are separate.[13] As Num. 28:16–17 explains, *pesaḥ* is offered on the fourteenth day of the first month; on the fifteenth day, the seven-day festival commences. The merger of the two is considered to have been an innovation of D.

The uncertain relationship of *pesaḥ* to *maṣṣōt* colors the interpretation of 12:14, which comes between material pertaining to each ritual. Verses 1-13 deal with the Egyptian Passover, with its instructions for acquiring and eating the *pesaḥ* lamb and painting the doorposts with its blood prior to the final plague and departure from Egypt, while verses 15-20 are about the Festival of Unleavened Bread. Bridging the two topics is Exod. 12:14:

> This day will be for you a reminder. You will celebrate it (*w*^{e}*ḥaggōtem ʾōtô*); a festival to Yahweh through your generations; an eternal law. You will celebrate it.

Scholars differ as to whether this verse refers retrospectively to *pesaḥ*,[14] or prospectively to *maṣṣōt*.[15] In fact, Janus-like, the verse points to both rituals[16] and in doing so, solidifies their merger and interprets them anew.

According to Exod. 12:3-9, observance of *pesaḥ* takes place in the home.[17] Furthermore its connection to the exodus receives repeated confirmation, most explicitly by the etymology given in Exod. 12:13. The Festival of Unleavened Bread, on the other hand, is a pilgrimage (*ḥag*) festival, while its connection

Presentation at the Jewish Theological Seminary, March 2009. Thomas Dozeman divides the chapter between P (12:1-13; 12:28), the P Historian (12:14-20; 12:40-51), and non-P (12:21-27; 12:37-39). Thomas B. Dozeman, *Exodus*, Eerdmans Critical Commentary (Grand Rapids: Eerdmans, 2009), 260–86. I find Nihan's analysis most convincing. In common with most scholars, he attributes 12:1-13 to P, but like Knohl sees evidence of H in 12:14-20 and 43-49. Christophe Nihan, *From Priestly Torah to Pentateuch: A Study in the Composition of the Book of Leviticus*, FAT 2:25 (Tübingen: Mohr Siebeck, 2007), 564–65.

13. See Exod. 12:43-49; Exod. 34:18, 25; and Num. 28:16, 17-25.

14. Knohl, *Sanctuary of Silence*, 20.

15. George W. Coats, *Exodus 1–18*, FOTL 2A (Grand Rapids: Eerdmans, 1999), 80.

16. See Brevard Childs, *The Book of Exodus: A Critical, Theological Commentary*, OTL (Philadelphia: Westminster, 1974), 197; William H.C. Propp, *Exodus*. 2 vols., AB 2–2A (New York: Doubleday, 1999–2006), 1:402; Dozeman, *Exodus*, 262; and Nihan, *From Priestly Torah to Pentateuch*, 565.

17. Although it is called a "festival" (*ḥag*) once, in Exod. 34:26.

to the exodus as narrated is tenuous.[18] The connection is made with a loose rationale in Exod. 12:17:

> You shall observe the [Festival of] Unleavened Bread because in that same day I took your assembled forces out of the land of Egypt. Observe this day through your generations; an eternal law.[19]

Nevertheless, with the instruction to celebrate or "*ḥag*" the commemoration of the escape from Egypt, Exod. 12:14 implies both observances with two consequences. The day that is the "reminder" refers simultaneously to both, thus merging the two observances. The designation "remembrance" provides a historical basis for the pilgrimage festival, a matter of concern for the Holiness tradition that is unimportant to P.[20] Not only is *maṣṣōt* "proven" to have originated at the time of the departure from Egypt, it also represents the attenuation of *pesaḥ* observance over seven days. With its historical underpinnings and firm attachment to *pesaḥ* solidified, the festival retains its currency even though there is no longer a pilgrimage destination. Both transformations are facilitated via the "remembrance."

2. *"A ŠABBĀTÔN, A REMINDER OF THE SHOUTS . . ."*

The use of the rarer construct *zikrôn* in Leviticus 23 comes to reinterpret the practice for signaling the start of the seventh month found in Numbers:

> In the seventh month, on the first of the month, you shall have a holy convocation; you shall do no work;[21] it shall be a day of shouts of acclaim for you (*yôm tᵉrûʿâ yihyeh lākem*). (Num. 29:1)

18. The association of *maṣṣôt* with the exodus is achieved by two details that are circumstantial and somewhat extraneous to the event. First the *pesaḥ* must be eaten with *maṣṣôt* and bitter herbs (Exod. 12:8). The second is the report that the people took "their dough before it had leavened" (Exod. 12:34).

19. Nihan writes, "[T]he celebration of Passover and Unleavened Bread is now explicitly connected with the exodus (12:17), and it is even defined as a 'memorial' . . . of the latter." *From Priestly Torah to Pentateuch*, 565.

20. Grounding a ritual in history is more characteristic of H. See, for example, H's explanation of the Festival of Booths (Lev. 23:43). Like the example in Exod. 12:17, this may also reflect the influence of D on the Holiness tradition. The priestly tradition on the other hand appears to be uninterested in history, even though, as von Rad observes, its authors recognized the necessity of providing historical bases for the festivals (see, for instance, Exod. 34:18), even as that basis recedes in importance in terms of the observance of the festivals.

21. The expression *kol-mᵉleʾket ʿăbōdâ* is variously translated. Milgrom prefers "all laborious work," reading the second noun of the construct adjectively. *Numbers*, JPS (Philadelphia: JPS, 1990), 234.

The term *tᵉrûʿâ* conveys strong monarchical associations. Acclamation of the king as God's representative on earth was a practice that may have derived from the Mesopotamian New Year festival. Formulaic expressions of this idea can be found in Psalms 2, 45, and 72 in addition to Num. 29:1. However, although the practice may have suited the monarchical period, it was no longer appropriate to a postmonarchical period nor politically wise once Judah was reduced to a province of Babylon and then Persia.[22] Hence, in the Leviticus version, the instruction reads:

> [I]n the seventh month on the first of the month you shall have a *šabbātôn*, a reminder of the shouts (*zikrôn tᵉrûʿâ*), a holy convocation (*miqrāʾ qōdeš*). (Lev. 23:24)[23]

The New Year may have been too important to the priestly calendar to be ignored completely. So in its place, the Holiness writers employ the newly introduced *šabbātôn*.[24] Instead of acclamation, the complete rest of the Sabbath will be a memorial of the new year. As a "reminder of the shouts," the *zikrôn tᵉrûʿâ* compensates for the loss of the former practice while at the same time furthers the process of ending it.

The "reminders" employed by H in Exod. 12:14 and Lev. 23:24 differ from those of the priestly school. Their purpose appears to be both to break from the past and relate to it. In his book *How Societies Remember*, Paul Connerton describes this evolutionary process using as a model the public and deliberately

HALOT proposes "daily work." I have chosen simply to use "work," as the nature of the work is not germane to this discussion.

22. On the Mesopotamian New Year, see Henri Frankfort, *Kingship and the Gods: A Study of Ancient Near Eastern Religion as the Integration of Society and Nature* (Chicago: University of Chicago Press, 1948), 313–33.

23. Rather than reading it as a construct noun, Milgrom and Levine respectively translate *zikrôn tᵉrûʿâ* as "commemorated with short blasts" and "commemorated with loud blasts." Milgrom, *Leviticus*, 3:2013; Levine, *Leviticus*, 60. Both understand *zikrôn* to refer to the trumpet blasts used to call attention to the new month. However, the Masoretic punctuation (trope markings) makes a break between "Speak to the Israelites saying: on the seventh month on the first of the month you will have a *šabbātôn*," and "a commemoration of the alarm blasts; a holy convocation." The second part of the verse is an adjectival clause composed of two construct nouns that describe the *šabbātôn*.

24. According to both Milgrom and Knohl, the term *šabbātôn* belongs to the Holiness tradition and is used to indicate that total rest is required. Knohl maintains that in Lev. 23:24, the Holiness school authors reframed the holiday to emphasize rest over blowing the shofar: "HS changed the title [of the day] to 'a complete rest, with commemorative shofar blasts.'" Knohl, *Sanctuary of Silence*, 35; Milgrom, *Leviticus*, 3:2014–16.

plebian execution of Louis XVI of France, which was, in his witty turn of phrase, "a royal funeral to end all royal funerals." The reason, Connerton argues, is that "a rite revoking an institution only makes sense by invertedly recalling the other rites that hitherto confirmed that institution."[25] In other words, rituals that seek to revoke or reinterpret old practices must nonetheless invoke the rejected form while at the same time debunking it. It appears that both Lev. 23:24 and, to a lesser extent, Exod. 12:14 seek to establish origins for newly conceptualized practices while putting an end to old understandings, and they do so through the novel reinterpretation of "reminder." In order to abolish the monarchical associations of the New Year celebration, its salient feature—the acclamation—becomes an echo of that sound, a mere "remembrance." In order to solidify the historical basis of the *maṣṣōt*, and at the same time elevate *pesaḥ* to the status of a festival, the initial day of the festival comes simultaneously to commemorate the event associated with Passover, namely the exodus from Egypt, and to function as its more complete observance. By designating the New Year and the Festival of Unleavened Bread as "reminders," H revises the old meanings associated with them and fills them with new, commemorative meaning.

3. *"AND A REMINDER BETWEEN YOUR EYES . . ."*

There is a third instance wherein Holiness material transforms a priestly practice. In Exod. 13:16, following a statement of the law of *peṭer reḥem* (dedication of firstlings), and a child's question about the practice, one is instructed to say

> [w]ith a strong arm Yahweh took us from Egypt, from the house of bondage. For he made it difficult for Pharaoh to send us out and Yahweh killed all the first-born in the land of Egypt, from the first-born person to the first-born animal. Therefore I am sacrificing to Yahweh all the first-delivered males of the womb, and all the first of my sons, I am redeeming. And it will be a sign on your arm and a *ṭôṭāpōt* between your eyes because with a strong hand Yahweh took us out of Egypt. (Exod. 13:14–16)[26]

The connection between the object on the arm and its exegesis is fairly straightforward. The semantic meaning of the second part, complicated in part by the obscurity of the term *ṭôṭāpōt*,[27] is far less obvious. Possibly the instruction

25. Paul Connerton, *How Societies Remember* (Cambridge: Cambridge University Press, 1989), 7–9.

26. The point of the "sign" in these passages will be taken up in the next chapter.

is a hendiadys with the sign and remembrance referring to a single worn object, or possibly there are two objects having the same function. But whether that function is directed to God's consciousness, to Israel's, or to both is also unclear. Most scholars agree that the statement in Exod. 13:16 requires literally wearing an armband or amulet on the body, even though other biblical references to placing words and other signs on the body are metaphorical (e.g., Song 8:6; Prov. 3:3; Isa. 44:5.[28] Some commentators suggest that the verse reflects an older practice that has been brought into Israelite religious practice.[29] The text, in any case, leaves much unexplained.

The instruction occurs as well in Exod. 13:9 following the rules for the Festival of Unleavened Bread, with *zikkārôn* replacing the otherwise obscure term *ṭôṭāpōt*.

> And you shall tell your child on that day saying because of this [which] Yahweh did for me when I came out of Egypt. And it shall be a sign (*ʾôt*) on your hand and a reminder (*zikkārôn*) between your eyes so that the Torah of Yahweh will be in your mouth. (Exod. 13:8–9)

On first glance, it would seem that Exod. 13:9 simply reformulates or clarifies the instruction in verse 16. But the two versions are contextually associated with two distinct practices—dedication of firstlings in verse 16 and eating unleavened bread in verse 9. Which practice is the ornament to commemorate? In fact, Exod. 13:9 refers to neither, for it offers as new primary purpose for the commemoration and a new understanding of it, to keep "the Torah of Yahweh in your mouth."

The word pair "sign" and *ṭôṭāpōt* is also found in Deut. 6:8 and 11:18 where it too refers to all the laws and commandments. Because it is presented

27. The precise meaning of *ṭôṭāpōt* remains unknown. The translation "phylactery" (amulet) derives from Greek translations. See the discussion in Weinfeld, *Deuteronomy 1–11*, AB 5 (New York: Doubleday, 1991), 334–35, and 343.

28. In contrast with the parallel statements in Deut. 6:8 and 11:18, which most likely are meant figuratively. According to Weinfeld, "Exodus 13 uses the term 'to be a sign' היה לאות which usually occurs in a sacerdotal context (e.g., Gen 9:13, 17:11, Exod 12:13, Num 17:3) and which has the meaning of a real physical token. These . . . observations apply also to the term 'to be a remembrance.'" Weinfeld, *Deuteronomy and the Deuteronomic School* (Oxford: Clarendon, 1972; repr., Winona Lake, IN: Eisenbrauns, 1992), 301–2. See also Tigay, *Deuteronomy*, JPS (Philadelphia: Jewish Publication Society, 1996), 359, n. 30; Weinfeld, *Deuteronomy 1–11*, 341–42. It is possible however that in Deuteronomy, where the sign is the teaching, its being literally bound to the body is a sign of loyalty.

29. For instance, Noth, *Exodus*, 101.

in the context of oral instruction, it is reasonable to interpret the deuteronomic version as a metaphor for remembering and transmitting the teaching to the next generation. The Holiness writers incorporate Deuteronomy's detachment of purpose from the act, but they do not necessarily dismiss the act of wearing whatever amulet or object is intended. Instead, by replacing the older priestly obscure word *ṭôṭāpōt* with *zikkārôn*, they simultaneously commemorate the practice required by Exod. 13:16 and transform it. No longer a prompt for either firstlings or unleavened bread, the twin ornaments, like the fringes, will remind Israel to obey the law. And like the fringes, the new reminder makes use of sight and touch to prompt memory, rather than rely on semantic dependence found in Exod. 13:6.

God's Memory in the Holiness Tradition

When it comes to God's memory, the Holiness writers conceptualize God's memory differently than does the priestly tradition. In the priestly tradition, as we saw earlier, there is always an external prompt, some external factor that fuels God's memory, which in turn precipitates God's action or engagement with Israel or the world. The material attributed to H does not exhibit the pattern of external prompt->memory->action in connection with God. Instead, God's memory is roused without reference to an external trigger and may even be assumed to be as constant as is the case in deuteronomic literature. In Lev. 26:40-45, a passage that follows the rehearsal of blessings (26:3-13) and curses (26:14-39) concluding the Holiness Code, God explains the stirrings of God's memory in terms of the enduring attachment to Israel:

> If they confess their iniquity and the iniquity of their ancestors . . . Then I will remember my covenant with Jacob (*wᵉzākartî ʾet-bᵉrîtî yaʿăqôb*), and even more, my covenant with Isaac, and still more my covenant with Abraham I will remember (*ʾezkōr*) and the land I will remember (*ʾezkōr*). (Lev. 26:40, 42)[30]

One might argue that it is the Israelites' confession that kindles God's memory of the eternal promise, but the interruption created by verse 41 undermines this explanation. Instead of contrite confession, the precursor to God's remembering

30. Milgrom translates: "namely, I will remember the land." In his interpretation, the land is the primary object of God's memory because it is implied in the patriarchal covenant, which alone among the covenants "specifies the promise of *land* and *seed*" (italics in original). Milgrom, *Leviticus,* 3:2335.

the covenant is, first, God's recall of having justly responded in kind to Israel's faithlessness, and second, Israel's *receipt* of its punishment:

> If they confess their iniquity and the iniquity of their ancestors—their unfaithfulness, when they were unfaithful to me, and they walked with me faithlessly. And I, had to continue to walk[31] faithlessly toward them and deliver them into the land of their enemies. If then they humble their uncircumcised hearts and they accept their punishment[32]—I will remember . . . (Lev. 26:40–42)

Israel's repentance after the long period of punishment encourages God to remember and reinstate God's covenant with them.[33] In fact, since God claims to have kept the covenant in mind during the period of punishment, God's memory of the covenant is not really newly aroused:

> Yet for all that, while they were in the land of their enemies, I did not reject them and I did not loathe them such that I would destroy them and annul my covenant with them, for I am Yahweh their God, and I will remember for their sake the covenant with the former ones (*wᵉzākartî lāhem bᵉrît riʾšōnîm*) whom I brought out of the land of Egypt in the eyes of all the nations that I might be their God. I am Yahweh. (Lev. 26:44–45)

31. The sense of the verb *ʾēlēk* is ambiguous. The NRSV interprets it as completed or past action but the morphology—it is a prefix (i.e., imperfect) form without the conversive waw—suggests on-going or future action, I have followed Milgrom who renders it as "had to continue to walk" (*Leviticus*, 3:2332).

32. I have followed Milgrom's translation of *ʿăwōnām* as "their punishment" on the basis of Isa. 40:2: *kî nirṣâ ʿăwōnāh* ("for their punishment has been accepted"). Ibid., 2333.

33. The requirement that Israel remember its former behavior prior to God's renewal of the covenant shows close affinity with Ezekiel, who maintains that it is through memory that Israel will come to acknowledge God, hate itself, and repent of its failings. See Lapsley, "Shame and Self-Knowledge: The Positive Role of Shame in Ezekiel's View of the Moral Self," in *The Book of Ezekiel: Theological and Anthropological Perspectives*, ed. M. S. Odell and J. T. Strong (Atlanta: SBL, 2000), 154–57. Memory and the shame that accompanies it will combine to make Israel see its unworthiness before God, who disinterestedly and magnanimously forgives and reestablishes the covenant (see in particular Ezekiel 16). God does this so that "[y]ou will know that I am Yahweh, so that you will remember and be ashamed and no longer protest your insult when I have forgiven you for all you did" (Ezek. 16:63). Although the authors of H do not make memory as central an element of their theology as does Ezekiel, they appreciate the potential of memory to effect repentance in cognitive and emotional terms.

8

Signs for God

Signs, as demonstrations of God's presence and power, dominate the beginning of Israel's national story as related by the priestly tradition. God instructs Moses to perform signs before the Israelites as proof of God's readiness to save them (Exod. 4:4–8) and before Pharaoh to demonstrate God's superior power (Exod. 4:17, 28, 30). As God prepares to carry out the onslaught of demonstrations, God declares, "I will harden the heart of Pharaoh and I will multiply my signs and wonders (*'et-'ōtōtay wᵉ'et-môpᵉtay*) in Egypt" (Exod. 7:3). With that declaration, God also provides the terminology that will define the plagues and other demonstrations of divine power in Israel's historiography.[1] A second category of sign is the apotropaic blood intended to ward off God's destructive force as God moves through Egypt killing all of the firstborn (Exod. 12:13). This sign is a one-time event that nevertheless proves that God can be affected or swayed by such cues and triggers. The most important category of sign includes the permanent ones, all of which refer to the covenant.

Signs of the Covenant

As we saw, the priestly tradition establishes the crucial function of "signs" as the instrument securing God's memory in the priestly account of [re-]creation with the "sign" that God fashions: the bow of Genesis 9. Once God has entered into a covenant with Israel, however, the people and the cult provide the requisite signs. They are circumcision (Genesis 17), the Sabbath (Exodus 31), and the combination of the plating and Aaron's rod, preserved after the high priest's singular status was reconfirmed in Numbers 17. Both of the latter two "signs" represent the reinterpretation of practices or instruments. As well, each covenantal "sign" has a worldly significance and a cosmic meaning.

1. For example, in Deuteronomy where such "signs" existed in the past and are to be recalled, not present and observable.

Each, therefore, represents the real meaning of God's relationship with Israel, a relationship for the sake of the world.

1. *Circumcision*

In the priestly tradition God establishes an eternal covenant with Abraham, promising that Abraham will be a "father of a multitude of nations" (*'ab-hămôn gōyîm*) and that his descendants will possess the land of Canaan as an "eternal land-hold" (*'ăḥuzzat 'ôlām*) (Gen. 17:4-8). The covenant is eternal—it is a *b^e^rît 'ôlām*—and as a sign of this covenant, Abraham and his descendants must be circumcised on the eighth day following birth. But God does not explain to Abraham how or why circumcision is a sign, and the reason for the practice has perplexed many readers.[2] As a sign of the first half of the covenantal promise, progeny, the circumcised penis may be a reasonable mnemonic, but we cannot determine for whom or how. There appears to be no connection to the second part of the promise, namely the land.

Attempts to understand the signatory value of circumcision have led in many directions. Some historians argue that the practice of circumcision entered Israelite life in exile, as a way to distinguish the Judeans from their Babylonian neighbors, while others propose it was to differentiate Israelites from the Philistines in the first half of the first millennium BCE.[3] An explanation popular in the mid-twentieth century suggests that circumcision was introduced as a substitute for sacrifice of the firstborn.[4] In the previous chapter, I mentioned the possibility that circumcision gained importance in the context

2. Michael V. Fox, "The Sign of the Covenant: Circumcision in the Light of the Priestly *'ôt* Etiologies," *RB* 81 (1974): 590–91, 595.

3. Cf. Judges 13–16, in particular 14:1-4; 1 Samuel 13. On the importance of circumcision as a meaningful "ethnic marker," see Elizabeth Bloch-Smith, "Israelite Ethnicity in Iron I: Archaeology Preserves What Is Remembered and What Is Forgotten in Israel's History," *JBL* 122, no. 3 (2003): 415; Rainer Albertz, *History of Israelite Religion* (Louisville: Westminster John Knox, 1994), 407–8; Meir Sternberg, *Hebrews Between Cultures: Group Portraits, National Literature* (Bloomington: Indiana University Press, 1998), 93–94, 109, 196–205. Fox however dismisses this possibility ("The Sign of the Covenant," 595). Kenton L. Sparks points out that circumcision distinguished the Israelites only from selected neighbors—the Assyrians, Elamites, and Sidonites. Nevertheless, such texts as Jer. 9:24-25 evince the idea that "one should be pitied if he is either uncircumcised or if he is compelled to associate with the uncircumcised" (*Ethnicity and Identity in Ancient Israel: Prolegomena to the Study of Ethnic Sentiments and Their Expression in the Hebrew Bible* [Winona Lake, IN: Eisenbrauns, 1998], 281–82).

4. See, for example, Jon Levenson, *Death and Resurrection of the Beloved Son: The Transformation of Child Sacrifice in Judaism and Christianity* (New Haven: Yale University Press, 1993), 43–54; Omri Boehm, "Ethical Responsibility and the Existence of the People of Israel," *VT* 54 (2004): 145–56; William H.C. Propp, "The Bloody Bridegroom: Exod IV 24-6," *VT* 43 (1993): 495–518.

of the Holiness program of inclusive sacredness. That may be true, but it does not explain the stated connection between circumcision and the covenant with Abraham or the theological implications of Abraham's descendants bearing a sign upon their flesh.

The very requirement of circumcision would seem to belie the eternality of the covenant, as does the consequence of failing to fulfill it: any male who is not circumcised will be "cut off from his people" and will have invalidated the covenant. The ruling is harsh. If boys are to be circumcised within a week of being born, why is the failure to be circumcised placed on them? Should not the father be the one "cut off from his people"? The signatory function of circumcision provides the explanation. Circumcision is not a requirement of the covenant, but as God's covenanted people, the Israelites are chosen to provide the sign for God, in analogy to the sign of the bow. A male who does not bear the sign is incapable of fulfilling the covenantal role.

Circumcision is a condition for life. The element that gives it its *signatory* capacity is the blood.[5] In addition to the importance that P gives to blood in general, two related passages confirm this to be so. Exodus 4:24-26 reports, "At a lodging on the road, Yahweh encountered [Moses] and sought to kill him" (*waybaqqēš hămîtô*). The danger is averted when Moses' wife Zipporah swiftly circumcises their son with a flint [knife] (*ṣōr*) and wipes [lit. "touches"—*wattaggaʿ*] Moses' or her son's leg with the blood. This archaic episode,[6] wholly uncharacteristic of P, nevertheless foreshadows the exodus night when, once again, blood saves the Israelites from the "destroyer" killing all of the firstborn. In the second instance, the blood is a "sign" (*ʾôt*). God says, "I will see the blood and rescue them (*wᵉrāʾîtî ʾet-haddām ûpāsaḥtî ʿălêkem*)" (Exod. 12:13).[7] By dint of that rescue, Israel comes into being as a nation with which Yahweh will [re-]establish the covenant. As a "sign," the condition of circumcision stands for the *blood* of circumcision that recalls God to God's promise.[8]

5. On the importance of blood in priestly theology, see Stephen A. Geller, "Blood Cult: An Interpretation of the Priestly Work of the Pentateuch," in *Sacred Enigmas: Literary Religion in the Hebrew Bible* (New York: Routledge, 1996).

6. The antiquity of the practice recounted here is further suggested by the account in Josh. 5:2-3 where, at God's command, Joshua fashions flint knives (*ṣurîm*) in order to circumcise the Israelite males.

7. See Chapter 6, note 23.

8. That the covenantal sign should be blood makes sense in terms of its central part in priestly ritual. On the purgative function of blood, its status as the part of life belonging to God, and its centrality to priestly religion, see Geller, "Blood Cult," 75–77, 83–84.

It is worth pointing out that in both of the Exodus passages just mentioned, blood protects against the destructive power of God. At the inn, it saves Moses from God's homicidal intent. On the exodus night when the blood is a called a "sign," it protects the Israelites from the massive destruction God wreaks on Egypt. With the blood its signature aspect, the possibility of circumcision also serving an apotropaic function must be considered. Furthermore, the designation "sign" associates circumcision with the bow, which similarly protects the world against the possibility that God may once again unleash devastation.

2. *The Sabbath*

The importance given to Israel's observance of the Sabbath in the Holiness tradition was discussed in the preceding chapter, where we considered its utility for Israel's spiritual sake. As the later strata of priestly writing reinterpreted circumcision, so it did with the Sabbath, in cultic terms and in accordance with their creation theology.

The Sabbath is introduced as a *sign* of the covenant in Exod. 31:13–17, at the very end of the Sinai revelation.[9] At the same time, the Sabbath is shown to have been established at creation:

> You speak to the Israelites saying, "My Sabbaths you shall preserve, for it is a sign between me and you through all generations that you may know that I am Yahweh who sanctifies you. . . . The Israelites shall preserve the Sabbath to make (*laʿăśôt*) the Sabbath through all generations—an eternal covenant. Between me and between the Israelites it is an eternal sign (*ʾôt hi[w]ʾ lᵉʿōlām*), because six days Yahweh made (*ʿāśâ*) the heavens and the earth and on the seventh day he desisted (*šābat*) and refreshed (*wayyinnāpaš*) himself. (Exod. 31:13, 16–17)

This is not the first time the Israelites learn about the Sabbath, nor of its basis in creation. We saw earlier that the *manna* introduced this concept shortly after the Israelites crossed the Sea of Reeds. At Sinai, God explained the Sabbath in connection to creation. Now, the intimacy of the relationship between the two is "proven" through the assonance between the noun *šabbāt* and the (possibly etymologically distinct) verb *šābat*.[10] Israel's performance of the Sabbath "sign"

9. The revelation continues at Leviticus 1, but there, God speaks from the Tent of Meeting.

10. Exodus 20:11 says simply, "and he rested (*wayyānaḥ*)."

replicates God's resting on the seventh day and provides an earthly model of divine time.

Yet the priestly predilection for concrete signs argues for an alternative or additional explanation of the Sabbath's signatory nature. A solution proposed by Stephen Geller is that when P calls the Sabbath a "sign," it means the tabernacle.[11]

As noted earlier, the traditional conclusion of ancient Near Eastern creation legends has the deity remove him- or herself to an abode (temple) that will be the divine resting place. The priestly version of creation has God rest, but provides no dwelling to which God may retire . . . until the tabernacle is built and erected. Beyond its association with creation in this sense, Geller suggests that it is also "the visible aspect of the sign of the Sabbath."[12] Geller points to the "strong cultic resonances," of the root *npš* from which *wayyinnāpaš* (Exod. 31:13) derives, and the general pattern by which "[a]ccording to the mythically rooted religions of the ancient world in general, creation should end with cult." These twin factors, he maintains, mean that the tabernacle is not only the actual end of the creation story, but also the concretization of the heavenly seventh day of Gen. 2:1–3 on which God rested.

However, it may be that both solutions are correct. If the tabernacle provides the sacred locus for the cult, Israel's observance of the Sabbath concretizes the sacred time in which to enact it. Further, the Sabbath is more than a simple imitation of God's creation and more than a model of the cosmos. It is also the scaffolding on which the temporal cultic calendar hangs, with its recurring pattern of seven days, weeks, and years. By observing the Sabbath rites, and indeed all the rites of the year, Israel lives according to divine time. When its people observe the Sabbath, they enact and embody the sign of its (covenantal) status as the one people that participates in divine time as well as divine space on earth. Like circumcision, observance of the Sabbath reminds God of the covenant with Israel and God's corresponding obligations toward them. Like the bow, Sabbath observance keeps God attuned to creation and continuation. As the cornerstone of the cult, Sabbath observance participates ritually in sustaining creation by replicating it on earth.

11. Stephen A. Geller, "Sabbath and Creation: A Literary-Theological Analysis," *Interpretation* (forthcoming).

12. Ibid.

3. *The Altar Plating and Aaron's Rod*

The plating on the altar and Aaron's rod were discussed earlier in terms of their commemorative function, indicated by their respective designations as *zikkārôn* and *mišmeret*. Both, however, are also called "signs," and in this capacity they operate on a symbolic level, directed toward God's consciousness. The symbolic function of each may have been recognized, though I have not come across evidence to that effect in the literature. Their symbolic value as a unity has not been appreciated. Taken together, the rod and the plating represent the unity of creation and Israel's cult. It is relatively easy to recognize the symbolic representation of the cult in the plating. Because it is affixed to the bronze altar, the plating is literally connected to the daily offerings, festival offerings, and individual sacrifices. The symbolic dimension of the rod is more obscure but can be found in the account of the miracle surrounding it.

> The next day, Moses went into the tent of the testament and, behold! The rod of Aaron of the House of Levi flowered (*w^{e}hinnēh pāraḥ maṭṭēh ʾahărōn l^{e}bêt lēwî*). Flowers burst and blossoms bloomed (*wayyōṣēʾ peraḥ wayyāṣēṣ ṣîṣ*) and it bore ripe almonds. (Num. 17:23)

Sprouting blossoms (*ṣîṣ*) and almonds, Aaron's rod enacts a miniature creation drama. Reminiscent of the seed-bearing grasses and fruit-bearing trees created on day three, the rod ties creation to the Aaronide priesthood. It does so both explicitly ("Aaron of the House of Levi") and implicitly by the blossoms (*ṣîṣ*), which recall the diadem on the high priest's turban (Exod. 28:36) that pronounced Aaron's unique status with the inscription "consecrated to Yahweh." With the two "signs" introduced together and housed within the tabernacle, the plating and the rod signal the actual connection between enactment of the cult and creation. Thus at the same time that they function as reminders for Israel, warning the people to let priests remain in charge, they also serve as signs that remind God of the cosmic implications of the cult as the means of ensuring God's presence in the world and the constancy and permanence of the cosmic order.

4. *"A Sign on Your Arm . . ."*

Like the plating and the rod, the item or ornament that the Israelites are to wear on their arm and head in Exod. 13:16 and its parallel in 13:9 is doubly named. As discussed in the previous chapter, Exod. 13:16 is likely the earlier formulation and probably refers to an actual worn item. The functions assigned it—"sign" and *ṭôṭāpōt*—may be redundant or may denote two functional qualities. In either case, it seems likely that the whole is meant solely as a reminder for Israel. In the hand of the Holiness writers, Exod. 13:16 is reinterpreted as a reminder of the archaic practice in Exod. 13:9 through the substitution of *zikkārôn* for *ṭôṭāpōt*. The purpose of the "sign" in the reformulated version has not yet been explained.

With the "sign on your arm" (*'ôt 'al yādᵉkâ*) of 13:16 corresponding to the strong arm (*ḥōzeq yād*) with which God delivered the Israelites from Egypt, the semantic link between visual cue and its exegesis is strong, and imparts the object with effective deictic capacity characteristic of priestly mnemonics.[13] The Holiness version may have retained it in that capacity; however, given the metaphorical meaning H ascribes to the worn reminder, the need for two objects is clearly redundant. Thus it seems to me more likely that the "sign on your arm" in Exod. 13:9 represents a priestly reinsertion of the older formulation, now with the sign serving God. The sign on the arm would thus be analogous to other visible signs like the blood on the doorposts that saved the Israelites on the night of the exodus, or to circumcision. If the former, the one-time sign would then be translated into a perpetual visual cue reminding God of Israel's relationship to God. If the latter, then the "sign" would be an outward manifestation of the circumcised penis. It would moreover be a mark not just of the patriarchal covenant, but of the covenant God makes with Israel.

The priestly tradition thus invests Israel with four opportunities to provide God the sign needed to keep God cognizant of the covenant made when the world was re-created. In Genesis 9, the sign positively keeps God true to the promise and negatively ensures that "never again will the waters flood the earth and destroy all flesh." The signs that the Israelites provide likewise both preserve and protect, while the rod housed in the tabernacle in tandem with the plating affirms the unity of creation and cult. The Sabbath is the enduring positive sign that models and preserves creation. Positively, the blood of circumcision and its analog, the sign on the arm, mark Israel as God's chosen partner. Negatively they keep God's destructive force at bay.

13. On semantic dependence between a mnemonic and what is to be recalled, see Anita Kasabova, "Memory, Memorials and Commemoration," *History and Theory* 47 (2008): 345–47. Drawing on work by linguist and psychologist Karl Bühler, Kasabova discusses signs that have a "semantic dependence relation between the antecedent [the event, idea, or object recalled from the past] and a consequent where the antecedent grounds the consequent." Because they stand for the consequent, such signs are synecdoche for what is recalled. They facilitate retrieval of the memory and they encapsulate it in a concrete fashion.

Conclusion

God's attention and God's response to Israel's worship are a pressing concern in priestly religion, and the rites and instruments of the cult function primarily to keep God mindful of the covenant and attentive to God's people. Foremost among all of them is the "sign" that recalls the world-saving sign of the bow.

The development of this particular reminder, with its symbolic rather than actual operation, may be a consequence of the priestly tradition's incorporation of the idea of a transcendent God within its innate theology of immanence. After the encounter with deuteronomic theology and the experience of the exile, the idea of a truly immanent God became less tenable. The postmonarchical priesthood responded with what Geller felicitously terms a theology of "transcendent immanence." This adaptation, however, comes at a cost, as transcendence makes God's reality more difficult to experience with certainty. Additionally, a transcendent God may well be imagined to have a wider mandate than simply providing for one people. The Israelites waiting to return to their land may fear that Yahweh, as a transcendent deity, will remain distant and preoccupied with larger matters. The convergence of Israel's covenant and creation resolves these anxieties. God is responsible for maintaining the created world, but Israel is God's vital partner, ensuring that God remains mindful of God's covenantal obligation. Hence this group establishes the "sign," which Israel provides threefold, as the most important trigger for God's memory, equal in importance to the bow that secures [re-]creation. Yet the cult, the priesthood, and the high priest in particular remain crucial, as the unity of the rod and the plating as "signs" affirms. In fact, Israel's covenantal role as sign-bearer elevates the importance of the high priest because with the stakes so very high, the cult must be perfectly performed.

When carried out properly by the priesthood, Israel's worship provides an ongoing sign of creation, and the sensory panoply it provides keeps it alive in God's mind. But the people through their observance of the two rites that God defines as signs—observance of the Sabbath and circumcision—also keep God mindful of creation and its maintenance. In this sense the Israelites are indeed a "kingdom of priests," for the world.

9

Conclusion and Comments

The summer after I finished my dissertation, I took myself to Rome for a month to celebrate. My last day was August 5, which is also the Feast Day of Our Lady of the Snows celebrated at Santa Maria Maggiore, the largest church in Rome and one of the Papal Basilicas. According to legend, in 356 CE Pope Liberio received a vision of the Virgin Mary instructing him to build a church in her name. On August 5 of that year a rectangle of snow appeared on the Esquiline Hill describing the outline of the church to be constructed. The festival is celebrated annually with High Mass. At the climax of the service, rose petals are scattered from the dome of the basilica in imitation of the snow that provided the church with its blueprint.

I wanted to see this festival and decided to attend the mass. The church was filled to capacity. The Pontifical Mass was conducted by the Cardinal Archbishop of the basilica. And just before the close of the service, white rose petals fell from the dome as a choir sang. The sight was stunning and, indeed, magical. Many in the congregation wept. Many held out their hands in reverent application. There was a powerful sense of divine presence.

The celebration was, in short, ritual of the highest order, commemorative and stirring, sensually gratifying and profoundly transporting. Everyone present knew that what fell from the dome were rose petals and not snow. A majority probably did not take the legend seriously as fact. Yet the power of the incense, the music, the priestly vestments, and above all the imitation of the miracle celebrated *as an experience* was able to capture the imagination and the emotion of the believers present.

The celebration of the Festival of Our Lady of the Snows makes no claim on the rational self. Therein lie both its power and its limitation. For all that the ceremony stirred intense feelings of devotion in the moment, I think it safe to say that within a few days, the experience receded, and the intense devotion lay waiting until reawakened by the next sensory symphony performed by the church.

This experience stayed with me in part because it so well matched the priestly idea of ritual. Its purpose was neither to teach theology nor to instruct on pious practice. Its purpose was to inspire awe on the part of the congregation and to demonstrate reverence for the saint in whose honor it was performed.

In the Jewish tradition, only one ritual begins to approximate the festival at Santa Maria Maggiore: the *Avodah* service for the Day of Atonement. But in contrast to the Catholic rite, with its symbolic replication of a miracle, in the Jewish service the centerpiece is a recitation from the *Mishna* that quotes the confessions of the high priest and narrates his and the congregation's prostration before God. Although prostration is replicated three times by the cantor, who also chants the recitation, the service is verbal and explanatory. The *Avodah* service is a pentimento, a priestly ghost within a didactic and mnemonic exercise.

This investigation of memory and the Pentateuch has demonstrated the importance of this concept in both Deuteronomy and priestly literature and in the religious program each sought to promote. It also gave evidence of two different emphases with respect to the kind of memory privileged and whose memory matters most.

Memory in deuteronomic religion is an explicit instrument of covenant maintenance. It serves the twofold function of keeping Israel's covenantal obligation always in mind and of connecting historical periods so that subsequent generations are as absolutely and completely bound to the covenant as was the first generation to enter into it. Memory in deuteronomic religion is not only cognitive, but also performative; it is the catalyst to action, especially the fulfillment of covenantally prescribed obligations. What is more, memory is crucial in Deuteronomy, because in its absence, Israel turns to idolatry and apostasy. Moreover, the tendency to forget is overwhelming. Indeed, forgetting seems to be Israel's default condition. The people must be repeatedly and continually prompted to remember as demonstrated by Moses' repeated urgings in Deuteronomy. Moses' promptings do more than just impress upon his generation the importance of memory for covenant maintenance. They provide a model for the transmission of memory from one generation to the next.

The priestly tradition emphasizes the sensory aspects of memory, an emphasis that informs both its rituals and ritual objects, and the literary presentation of its religious program. These are designed on the one hand, to sustain God's memory of the covenant bestowed upon Israel, and on the other hand, to ensure that cultic activity is properly executed. The first of these objects is primary because, for this tradition, God's covenant with Israel replicates God's covenant with the world.

This investigation has also demonstrated that the Pentateuch offers two models of religious practice and two approaches to the relationship between Israel and God. One depends on memory that is semantic and verbal; the other looks to specific episodes sufficiently charged to be retrieved with a simple cue. One relies on speaking and hearing what is to be done to ensure that the congregation remembers and understands its obligations. The other eschews explanation so far as the congregation is concerned and trusts drama and terror to inscribe its truths, while it offers a near-constant array of sights, smells, and sounds to keep God engaged, aware, and present.

By emphasizing the differences between the two religious and literary traditions of the Pentateuch, I have run the risk of drawing too sharp a dichotomy. As I said at the outset, both traditions share the certainty in Israel's unique relationship with God. The inclusion of both in the Pentateuch also suggests that the editors recognized the contributions of both. The delineations between the kinds of memory, and consequently the religions exemplified in Deuteronomy and in the priestly tradition, may not be so sharp in practice. In reality, human beings make use of both semantic and episodic memory and respond to both didactic and experiential practices, and most religious traditions engage, or seek to engage, both mind and emotion.

A frequent complaint in both synagogues and churches is the absence of "spirituality," a catchall for the emotional, experiential aspect of religious practice, in favor of rote recitation of prayer and liturgy. Figuring out how to incorporate this elusive goal of modern religious practice vexes clergy and lay leadership alike. The hard truth, however, is that the emotional and experiential aspects of religion wilt in the face of our post-Enlightenment rational examination. Ultimately, we seek explanations for the practices we observe, even though explanation deprives ritual of its essential *mysterium tremendum* quality.

Deuteronomy provides the cognitive underpinnings for religious life. It is addressed to the rational mind that requires justification for enjoined practices. But it offers little drama and like the intellectualization of western religion today, can leave its practitioners emotionally empty. The priestly model offers sensual, experiential religion but minimal explanation. The drama is credible for only so long before one demands justification. Together, the two traditions anticipate the tension between "spirituality" and rational theology that exists in contemporary churches and synagogues. But as well, they show that this dichotomy is actually false, for the presence of both traditions in a single sacred text points ultimately to a belief in their complementary and dialogical coexistence, which as a totality offers a religious model of value today.

Bibliography

Ackerman, Susan. "Coming-of-Age Rituals in Ancient Israel." Paper presented at the annual meeting of the Society of Biblical Literature, Atlanta, November 21, 2010.

———. "Cult Centralization, the Erosion of Kin-Based Communities, and the Implications for Women's Religious Practices." Pages 19–40 in *Social Theory and the Study of Israelite Religion: Essays in Retrospect and Prospect.* Edited by S. M. Olyan. Atlanta: Society of Biblical Literature, 2012.

———. "The Personal Is Political: Covenantal and Affectionate Love (*ʾāhēb, ʾahăbâ*) in the Hebrew Bible." *Vetus Testamentum* 52 (2002): 437–58.

———. "Women's Rites of Passage in Ancient Israel: Three Case Studies (Birth, Coming of Age, and Death)." In *Family and Household Religion: Toward a Synthesis of Old Testament Studies, Archaeology, Epigraphy, and Cultural Studies.* Edited by R. Albertz, B. Alpert-Nakhai, S. M. Olyan, and R. Schmitt. Winona Lake, IN: Eisenbrauns, forthcoming.

Ackroyd, Peter R. *Exile and Restoration: A Study of Hebrew Thought of the Sixth Century B.C.* Philadelphia: Westminster, 1968.

Albertz, Rainer. "Exodus: Liberation History against Charter Myth." Pages 128–43 in *Religious Identity and the Invention of Tradition: Papers read at a NOSTER Conference in Soesterberg, January 4–6, 1999.* Edited by J. W. V. Henten and A. Houtepen. STAR 3. Assen: Royal Van Gorcum, 2001.

———. *History of Israelite Religion.* Louisville: Westminster John Knox, 1994.

———. *Israel in Exile: The History and Literature of the Sixth Century B.C.E.* Atlanta: Society of Biblical Literature, 2003.

Albrektson, Bertil. *History and the Gods: An Essay on the Idea of Historical Events as Divine Manifestations in the Ancient Near East and in Israel.* Coniectanea biblica: Old Testament Series 1. Lund: CWK Gleerup, 1967.

Albright, W. F. "Anath and the Dragon." *Bulletin of the American Schools of Oriental Research* 84 (1941): 14–17.

Allen, George. *The Importance of the Past: A Meditation on the Authority of Tradition.* Albany: State University of New York Press, 1985.

Alt, Albrecht. "The God of the Fathers." Pages 1-86 in *Essays on Old Testament History and Religion.* Translated by R. A. Wilson. Garden City, NY: Anchor, 1968.

Alter, Robert. *The Five Books of Moses: A Translation with Commentary*. New York: W. W. Norton, 2004.

Anderson, Bernhard. "Exodus and Covenant in Second Isaiah and the Prophetic Tradition." Pages 339–60 in *Magnalia Dei: Essays on the Bible and Archaeology in Memory of G. Ernest Wright*. Edited by F. M. Cross, W. E. Lemke, and P. D. Miller Jr. Garden City, NY: Doubleday, 1976.

______. "From Analysis to Synthesis: The Interpretation of Genesis 1-11." *Journal of Biblical Literature* 97 (1978): 23–39.

Anderson, Edward B. "City Names as Memorials in Old Testament Theology." Ph.D. diss., Dallas Theological Seminary, 2002.

André, G. "פָּקַד *pāqaḏ*, פָּקִיד *pāqîḏ*, פִּקָּדוֹן *piqqāḏôn*, פִּקּוּדִים *piqqûḏîm*, פְּקוּדִים *p^{e}qûḏîm*, פְּקֻדֻת *p^{e}qiduṯ*, פְּקֻדָּה *p^{e}quddâ*, מִפְקָד *mipqāḏ*." Pages 50–63 in vol. 14 of *Theological Dictionary of the Old Testament*. Edited by G. J. Botterweck and H. Ringgren. Translated by J. T. Willis, G. W. Bromiley, and D. E. Green. 14 vols. Grand Rapids: Eerdmans, 1974–.

Ashley, Timothy R. *The Book of Numbers*. Grand Rapids: Eerdmans, 1993.

Assmann, Jan. "Guilt and Remembrance: On the Theologization of History in the Ancient Near East." *History and Memory* 2 (1990): 5–33.

______. *Moses the Egyptian: The Memory of Egypt in Western Monotheism*. Cambridge, MA: Harvard University Press, 1997.

______. *Religion and Cultural Memory: Ten Studies*. Translated by R. Livingstone. Stanford: Stanford University Press, 2006.

Assmann, Jan, and John Czaplicka. "Collective Memory and Cultural Identity." *New German Critique* 65 (1995): 124–33.

Balentine, Samuel E. *The Torah's Vision of Worship*. Minneapolis: Fortress Press, 1999.

Baltzer, Klaus. *The Covenant Formulary in Old Testament, Jewish and Early Christian Writings*. Translated by David E. Green. Philadelphia: Fortress Press, 1971.

Barash, Jeffrey Andrew. "The Sources of Memory." *Journal of the History of Ideas* 58 (1997): 707–17.

Bar-Efrat, Shimon. *1–2 Samuel*. 2 vols. Miqra' L^{ə}yisrael. Tel Aviv: Obed, 1996 (Hebrew).

Barmash, Pamela. "At the Nexus of History and Memory: The Ten Lost Tribes." *Association for Jewish Studies Review* 29 (2005): 207–36.

Barr, James. *History and Ideology in the Old Testament: Biblical Studies at the End of a Millennium*. Oxford: Oxford University Press, 2000.

_____. "Some Semantic Notes on the Covenant." Pages 23–38 in *Beiträge zur Alttestamentlichen Theologie: Festschrift für Walther Zimmerli zum 70. Geburtstag.* Edited by H. Donner, R. Hanhart, and R. Smend. Göttingen: Vandenhoeck & Ruprecht, 1977.

Barth, Fredrik. *Ritual and Knowledge among the Baktaman of New Guinea.* New Haven: Yale University Press, 1975.

Barton, John. "Forgiveness and Memory in the Old Testament." Pages 987–95 in *Gott und Mensch im Dialog.* Edited by M. Witte. Berlin: Walter de Gruyter, 2004.

Bell, Catherine. *Ritual: Perspectives and Dimensions.* New York: Oxford University Press, 1997.

_____. *Ritual Theory, Ritual Practice.* New York: Oxford University Press, 1992.

Ben-Dov, Jonathan. "Writing as Oracle and as Law: New Contexts for the Book-Find of King Josiah." *Journal of Biblical Literature* 127 (2008): 223–39.

Bergen, Wesley J. *Reading Ritual: Leviticus in Postmodern Culture.* Journal for the Study of the Old Testament: Supplement Series 417. London and New York: T. & T. Clark, 2005.

Bergson, Henri. *Matter and Memory.* Translated by N. M. Paul and W. S. Palmer. London: Allen & Unwin, 1911. Repr., Mineola, NY: Dover, 2004.

Bernat, David A. *Sign of the Covenant: Circumcision in the Priestly Tradition.* Society of Biblical Literature Ancient Israel and Its Religion Series 3. Atlanta: Society of Biblical Literature, 2009.

Black, J., et al., eds. *A Concise Dictionary of Akkadian.* 2nd [corrected] printing. Wiesbaden: Harrassowitz, 2000.

Blenkinsopp, Joseph. *A History of Prophecy in Israel: From the Settlement in the Land to the Hellenistic Period.* Philadelphia: Westminster, 1983.

_____. "Memory, Tradition, and the Construction of the Past in Ancient Israel." *Biblical Theology Bulletin* 27 (1997): 76–82.

_____. "Structure of P." *Catholic Biblical Quarterly* 38 (1976): 275–92.

Bloch, Maurice. "Internal and External Memory: Different Ways of Being in History." Pages 215–33 in *Tense Past: Cultural Essays in Trauma and Memory.* Edited by P. Antze and M. Lambek. London: Routledge, 1996.

_____. "Symbols, Song, Dance and Features of Articulation: Is Religion an Extreme Form of Traditional Authority?" *Archives Européennes de Sociologie* 15 (1974): 55–81.

Bloch-Smith, Elizabeth. "Israelite Ethnicity in Iron I: Archaeology Preserves What Is Remembered and What Is Forgotten in Israel's History." *Journal of Biblical Literature* 122 (2003): 401–25.

Boehm, Omri. "Ethical Responsibility and the Existence of the People of Israel." *Vetus Testamentum* 54 (2004): 145–56.

Boling, Robert G. *Judges.* Anchor Bible 6. Garden City, NY: Doubleday, 1975.

Boston, J. R. "The Wisdom Influences upon the Song of Moses." *Journal of Biblical Literature* 87 (1968): 166–78.

Bottéro, Jean. "Les morts est l'au-delà dans les rituels en accadien contre l'action des 'revenants.'" *Zeitschrift für Assyriologie und vorderasiatische Archäologie* 73 (1983): 153–203.

Botterweck, G. Johannes, and Helmer Ringgren, eds. *Theological Dictionary of the Old Testament.* Translated by J. T. Willis, G. W. Bromiley, and D. E. Green. 14 vols. Grand Rapids: Eerdmans, 1974–.

Brakke, David, Michael L. Satlow, and Steven Weitzman, eds. *Religion and the Self in Antiquity.* Bloomington: Indiana University Press, 2005.

Bréal, Michel. *Semantics: Studies in the Science of Meaning, with a new introduction by Joshua Whatmough.* New York: Dover, 1964. Reprint of *Semantics: Studies in the Science of Meaning.* Translated by Mrs. H. Cust. New York: Henry Holt, 1900.

Breisach, Ernst. "Historiography: An Overview." Pages 370–83 in vol. 6 of *The Encyclopedia of Religion.* Edited by M. Eliade. 16 vols. New York: Macmillan, 1987.

Brettler, Marc Zvi. *The Creation of History in Ancient Israel.* London and New York: Routledge, 1995.

______. "Memory in Ancient Israel." Pages 1–17 in *Memory and History in Christianity and Judaism.* Edited by M. A. Signer. Notre Dame: University of Notre Dame Press, 2001.

Brichto, Herbert Chanan. "The Case of the *Śōṭā* and a Reconsideration of Biblical 'Law.'" *Hebrew Union College Annual* 46 (1975): 55–70.

Brill, Adolf, ed. *Das samaritanische Targum zum Pentateuch.* Frankfurt am Main: Wilhelm Erras, 1876. Repr., Hildesheim, NY: Georg Olms, 1871.

Brown, F., S. R. Driver, and C. A. Briggs. *A Hebrew and English Lexicon of the Old Testament with an Appendix Containing the Biblical Aramaic.* Boston: Houghton Mifflin, 1907.

Brown, R., and J. Kulik. "Flashbulb Memory." Pages 50–65 in *Memory Observed: Remembering in Natural Contexts.* Edited by U. Neisser and I. E. Hyman. San Francisco: W. H. Freeman, 1982.

Brueggemann, Walter. *Deuteronomy*. Abingdon Old Testament Commentaries. Nashville: Abingdon, 2001.

_____. *Theology of the Old Testament: Testimony, Dispute, Advocacy*. Minneapolis: Fortress Press, 1997.

Buis, Pierre, and Jacques LeClercq. *Le Deutéronome*. Sources bibliques. Paris: J. Gabalda, 1963.

Burke, Peter. "History as Social Memory." Pages 97–113 in *Memory: History, Culture and Mind*. Edited by T. Butler. Oxford: Blackwell, 1989.

Camp, Claudia. *Wisdom and the Feminine in the Bible and Proverbs*. Decatur, GA: Almond Press, 1985.

_____. *Wise, Strange and Holy: The Strange Woman and the Making of the Bible*. Sheffield: Sheffield Academic, 2000.

Carasik, Michael. *Theologies of the Mind in Biblical Israel*. Studies in Biblical Literature 85. New York: Peter Lang, 2006.

Carmichael, Calum. "A New View of the Origin of the Deuteronomic Credo." *Vetus Testamentum* 19 (1969): 273–89.

Carr, David M. *Writing on the Tablet of the Heart: Origins of Scripture and Literature*. Oxford: Oxford University Press, 2005.

Carroll, Robert R. "Prophecy and Society." Pages 203–25 in *The World of Ancient Israel: Sociological, Anthropological, and Political Perspectives*. Edited by R. E. Clements. Cambridge: Cambridge University Press, 1989.

Cassuto, Umberto. *A Commentary on the Book of Genesis. Part One: From Adam to Noah*. Translated by I. Abrahams. Jerusalem: Magnes, 1998.

_____. *A Commentary on the Book of Genesis. Part Two: From Noah to Abraham*. Translated by I. Abrahams. Jerusalem: Magnes, 1997.

_____. *A Commentary on the Book of Exodus*. Translated by I. Abrahams. Jerusalem: Magnes, 1997.

Chavel, Simeon. "Numbers 15:32-36—A Microcosm of the Living Priesthood and Its Literary Production. Pages 45–56 in *The Strata of the Priestly Writing: Contemporary Debate and Future Directions*. Edited by S. Shectman and J. S. Baden. Abhandlungen zur Theologie des Alten und Neuen Testaments 95. Zürich: Theologischer, 2009.

Childs, Brevard. *Biblical Theology of the Old and New Testaments: Theological Reflections on the Christian Bible*. Minneapolis: Fortress Press, 1992.

_____. *The Book of Exodus: A Critical, Theological Commentary*. Old Testament Library. Philadelphia: Westminster, 1974.

_____. *Introduction to the Old Testament as Scripture*. Minneapolis: Fortress Press, 1979.

______. *Memory and Tradition in Israel.* Studies in Biblical Theology. Naperville, IL: Alec R. Allenson, 1962.

Clark, Anne L. "Testing the Two Modes Theory: Christian Practice in the Later Middle Ages." Pages 125–42 in *Theorizing Religions Past: Archaeology, History, and Cognition.* Edited by H. Whitehouse and L. H. Martin. Walnut Creek, CA: AltaMira, 2004.

Clements, R. E., ed. *The World of Ancient Israel: Sociological, Anthropological and Political Perspectives.* Cambridge: Cambridge University Press, 1989.

Clifford, Richard J. "Mot Invites Baal to a Feast: Observations on a Difficult Ugaritic Text (CTA 5.i. = KTU 1.5.1.)." Pages 55–64 in *Working with No Data: Semitic and Egyptian Studies Presented to Thomas O. Lambdin.* Edited by D. M. Golomb and S. T. Hollis. Winona Lake, IN: Eisenbrauns, 1987.

Coats, George W. *Exodus.* 2 vols. Forms of the Old Testament Literature. Grand Rapids: Eerdmans, 1999.

Cochran, Clarke E. "Joseph and the Politics of Memory." *Review of Politics* 64 (2002): 42–46.

Collingwood, R. G. *The Idea of History.* Oxford: Clarendon, 1946.

Collins, John J. "The Development of the Exodus Tradition." Pages 144–55 in *Religious Identity and the Invention of Tradition: Papers read at a NOSTER Conference in Soesterberg, January 4–6, 1999.* Edited by J. W. Van Henten and A. Houtepen. STAR 3. Assen: Royal Van Gorcum, 2001.

______. "The Zeal of Phinehas and the Legitimization of Violence." *Journal of Biblical Literature* 122 (2003): 3–21.

Connerton, Paul. *How Societies Remember.* Cambridge: Cambridge University Press, 1989.

Cooper, Alan M., and Bernard R. Goldstein. "At the Entrance to the Tent: More Cultic Resonances in Biblical Narrative." *Journal of Biblical Literature* 116 (1997): 201–15.

______. "The Development of the Priestly Calendar (I): The Daily Sacrifice and the Sabbath." *Hebrew Union College Annual* 74 (2003): 1–20.

______. "Exodus and *Maṣṣôt* in History and Tradition." *Maarav* 8 (1992): 15–37.

______. "The Festivals of Israel and Judah and the Literary History of the Pentateuch." *Journal of the American Oriental Society* 110 (1990): 19–31.

Cowley, A. E. *Aramaic Papyri of the Fifth Century B.C.* Oxford: Clarendon, 1923.

Craigie, Peter C. *The Book of Deuteronomy.* New International Commentary on the Old Testament. Grand Rapids: Eerdmans, 1976.

Crenshaw, James L. *Old Testament Wisdom: An Introduction.* Rev. and enlarged ed. Louisville: Westminster John Knox, 1998.

Cross, Frank Moore. *Canaanite Myth and Hebrew Epic: Essays in the History of the Religion of Israel.* Cambridge, MA: Harvard University Press, 1973.

Crüsemann, Frank. *The Torah: Theology and Social History of Old Testament Law.* Translated by Allan W. Mahnke. Minneapolis: Fortress Press, 1996. Originally published in German, 1992.

Dahood, Mitchell. *Psalms.* 3 vols. Anchor Bible 16–17A. Garden City, NY: Doubleday, 1966–70.

Damrosch, David. *The Narrative Covenant: Transformation of Genre in the Growth of Biblical Literature.* Ithaca: Cornell University Press, 1987.

Dauenhauer, Bernard. "Paul Ricoeur." *The Stanford Encyclopedia of Philosophy (Winter 2005 Edition).* Edited by E. N. Zalta. No pages. Online: http://plato.stanford.edu/archives/ win2005/entries/riceour/.

Davidson, Robert. "Covenant Ideology in Ancient Israel." Pages 323–47 in *The World of Ancient Israel: Sociological, Anthropological and Political Perspectives.* Edited by R. E. Clements. Cambridge: Cambridge University Press, 1989.

Davies, Philip R. *In Search of 'Ancient Israel.'* Journal for the Study of the Old Testament: Supplement Series. Sheffield: Sheffield Academic, 1992.

Davis, Douglas. "An Interpretation of Sacrifice in Leviticus." *Zeitschrift für die alttestamentliche Wissenschaft* 89 (1977): 387–99.

Day, Peggy L. "From the Child Is Born the Woman: The Story of Jephthah's Daughter." Pages 58–74 in *Gender and Difference in Ancient Israel.* Edited by P. L. Day. Minneapolis: Fortress Press, 1989.

Deeley, Mary Kathleen. "The Rhetoric of Memory in the Stories of Saul and David." *Society of Biblical Literature Seminar Papers* 25 (1998): 285–92.

De Vries, Simon J. "Remembrance in Ezekiel: A Study of an Old Testament Theme." *Interpretation: A Journal of Bible and Theology* 16 (1962): 58–64.

______. *Yesterday, Today and Tomorrow: Time and History in the Old Testament.* Grand Rapids: Eerdmans, 1975.

Dewey, Russel A. "Flashbulb Memory." In *Psychology: An Introduction.* Online: http://www.psywww.com/intropsych/ch06_memory/ flashbulb_memory.html.

Dick, Michael Brennan. "Job XXVIII 4: A New Translation." *Vetus Testamentum* 29 (1979): 216–21.

Dijkstra, Meindert. "The Law of Moses: The Memory of Mosaic Religion In and After the Exile." Pages 70–98 in *Yahwism After the Exile: Perspectives on Israelite Religion in the Persian Era.* Edited by R. Albertz and B. Becking. Assen: Van Gorcum, 2003.

Douglas, Mary. *Into the Wilderness: The Doctrine of Defilement in the Book of Numbers.* Sheffield: Sheffield Academic, 1993. Repr., Oxford: Oxford University Press, 2001.

______. *Leviticus as Literature.* Oxford: Oxford University Press, 1999.

______. *Purity and Danger: An Analysis of the Concept of Pollution and Taboo.* London: Routledge, 1966. Repr., New York: Routledge, 2004.

Dozeman, Thomas B. *Exodus.* Eerdmans Critical Commentary. Grand Rapids: Eerdmans, 2009.

Ehrlich, Arnold B. *Mikrâ ki-Pheshutô.* 3 vols. First published, 1899. Repr., with Prolegomenon by H. M. Orlinsky. New York: Ktav, 1969.

Eisenstadt, Shmuel Noah, ed. *The Origins and Diversity of Axial Age Civilizations.* SUNY Series in Near East Studies. Albany: State University of New York Press, 1986.

Eising, H. "זָכַר *zākhar;* זֵכֶר *zēkher;* זִכָּרוֹן *zikkārôn;* אַזְכָּרָה *ʾazkārāh.*" Pages 64–82 in vol. 4 of *Theological Dictionary of the Old Testament.* Edited by G. J. Botterweck and H. Ringgren. Translated by J. T. Willis, G. W. Bromiley, and D. E. Green. 14 vols. Grand Rapids: Eerdmans, 1974–.

Eitan, Israel. "An Identification of *tiškaḥ yĕmīnī*, Ps 137:5." *Journal of Biblical Literature* 47 (1928): 193–95.

Eliade, Mircea. "Australian Religions. Part III: Initiation Rites and Secret Cults." *History of Religions* 7 (1967): 61–90.

______. *Cosmos and History: The Myth of the Eternal Return.* Translated by W. R. Trask. New York: Bollingen-Pantheon, 1954.

______. *The Sacred and the Profane: The Nature of Religion.* Translated by W. R. Trask. New York: Harcourt Brace Jovanovich, 1959.

Eliade, Mircea, ed. *The Encyclopedia of Religion.* 16 vols. New York: Macmillan, 1987.

Elliger, K., and W. Rudolph, eds. *Biblia Hebraica Stuttgartensia.* Stuttgart: Deutsche Bibelgesellschaft, 1983.

Elliot, John H. *What Is Social Scientific Criticism?* Minneapolis: Fortress Press, 1993.

Ellman, Barat. "Memory and Religious Praxis: The Meaning and Function of Memory in Deuteronomic and Priestly Religion." Ph.D. diss., Jewish Theological Seminary, 2011.

______. "Is שכח a Technical Term for Covenantal Disloyalty?" Paper presented at the international meeting of the SBL, London, June 2011.

Evans, Richard J. *In Defense of History.* New York: W. W. Norton, 1999.

Even-Shoshan, A., ed. *A New Concordance of the Bible: Thesaurus of the Language of the Bible, Hebrew and Aramaic Roots, Words, Proper Names, Phrases and Synonyms.* Jerusalem, Kiryat-Sefer, 1988.

Farber, Walter. *Beschwörungsrituale an Ištar und Dumuzi: Attī Ištar ša ḫarmaša Dumuzi.* Akademie der Wissenschaften und der Literatur. Veröffentlichungen der Orientalischen Kommission Bd. 30. Wiesbaden: Franz Steiner, 1977.

Fisch, Harold. *Poetry with a Purpose: Biblical Poetics and Interpretation.* Indiana Studies in Biblical Literature. Bloomington: Indiana University Press, 1988.

Fishbane, Michael. "Accusations of Adultery: A Study of Law and Scribal Practice in Numbers 5:11-31." *Hebrew Union College Annual* 45 (1974): 25–45.

______. *Biblical Interpretation in Ancient Israel.* Oxford: Clarendon, 1985.

_____. *The Garments of Torah: Essays in Biblical Hermeneutics.* Bloomington: Indiana University Press, 1989.

______. "On Biblical Omina." *Shnaton Ha-Miqra*ʾ1 (1976): 213–34 (Hebrew).

Fleming, Daniel. "Mari and the Possibility of Biblical Memory." *Revue d'assyriologie et d'archéologie orientale* 92 (1998): 41–78.

Fox, Everett. *The Five Books of Moses.* New York: Schocken, 1995.

Fox, Michael V. "The Sign of the Covenant: Circumcision in the Light of the Priestly *ʾôt* Etiologies." *Revue biblique* 81 (1974): 557–96.

Frankfort, Henri. *Kingship and the Gods: A Study of Ancient Near Eastern Religion as the Integration of Society and Nature.* Chicago: University of Chicago Press, 1948.

Freedman, David Noel. "The Structure of Psalm 137." Pages 187–205 in *Near Eastern Studies in Honor of William Foxwell Albright.* Edited by H. Goedicke. Baltimore: Johns Hopkins University Press, 1971.

Freedman, David Noel, ed. *The Anchor Bible Dictionary.* 6 vols. New York: Doubleday, 1992.

Fried, Lisbeth S. "The High Places (*Bāmôt*) and the Reforms of Hezekiah and Josiah: An Archaeological Investigation." *Journal of the American Oriental Society* 122 (2002): 437–65.

Frymer-Kensky, Tikva. "The Atrahasis Epic and Its Significance for Our Understanding of Genesis 1-9," *Biblical Archaeologist* 40 (1977): 147–54.

______. "The Strange Case of the Suspected Sotah (Numbers V 11-31)." *Vetus Testamentum* 34 (1984): 11–26.

Funkenstein, Amos. *Perceptions of Jewish History.* Berkeley: University of California Press, 1993.

Galpaz-Feller, Prina. "Private Lives and Public Censure: Adultery in Ancient Egypt and Biblical Israel." *Near Eastern Archaeology* 67 (2004): 152–61.

Gandulla, Bernardo. "Memory and Remembrance in Patriarchal Tradition: Two Cases of Resignification for the Presence of Absence." *Holy Land Studies* 6 (2007): 163–75.

Gane, Roy. *Cult and Character: Purification Offerings, Day of Atonement and Theodicy*. Winona Lake, IN: Eisenbrauns, 2005.

Gedi, Noa, and Yigal Elam. "Collective Memory: What Is It?" *History and Memory* 8 (1996): 30–50.

Geertz, Clifford. *The Interpretation of Cultures*. New York: Basic Books, 1973.

______. *Thick Descriptions: Toward an Interpretive Theory of Culture*. New York: Basic Books, 1973.

Gelb, Ignace J., Benno Landsberger, and A. Leo Oppenheim, eds. *The Assyrian Dictionary of the Oriental Institute of the University of Chicago*. Oriental Institute. Chicago: University of Chicago Press, 1956–.

Geller, Stephen A. "Blood Cult: An Interpretation of the Priestly Work of the Pentateuch." Pages 62–86 in *Sacred Enigmas: Literary Religion in the Hebrew Bible*. New York: Routledge, 1996.

______. "Fiery Wisdom: The Deuteronomic Tradition." Pages 30–61 in *Sacred Enigmas: Literary Religion in the Hebrew Bible*. New York: Routledge, 1996.

______. "God, Humanity, and Nature in the Pentateuch." Pages 421–65 in *Gazing on the Deep: Ancient Near Eastern and Other Studies in Honor of Tzvi Abusch*. Edited by J. Stackert, B. N. Porter, and D. P. Wright. Bethesda, MD: CDL, 2010.

______. "Manna and Sabbath: A Literary-Theological Reading of Exodus 16." *Interpretation: A Journal of Bible and Theology* 59 (2005): 5–16.

______. "The Religion of the Bible." Pages 2121–40 in *The Jewish Study Bible*. Edited by M. Z. Brettler and A. Berlin. New York: Oxford University Press, 2004.

______. "Sabbath and Creation: A Literary-Theological Analysis." *Interpretation: A Journal of Bible and Theology*. Forthcoming.

______. *Sacred Enigmas: Literary Religion in the Hebrew Bible*. New York: Routledge, 1996.

George, A. R., ed. *The Babylonian Gilgamesh Epic: Introduction, Critical Edition and Cuneiform Texts*. 2 vols. Oxford: Oxford University Press, 2003.

Gerstenberger, Erhard S. *Leviticus: A Commentary*. Old Testament Library. Louisville: Westminster John Knox, 1996.

Gillis, John R. *Commemoration: The Politics of Identity*. Princeton: Princeton University Press, 1994.

Ginsberg, H. L. *The Israelian Heritage of Judaism*. Texts and Studies of the Jewish Theological Seminary of America 24. New York: Jewish Theological Seminary, 1982.

Gittlen, Barry M. *Sacred Time, Sacred Place: Archaeology and the Religion of Israel*. Winona Lake, IN: Eisenbrauns, 2002.

Goetze, Albrecht. "Historical Allusion in Old Babylonian Omen Texts." *Journal of Cuneiform Studies* 1 (1947): 253–71.

Goody, Jack. "Religion and Ritual: The Definitional Problem." *The British Journal of Sociology* 12 (1961): 142–64.

Gordon, Cyrus H. *Ugaritic Textbook: Grammar, Texts and Translations, Cuneiform Selections, Glossary, Indices*. Analecta orientalia 38. Rome, Pontifical Biblical Institute, 1965.

Gorman, Frank H. *The Ideology of Ritual: Space, Time and Status in the Priestly Theology*. Journal for the Study of the Old Testament: Supplement Series 91. Sheffield: JSOT, 1990.

______. "Priestly Rituals of Founding: Time, Space, and Status." Pages 47–64 in *History and Interpretation: Essays in Honor of John H. Hayes*. Edited by M. P. Graham, W. P. Brown, and J. K. Kuan. Journal for the Study of the Old Testament: Supplement Series 173. Sheffield: Sheffield Academic, 1993.

______. "Ritual Studies and Biblical Studies: Assessment of the Past, Prospects for the Future." *Semeia* 67 (1994): 12–36.

Graham, William Albert. *Beyond the Written Word: Oral Aspects of Scripture in the History of Religion*. Cambridge: Cambridge University Press, 1993.

Grayson, A. Kirk. "History and Historians of the Ancient Near East: Assyria and Babylon." *Orientalia* (NS) 49 (1980): 140–94.

Green, Thomas A. "Folk History and Cultural Resurgence: A Tigua Example." *Journal of American Folklore* 89 (1976): 310–18.

Greenberg, Moshe. *Biblical Prose Prayer as a Window into the Popular Religion of Israel*. Berkeley: University of California Press, 1983.

______. *Ezekiel 1–20*. Anchor Bible 22. Garden City, NY: Doubleday, 1983.

Greenstein. Edward L. "Mixing Memory and Design: Reading Psalm 78." *Prooftexts: A Journal of Jewish Literary History* 10 (1990): 197–218.

Gruenwald, Ithamar. *Rituals and Ritual Theory in Ancient Israel*. Leiden: Brill, 2003.

Haag, H. "חָמָס, *chāmās*." Pages 478–86 in vol. 4 of *Theological Dictionary of the Old Testament*. Edited by G. J. Botterweck and H. Ringgren. Translated by J. T. Willis, G. W. Bromiley, and D. E. Green. 14 vols. Grand Rapids: Eerdmans, 1974–.

Hahn, Scott. "Covenant in the Old and New Testaments: Some Current Research (1994–2004)." *Currents in Biblical Research* 3 (2005): 263–92.

Hahn, Sidney Mayfield. "The Effect of Music in the Learning and Retention of Lexical Items in German." Online: http://eric.ed.gov/PDFS/ED119455.pdf.

Halbwachs, Maurice. *Les cadres sociaux de la mémoire.* Paris: F. Alcan, 1925. Repr., New York: Arno, 1975.

______. *The Collective Memory.* Translated by F. J. Ditter and V. Y. Ditter. New York: Harper & Row, 1980. Translation of *Le mémoire collective.* Paris: Presses Universitaires de France, 1950.

______. *La topographie légendaire des évangiles en Terre sainte: Études de mémoire collective.* Paris: Presses Universitaires de France, 1941.

Hallo, W. W., ed. *The Context of Scripture.* 3 vols. Leiden: Brill, 2003.

Halpern, Baruch. *The First Historians: The Hebrew Bible and History.* San Francisco: Harper & Row, 1988.

Hanchett, Suzanne. "Review: Five Books in Symbolic Anthropology." *American Anthropologist* New Series 80 (1978): 613–21.

Haran, Menahem. "The Character of the Priestly Source: Utopian and Exclusive Features." *Proceedings of the Eighth World Congress of Jewish Studies* (1983): 131–38.

______. "The Holiness Book." Pages 1094–96 in vol. 5 of *ʾEnṣîqlōppedia Miqraʾit.* Edited by B. Mazer et al. 9 vols. Jerusalem: Bialik, 1950–88 (Hebrew).

______. "Minḥa." Pages 23–30 in vol. 5 of *ʾEnṣîqlōppedia Miqraʾit.* Edited by B. Mazer et al. 9 vols. Jerusalem: Bialik, 1950–88 (Hebrew).

______. *Temples and Temple Service in Ancient Israel: An Inquiry into Biblical Cult Phenomena and the Historical Setting of the Priestly School.* Oxford: Clarendon, 1978. Repr., Winona Lake, IN: Eisenbrauns, 1985.

Harrelson, Walter. *From Fertility to Cult.* New York: Doubleday, 1969.

Heiser, Michael S. "Deuteronomy 32:8 and the Sons of God." *Bibliotheca sacra* 158 (2001): 52–74.

Helfmeyer, F. J. "אוֹת ʾôth." Pages 167–88 in vol. 1 of *The Theological Dictionary of the Old Testament.* Edited by G. J. Botterweck and H. Ringgren. Translated by J. T. Willis, G. W. Bromiley, and D. E. Green. 14 vols. Grand Rapids: Eerdmans, 1974–.

Hemmer Gudme, Anne Katrine de. "How Should We Read Hebrew Bible Ritual Texts?: A Ritualistic Reading of the Law of the Nazirite (Num 6,1-21)." *Scandinavian Journal of the Old Testament* 23 (2009): 64–84.

Hendel, Ronald. "The Exodus in Biblical Memory." *Journal of Biblical Literature* 120, no. 4 (2001): 601–22.

______. "Israel Among the Nations: Biblical Culture in the Ancient Near East." Pages 43–75 in *Culture of the Jews: A New History*. Edited by D. Biale. New York: Schocken, 2002.

______. "Purity and Danger in the Temple Court." Forthcoming.

______. *Remembering Abraham: Culture, Memory, and History in the Hebrew Bible.* Oxford: Oxford University Press, 2005.

Hens-Piazza, Gina. *The New Historians.* Minneapolis: Fortress Press, 2002.

Hervieu-Léger, Danièle. *Religion as a Chain of Memory.* Translated by S. Lee. New Brunswick, NJ: Rutgers University Press, 2000. Originally published as *La religion pour mémoire.* Paris: Cerf, 1993.

Hillers, Delbert R. *Covenant: The History of a Biblical Idea.* Baltimore: Johns Hopkins University Press, 1969.

Hobsbawm, Eric, and Terence Ranger. *The Invention of Tradition.* Cambridge: Cambridge University Press, 1983.

Hoffman, Yair. *Jeremiah.* 2 vols. Miqra' Lᵊyisrael. Tel Aviv: Obed, 2004 (Hebrew).

Hoftijzer, J., and K. Jongeling, eds. *Dictionary of North-West Semitic Inscriptions.* 2 vols. Leiden: E. J. Brill, 1995.

Hurowitz, Victor. "From Storm God to Abstract Being: How the Deity Became More Distant from Exodus to Deuteronomy." *Biblical Research* 14 (1998): 40–47.

______. "The Priestly Account of Building the Tabernacle." *Journal of the American Oriental Society* 105 (1985): 21–30.

Hurvitz, Ari. *A Linguistic Study of the Relationship between the Priestly Source and the Book of Ezekiel.* Cahiers de la Revue biblique 20. Paris: Gabalda, 1982.

Hwang, Jerry. *The Rhetoric of Remembrance: An Investigation of the "Fathers" in Deuteronomy*. Winona Lake, IN: Eisenbrauns, 2012.

Jacobsen, Thorkild. "Oral to Written." *Studies Diakonoff* (1982): 129–37.

______. *Treasures of Darkness: A History of Mesopotamian Religions.* New Haven: Yale University Press, 1976.

Janzen, J. Gerald. "The 'Wandering Aramean' Reconsidered." *Vetus Testamentum* 44 (1994): 359–75.

Jaspers, Karl. *The Origin and Goal of History.* New Haven: Yale University Press, 1954.

Jastrow, Marcus. *A Dictionary of the Targumim, the Talmud Babli and Yerushalmi, and the Midrashic Literature.* 2nd ed. New York: G. B. Putnam, 1903. Reprint, New York: Judaica, 1971.

Jenni, Ernst (with assistance from Claus Westermann), ed. *Theological Lexicon of the Old Testament.* Translated by M. E. Biddle. 3 vols. Peabody, MA: Hendrickson, 1997.

Jenson, Philip Peter. *Graded Holiness: A Key to the Priestly Conception of the World.* Journal for the Study of the Old Testament: Supplement Series 106. Sheffield: Sheffield Academic, 1992.

Jonker, Gerdien. *The Topography of Remembrance: The Dead, Tradition and Collective Memory in Mesopotamia.* Leiden: E. J. Brill, 1995.

Jonker, L. C. "Religious Polemics in Exile: The Creator God of Genesis 1," in *Religious Polemics in Context: Papers Presented to the Second International Conference of the Leiden Institute for the Studies of Religions (LISOR) held at Leiden, 27–28, April 2000.* Edited by T. L. Hettema and A. van der Kooij (Assen: Van Gorcum, 2004), 235–54.

Joüon, P. *A Grammar of Biblical Hebrew.* Translated and revised by T. Muraoka. 2 vols. Subsidia biblica 14/1–2. Rome: Editrice Pontificio Istituto Biblico, 1991.

Kaminsky, Joel. Review of Rolf Rendtorff, *The Covenant Formula: An Exegetical and Theological Investigation.* Old Testament Studies. Edinburgh: T. & T. Clark, 1998. *Journal of Religion* 80, no. 3 (2000): 485–86.

Kasabova, Anita. "Memory, Memorials and Commemoration." *History and Theory* 47 (2008): 331–50.

Katzenellenbogen, Mordechai Leib, ed. *Torat Ḥayim: ḥamishah ḥumshe Torah: mugahim ʿal-pi ha-nusaḥ veha-mesorah shel Keter Aram Tsovah ve-khitve-yad ha-kerovim lo, ʿim Targum Onkelos mugah ʿal-pi ha-Tag' ; ʿim perushe Rasag, Raḥ, Rashi … ; yotsʾim le-or ʿal-pi kitve-yad u-defusim rishonim ʿim tsiyune meḳorot, heʿarot u-veʾurim.* 7 vols. Jerusalem: Mosad Harav Kook, 1986–93 (Hebrew).

______. *Haggadah Shel Pesach:Torat Chaim im Perushei Harishonim.* Jerusalem: Mosad Harav Kook, 1998 (Hebrew).

Kautzsch. E., ed. *Gesenius' Hebrew Grammar.* Translated by A. E. Cowley. 2nd ed. Oxford: Clarendon, 1910.

Kippenberg, Hans G. "Name and Person in Ancient Judaism and Christianity." Pages 103–24 in *Concepts of the Person in Religion and Thought.* Edited by H. G. Kippenberg. Berlin: Mouton de Gruyter, 1990.

Knierim, Rolf P., and George W. Coats. *Numbers*. Forms of the Old Testament Literature 4. Grand Rapids: Eerdmans, 2005.

Knohl, Israel. *The Sanctuary of Silence: The Priestly Torah and the Holiness School*. Minneapolis: Augsburg Fortress Press, 1995. Repr., Winona Lake, IN: Eisenbrauns, 2007.

Knoppers, Gary N., and J. Gordon McConville, eds. *Reconsidering Israel and Judah: Recent Studies on the Deuteronomistic History*. Winona Lake, IN: Eisenbrauns, 2000.

Koehler, L., W. Baumgartner, and J. J. Stamm. *The Hebrew and Aramaic Lexicon of the Old Testament*. Translated and edited under the supervision of M. E. J. Richardson. 5 vols. Leiden: Brill, 1994–99.

Koeping, Klaus-Peter. "Anamnesis." Pages 253–61 in vol. 1 of *The Encyclopedia of Religion*. Edited by M. Eliade. 16 vols. New York: Macmillan, 1987.

Kofoed, Jens Bruun. *Text and History: Historiography and the Study of the Biblical Text*. Winona Lake, IN: Eisenbrauns, 2005.

Kraus, Hans-Joachim. *Worship in Israel: A Cultic History of the Old Testament*. Translated by Geoffrey Buswell. Richmond, VA: John Knox, 1966. German edition, 1962.

Krzysztof, Pomian. "De l'histoire, partie de la mémoire, à la mémoire, objet d'histoire." *Revue de métaphysique et de morales* 1 (1998): 63–110.

Labuschagne, Casper J. "The Pattern of Divine Speech Formulas in the Pentateuch: The Key to Its Literary Structure. *Vetus Testamentum* 32 (1982): 286–96.

Lambert, W. G., ed. *Babylonian Wisdom Literature*. Oxford: Oxford University Press, 1960.

Lambert, W. G., and A. R. Millard, eds. *Atra-Ḫasīs: The Babylonian Story of the Flood*. Winona Lake, IN: Eisenbrauns, 1999.

Lapsley, Jacqueline E. *Can These Bones Live? The Problem of the Moral Self in Ezekiel*. Berlin: Walter de Gruyter, 2000.

______. "Shame and Self-Knowledge: The Positive Role of Shame in Ezekiel's View of the Moral Self." Pages 143–73 in *The Book of Ezekiel: Theological and Anthropological Perspectives*. Society of Biblical Literature Symposium Series 9. Edited by M. S. Odell and J. T. Strong. Atlanta: Society of Biblical Literature, 2000.

______. "Feeling Our Way: Love for God in Deuteronomy." *Catholic Biblical Quarterly* 65 (2003): 350–69.

Lawlor, Leonard, and Valentine Moulard. "Henri Bergson." *The Stanford Encyclopedia of Philosophy (Spring 2008 edition).* Edited by E. N. Zalta. Rev. Jan. 12, 2010. http://plato.stanford.edu/entries/bergson/.

Lawrence, Peter. *Road Belong Cargo: A Study of the Cargo Movement in the Southern Madang District, New Guinea.* Melbourne: Melbourne University Press, 1964.

Leal, Robert Barry. *Wilderness in the Bible: Toward a Theology of Wilderness.* Society of Biblical Literature 72. New York: Peter Lang, 2004.

LeFebvre, Michael. *Collections, Codes and Texts: The Re-characterization of Israel's Written Law.* New York: T. & T. Clark, 2006.

Le Goff, Jacques. *History and Memory.* Translated by S. Rendall and E. Claman. New York: Columbia University Press, 1992.

Lemche, Niels Peter. *Ancient Israel: A New History of Israelite Society.* Sheffield: Sheffield Academic, 1988.

Leuchter, Mark. "Why Is the Song of Moses in the Book of Deuteronomy?" *Vetus Testamentum* 57 (2007): 295–317.

Leveen, Adriane. *Memory and Tradition in the Book of Numbers.* New York: Cambridge University Press, 2008.

Levenson, Jon D. *Creation and the Persistence of Evil: The Jewish Drama of Divine Omnipotence.* Princeton: Princeton University Press, 1988.

______. *Death and Resurrection of the Beloved Son: The Transformation of Child Sacrifice in Judaism and Christianity.* New Haven: Yale University Press, 1993.

______. *Sinai and Zion: An Entry into the Jewish Bible.* San Francisco: HarperCollins, 1995.

Levine, Baruch. "The Descriptive Tabernacle Texts of the Pentateuch." *Journal of the American Oriental Society* 85 (1965): 307–18.

______. *Leviticus.* The JPS Torah Commentary. Philadelphia: Jewish Publication Society, 1989.

______. *Numbers.* 2 vols. Anchor Bible 4A–B. New York: Doubleday, 1993–2000.

______. "Ritual as Symbol: Modes of Sacrifice in Israelite Religion." Pages 125–35 in *Sacred Time, Sacred Place: Archaeology and the Religion of Israel.* Edited by B. M. Gittlen. Winona Lake, IN: Eisenbrauns, 2002.

Levinson, Bernard M. *Deuteronomy and the Hermeneutics of Legal Innovation.* New York: Oxford University Press, 1997.

______. "The Hermeneutics of Tradition in Deuteronomy: A Reply to J. G. McConville." *Journal of Biblical Literature* 119 (2000): 269–86.

Lewis, Bernard. *History Remembered, Recovered, Invented.* Princeton: Princeton University Press, 1975.

Lewis, Gilbert. "Religious Doctrine or Experience: A Matter of Seeing, Learning, or Doing." Pages 155–72 in *Ritual and Memory: Toward a Comparative Anthropology of Religion.* Edited by H. Whitehouse and J. Laidlaw. Walnut Creek, CA: AltaMira, 2004.

Lewis, Theodore J. *Cults of the Dead in Ancient Israel and Ugarit.* Harvard Semitic Monographs 39. Atlanta: Scholars, 1989.

Linton, Ralph. "Nativistic Movements." Pages 497–503 in *Reader in Comparative Religion: An Anthropological Approach.* Edited by W. A. Lessa and E. Z. Vogt. 3rd ed. New York: Harper & Row, 1971. Repr., from *American Anthropologist* 45 (1943): 230–40.

Lipiński, Edward. *Semitic Languages: Outline of a Comparative Grammar.* Orientalia Lovaniensia Analecta 80. Leuven: Uitgeverij Peeters, 1997.

Liss, Hanna, "The Imaginary Sanctuary: The Priestly Code as an Example of Fictional Literature in the Hebrew Bible." Pages 663–89 in *Judah and the Judeans in the Persian Period.* Edited by O. Lipschits and M. Oeming. Winona Lake, IN: Eisenbrauns, 2006.

Lorberbaum, Yair. "The Rainbow in the Cloud: An Anger Management Device." *Journal of Religion* 89 (2009): 498–540.

Lord, Albert Bates. *Epic Singers and Oral Tradition.* Ithaca, NY: Cornell University Press, 1991.

______. *The Singer of Tales.* Cambridge, MA: Harvard University Press, 1960.

Lowenthal, David. *The Past Is a Foreign Country.* London: Cambridge University Press, 1985.

Lundbom, Jack R. "The Law Book of the Josianic Reform." *Catholic Biblical Quarterly* 38 (1976): 292–302.

Lyons, John. *Introduction to Theoretical Linguistics.* London: Cambridge University Press, 1968.

MacDonald, Nathan. "The Literary Criticism and Rhetorical Logic of Deut. I–IV," *Vetus Testamentum* 56 (2006): 203–12.

Mann, Thomas W. *Deuteronomy.* Westminster Bible Companion. Louisville: Westminster John Knox, 1995.

Marcus, Mordecai. "What Is an Initiation Story?" *Journal of Aesthetics and Art Criticism* 19 (1960): 221–28.

Margalit, Avishai. *The Ethics of Memory.* Cambridge, MA: Harvard University Press, 2002.

Mayes, Andrew D. H. "Deuteronomistic Ideology and the Theology of the Old Testament," *Journal for the Study of the Old Testament* 82 (1999): 57–82.

______. *The Story of Israel between Settlement and Exile: A Redactional Study of the Deuteronomic History*. London: SCM, 1983.

Mazer, B., et al., eds. *ʾEnṣîqlōppedia Miqraʾit*. 9 vols. Jerusalem: Bialik, 1950–88 (Hebrew).

McBride, S. Dean. "The Yoke of the Kingdom: An Exposition of Deuteronomy 6:4-5." *Interpretation: A Journal of Bible and Theology* 27 (1973): 273–306.

McCarthy, Dennis J. *Old Testament Covenant: A Survey of Current Opinion*. Richmond, VA: John Knox, 1972.

______. Review of Lothar Perlitt, *Bundestheologie im Alten Testament*. *Biblica* 53 (1972): 110–21.

McCauley, Robert N., and E. Thomas Lawson. *Bringing Ritual to Mind: Psychological Foundations of Cultural Forms*. New York: Cambridge University Press, 2002.

McConville, J. G. *Law and Theology in Deuteronomy*. Journal for the Study of the Old Testament: Supplement Series 33. Sheffield: JSOT, 1984.

McConville, J. G., and J. G. Miller, eds. *Time and Place in Deuteronomy*. Journal for the Study of the Old Testament: Supplement Series 179. Sheffield: Sheffield Academic, 1995.

McKay, J. W. "Man's Love for God in Deuteronomy and the Father/Teacher–Son/Pupil Relationship." *Vetus Testamentum* 22 (1972): 426–35.

McKenzie, Steven L. *Covenant*. St. Louis: Chalice, 2000.

______. "Deuteronomistic History." Pages 160–68 in vol. 2 of *The Anchor Bible Dictionary*. Edited by D. N. Freedman. 6 vols. New York: Doubleday, 1992.

______. *The Trouble with Kings: The Composition of the Book of Kings in the Deuteronomistic History*. Vetus Testamentum Supplements 42. Leiden and New York: E. J. Brill, 1991.

McKenzie, Steven L., and M. Patrick Graham, eds. *The History of Israel's Traditions: The Heritage of Martin Noth*. Journal for the Study of the Old Testament: Supplement Series 182. Sheffield: Sheffield Academic, 1994.

McNally, Robert N., and E. Thomas Lawson. *Bringing Ritual to Mind: Psychological Foundations of Cultural Forms*. New York: Cambridge University Press, 2002.

Medina, Suzanne L. "The Effects of Music upon Second Languages Vocabulary Acquisitions." School of Education. California State University Educational Resources Information Center Database. ERIC Document #ED 352-834.

Mendenhall, George. *Law and Covenant in Israel and the Ancient Near East.* Pittsburgh: Biblical Colloquium, 1955.

Mettinger, Tryggve N. D. *The Riddle of Resurrection: "Dying and Rising Gods" in the Ancient Near East.* Coniectanea biblica: Old Testament Series 50 Stockholm: Almqvist & Wiksell International, 2001.

Michalowski, Piotr. "History as a Charter: Some Observations on the Sumerian King List." *Journal of the American Oriental Society* 103 (1983): 237–48.

Milgrom, Jacob. "Encroaching on the Sacred: Purity and Polity in Numbers 1-10." *Interpretation: A Journal of Bible and Theology* 51 (1997): 241–53.

______. *Leviticus.* 3 vols. Anchor Bible 3–3B. New York: Doubleday, 1991–2001.

______. *Numbers.* The JPS Torah Commentary. Philadelphia: Jewish Publication Society, 1990.

______. *Studies in Levitical Terminology.* 2 vols. Near Eastern Studies 14. Berkeley: University of California Press, 1969.

Millard, Alan R. "A Wandering Aramean." *Journal of Near Eastern Studies* 39 (1980): 153–55.

Miller, Patrick D. *Deuteronomy.* Interpretation: A Bible Commentary for Teaching and Preaching. Louisville: Westminster John Knox, 1990.

Monroe, Lauren A. S. *Josiah's Reform and the Dynamics of Defilement.* Oxford: Oxford University Press, 2011.

Moran, William L. *The Amarna Letters.* Baltimore: Johns Hopkins University Press, 1987. Translation of *Les lettres d'El-Amarna.* Paris: Cerf, 1987.

______. "The Ancient Near Eastern Background of the Love of God in Deuteronomy." *Catholic Biblical Quarterly* 25 (1963): 77–87.

Moscati, Sabatino. *An Introduction to the Comparative Grammar of the Semitic Languages: Phonology and Morphology.* Wiesbaden: Otto Harrassowitz, 1964.

Müller, Hans-Peter. "History-oriented Foundation Myths in Israel and Its Environment." Pages 156–68 in *Religious Identity and the Invention of Tradition: Papers read at a NOSTER Conference in Soesterberg, January 4–6, 1999.* Edited by J. W. Van Henten and A. Houtepen. STAR 3. Assen: Royal Van Gorcum, 2001.

______. חָכָם "*chākham.*" Pages 364–85 in vol. 4 of *Theological Dictionary of the Old Testament.* Edited by G. J. Botterweck and H. Ringgren. Translated by J. T. Willis, G. W. Bromiley, and D. E. Green. 14 vols. Grand Rapids: Eerdmans, 1974–.

Naveh, Joseph. *On Stone and Mosaic: Aramaic and Hebrew Inscriptions from the Period of the Second Temple, the Mishna and the Talmud.* Jerusalem: Magnes, 1992 (Hebrew).

Nelson, Richard D. *Deuteronomy: A Commentary.* Old Testament Library. Louisville: Westminster John Knox, 2002.

Newsome, Carol A. "Meditations on Social and Cultural Memory–Hebrew Bible Studies." Paper presented at the annual meeting of the Society of Biblical Literature, Atlanta, November 21, 2010.

Nicholson, Ernest W. *Deuteronomy and Tradition.* Philadelphia: Fortress Press, 1967.

______. *God and His People: Covenant and Theology in the Old Testament.* Oxford: Clarendon, 1986.

Niehaus, Jeffrey J. *God at Sinai: Covenant and Theophany in the Bible and Ancient Near East.* Grand Rapids: Zondervan, 1995.

Nihan, Christophe. *From Priestly Torah to Pentateuch: A Study in the Composition of the Book of Leviticus.* Forschungen zum Alten Testament 2:25. Tübingen: Mohr Siebeck, 2007.

Nola, Alfonso M. di, and Robert D. Pelton, "Demythicization in Certain Primitive Cultures: Cultural Fact and Socioreligious Integration." *History of Religions* 12 (1972): 1–27.

Nöldeke, Theodor. "Wörter mit Gegensinn *(Aḍdād).*" Pages 67–108 in *Neue Beiträge zur semitischen Sprachwissenschaft.* Strassburg: Karl J. Trübner, 1910.

Nora, Pierre. "Between Memory and History: Les Lieux des Mémoire." *Representation* 26 (1989): 7–24.

Noth, Martin. *The Deuteronomistic History.* Translated by E. W. Nicholson. Journal for the Study of the Old Testament: Supplement Series 15. Sheffield: JSOT, 1981. Translation of pages 1–110 of *Überlieferungsgeschichtliche Studien,* 2nd ed. Tübingen: Max Niemeyer, 1957.

______. *Exodus: A Commentary.* Old Testament Library. Philadelphia: Westminster, 1962.

______. *A History of Pentateuchal Traditions.* Translated by B. W. Anderson. Englewood Cliffs, NJ: Prentice-Hall, 1972.

______. *Leviticus: A Commentary.* Old Testament Library. Philadelphia: Westminster, 1965.

Olick, Jeffrey K. "Collective Memory: The Two Cultures." *Sociological Theory* 17 (1999): 333–48.

Olson, Dennis T. *The Death of the Old and the Birth of the New: The Framework of the Book of Numbers and the Pentateuch.* Brown Judaic Studies 71. Chico, CA: Scholars, 1985.

Olyan, Saul M. *Biblical Mourning: Ritual and Social Dimensions.* Oxford: Oxford University Press, 2004.

______. "Exodus 31:12-17: The Sabbath According to H or the Sabbath According to P and H?" *Journal of Biblical Literature* 124 (2005): 201–9.

______. *Rites and Rank: Hierarchy in Biblical Representations of Cult.* Princeton: Princeton University Press, 2000.

______. "What Do Shaving Rites Accomplish and What Do They Signal in Biblical Ritual Contexts?" *Journal of Biblical Literature* 117 (1998): 611–22.

Olyan, Saul M., ed. *Social Theory and the Study of Israelite Religion: Essays in Retrospect and Prospect.* Atlanta: Society of Biblical Literature, 2012.

Otto, Rudolf. *The Idea of the Holy: An Inquiry into the Non-rational Factor in the Idea of the Divine and Its Relation to the Rational.* 2nd ed. Translated by J. W. Harvey. London: Oxford University Press, 1950.

Overholt, Thomas W. *Cultural Anthropology and the Old Testament.* Minneapolis: Fortress Press, 1996.

Pardes, Ilana. *The Biography of Ancient Israel: National Narratives in the Bible.* Berkeley: University of California Press, 2000.

______. *Countertraditions in the Bible: A Feminist Approach.* Cambridge, MA: Harvard University Press, 1992.

______. "Imagining the Birth of Ancient Israel: National Metaphors in the Bible." Pages 9–41 in *Cultures of the Jews: A New History.* Edited by D. Biale. New York: Schocken, 2002.

Patton, John Hastings. *Canaanite Parallels in the Book of Psalms.* Baltimore: Johns Hopkins University Press, 1944.

Perdue, Leo G. *The Collapse of History: Reconstructing Old Testament Theology.* Minneapolis: Fortress Press, 1994.

Person, Raymond F., Jr. *The Deuteronomic School: History, Social Setting, and Literature.* Leiden: Brill, 2002.

Phillips, Anthony. *Deuteronomy.* London: Cambridge University Press, 1973.

______. "A Fresh Look at the Sinai Pericope." Parts 1 and 2. *Vetus Testamentum* 34 (1984): 39–53 and 282–94.

Polen, Nehemiah. "God's Memory." Pages 139–53 in *Obliged by Memory.* Edited by S. Katz and A. Rosen. Syracuse: University of Syracuse Press, 2005.

Polzin, Robert. *Moses and the Deuteronomist: A Literary Study of the Deuteronomic History*. New York: Seabury, 1980.

_____. "Deuteronomy." Pages 92–101 in *The Literary Guide to the Bible*. Edited by R. Alter and F. Kermode. Cambridge, MA: Harvard University Press, 1987.

Pope, Marvin. Review of John Gray, *The Legacy of Canaan: The Ras Shamra Texts and Their Relevance to the Old Testament*. *Journal of Semitic Studies* 11 (1966): 228–41.

Popović, Anto. "The Bible as a Book of Memory." *Antonianum* 79 (2004): 441–43.

Powhida, Timothy. "Classroom Songs: Aiding in the Retention and Recall of Test Material with Fourth Grade Students." Masters Thesis. SUNY Potsdam, 2008. Online: http://hdl.handle.net/1951/43066.

Preuss, H. D. שָׁכַח, "*šākaḥ*." Pages 671–77 in vol. 14 of *Theological Dictionary of the Old Testament*. Edited by G. J. Botterweck and H. Ringgren. Translated by J. T. Willis, G. W. Bromiley, and D. E. Green. 14 vols. Grand Rapids: Eerdmans, 1974–.

Pritchard, James B., ed. *Ancient Near Eastern Texts Relating to the Old Testament*. Princeton: Princeton University Press, 1969.

Propp, William H. C. "The Bloody Bridegroom: Exod iv 24-6." *Vetus Testamentum* 43 (1993): 495–518.

_____. *Exodus*. 2 vols. Anchor Bible 2–2A. New York: Doubleday, 1999–2006.

Rad, Gerhard von. *Genesis: A Commentary*. Old Testament Library. Philadelphia: Westminster, 1972.

_____. *Old Testament Theology*. Translated by D. M. G. Stalker. 2 vols. New York: Harper & Row, 1963.

_____. *The Problem of the Hexateuch and Other Essays*. Translated by E. W. Dicken. Edinburgh and London: Oliver & Boyd, 1965.

_____. *Studies in Deuteronomy*. Translated by D. M. G. Stalker. Studies in Biblical Theology 9. London: SCM, 1953.

Regev, Eyal. "Priestly Dynamic Holiness and Deuteronomic Static Holiness." *Vetus Testamentum* 51 (2001): 243–61.

Reich, Wendy. "The Uses of Folklore in Revitalization Movements." *Folklore* 82 (1971): 233–44.

Rendsburg, Gary A., and Susan Rendsburg. "Physiological and Philological Notes to Psalm 137." *Jewish Quarterly Review* 83 (1993): 385–99.

Rendtorff, Rolf. "'Covenant' as a Structuring Concept in Genesis and Exodus." *Journal of Biblical Literature* 108 (1989): 385–93.

______. *The Covenant Formula: An Exegetical and Theological Investigation.* Old Testament Studies. Edinburgh: T. & T. Clark, 1998.

Retsö, Jan. *Diathesis in the Semitic Languages: A Comparative Morphological Study.* Leiden: Brill, 1989.

Richter, Sandra L. *The Deuteronomistic History and the Name Theology:* lᵊšakkēn šᵊmô šām *in the Bible and the Ancient Near East.* Berlin and New York: Walter de Gruyter, 2002.

Ricoeur, Paul. *Memory, History and Forgetting.* Translated by K. Blamey and D. Pellauer. Chicago: University of Chicago Press, 2004.

Ringgren, Helmer. "בִּין *bîn,* בִּינָה *bînāh,* תְּבוּנָה *tᵉbhûnāh.*" Pages 99–107 in vol. 2 of *The Theological Dictionary of the Old Testament.* Edited by G. J. Botterweck and H. Ringgren. Translated by J. T. Willis, G. W. Bromiley, and D. E. Green. 14 vols. Grand Rapids: Eerdmans, 1974–.

Roberts, J. J. M. "NIŠKAḤTÎ . . . MILLĒB, Ps. XXXI 13." *Vetus Testamentum* 25 (1971): 797–801.

Rogerson, John W. *Anthropology and the Old Testament.* Oxford: Blackwell, 1978.

Römer, Thomas C. *The So-Called Deuteronomistic History: A Sociological, Historical and Literary Introduction.* London and New York: T. & T. Clark, 2005.

Rose, Martin. "Names of God in the OT." Pages 1002–11 in vol. 4 of *The Anchor Bible Dictionary.* Edited by D. N. Freedman. 6 vols. New York: Doubleday, 1992.

Rosenbaum, Jonathan. "Hezekiah's Reform and the Deuteronomistic Tradition." *Harvard Theological Review* 22 (1979): 23–43.

Rosenfeld, Israel. *Invention of Memory: A New View of the Brain.* New York: Basic Books, 1988.

Roth, Cecil. "Ecclesiasticus in the Synagogue Service." *Journal of Biblical Literature* 71 (1952): 171–78.

Rowlands, Michael. "The Role of Memory in the Transmission of Culture." *World Archaeology* 25 (1993): 141–51.

Said, Edward W. "Invention, Memory and Place." *Critical Inquiry* 26 (2000): 175–92.

Sarna, Nahum. *Exodus.* The JPS Torah Commentary. Philadelphia: Jewish Publication Society, 1991.

_____. *Exploring Exodus: The Origins of Biblical Israel.* New York: Schocken, 1986.

_____. *Genesis.* The JPS Torah Commentary. Philadelphia: Jewish Publication Society, 2001.

_____. *Understanding Genesis: The Heritage of Biblical Israel.* New York: Schocken, 1970.

Sawyer, John F. A. *Semantics in Biblical Research: New Methods of Defining Hebrew Words for Salvation.* Studies in Biblical Theology 2/24. London: SCM, 1972.

Schenker, Adrian, et al., gen. eds. *Biblia Hebraica Quinta.* Stuttgart: Deutsche Bibelgesellschaft, 2004–.

Schmidt, Brian B. "Memory as Immortality: Countering the Dreaded 'Death After Death' in Ancient Israelite Society." Pages 87–100 in *Judaism in Late Antiquity IV.* Edited by A. J. Avery-Peck and J. Neusner. Leiden: E. J. Brill, 2000.

Schottroff, Willy. *"Gedenken" im Alten Orient und im Alten Testament: Die Wurzel* zākar *im semitischen Sprachkreis.* Neukirchen-Vluyn: Neukirchener, 1967.

_____. "זכר, *zkr*, to remember." Pages 381–88 in vol. 1 of *The Theological Lexicon of the Old Testament.* Edited by E. Jenni with assistance from C. Westermann. Translated by M. E. Biddle. 3 vols. Peabody, MA: Hendrickson, 1997.

_____. "שכח, *škḥ*, to forget." Pages 1322–26 in vol. 3 of *The Theological Lexicon of the Old Testament.* Edited by E. Jenni with assistance from C. Westermann. Translated by M. E. Biddle. 3 vols. Peabody, MA: Hendrickson, 1997.

Schulkind, M. D. "Is Memory for Music Special?" *Annals of the New York Academy of Sciences* 1169 (2009): 216–24.

Schulz, Kathryn. *Being Wrong: Adventures in the Margin of Error.* New York: HarperCollins, 2010.

Schuman, Howard, Vered Vinitzky-Seroussi, and Amiram D. Vinokur. "Keeping the Past Alive: Memories of Israeli Jews at the Turn of the Millennium." *Sociological Forum* 18 (2003): 101–36.

Schwartz, Baruch J. "The Priestly Account of the Theophany and Lawgiving at Sinai." Pages 103–34 in *Texts, Temples and Traditions: A Tribute to Menahem Haran.* Edited by M. V. Fox, V. A. Hurowitz, et al. Winona Lake, IN: Eisenbrauns, 1996.

Skehan, Patrick W. "A Fragment of the 'Song of Moses' (Deut. 32) from Qumran." *Bulletin of the American Schools of Oriental Research* 136 (1954): 12.

______. "The Structure of the Song of Moses in Deuteronomy." *Catholic Biblical Quarterly* 13 (1951): 153–63.

Sirat, René-Samuel. "Devoir de mémoir et mémoir d'avenir." Pages 231–43 in *Le Livre du Centenaire du Grand Rabbin Jacob Kaplan*. Edited by M-R. Hayoun, F. Kaplan, and R-S. Sirat. Paris: Noêsis, 1997.

Smith, Daniel L. *The Religion of the Landless: The Social Context of the Babylonian Exile*. Bloomington, IN: Meyer Stone, 1989.

Smith, Mark S. *The Memoirs of God: History, Memory, and the Experience of the Divine in Ancient Israel*. Minneapolis: Fortress Press, 2004.

______. *The Priestly Vision of Genesis 1*. Minneapolis: Fortress Press, 2010.

______. "Remembering God: Collective Memory in Israelite Religion." *Catholic Biblical Quarterly* 64 (2002): 631–51.

Snyman, Gerrie. "Collective Memory and Coloniality of Being as a Hermeneutical Framework: A Particularized Reading of Ezra-Nehemiah." *Old Testament Essays* 20 (2007): 35–83.

Sokoloff, Michael. *Dictionary of Jewish Palestinian Aramaic of the Byzantine Period*. Ramat Gan: Bar Ilan University Press, 1990.

Sommer, Benjamin D. *The Bodies of God and the World of Ancient Israel*. New York: Cambridge University Press, 2009.

Sparks, Kenton L. *Ethnicity and Identity in Ancient Israel: Prolegomena to the Study of Ethnic Sentiments and Their Expression in the Hebrew Bible*. Winona Lake, IN: Eisenbrauns, 1998.

______. "'Enūma Elish' and Priestly Mimesis: Elite Emulation in Nascent Judaism." *Journal of Biblical Literature* 126 (2007): 625–48.

Sperling, S. David. "Yahweh's *Berît* (Covenant): Which Came First—Sex or Politics?" Pages 61–74 in *The Original Torah: The Political Intent of the Bible*. New York: New York University Press, 1998.

Spiegel, Gabrielle M. "Memory and History: Liturgical Time and Historical Time." *History and Theory* 41 (2002): 149–62.

Stackert, Jeffrey. "The Holiness Legislation and its Pentateuchal Sources: Revision, Supplement, and Replacement." Pages 187-204 in *The Strata of the Priestly Writing: Contemporary Debate and Future Directions*. Edited by S. Shectman and J. S. Baden. Zürich: Theologischer, 2009.

______. *Rewriting the Torah: Literary Revisionism in Deuteronomy and the Holiness Legislation*. Tübingen: Mohr Siebeck, 2007.

Sternberg, Meir. *Hebrews Between Cultures: Group Portraits, National Literature*. Bloomington: Indiana University Press, 1998.

Sutton, John. "Memory." *The Stanford Encyclopedia (Summer 2004 Edition).* Edited by E. N. Zalta. Online: http://plato.stanford.edu/archives/sum2004/entries/ memory.

Sweeney, Marvin. *King Josiah of Judah: The Lost Messiah of Israel.* Oxford: Oxford University Press, 2001.

Tal, Abraham, ed. *Samaritan Targum of the Pentateuch: A Critical Edition.* 3 vols. Tel-Aviv: Tel-Aviv University Press, 1981.

Talmon, Shemaryahu. Review of Brevard Childs, *Memory and Tradition in Ancient Israel. Journal of Biblical Literature* 82 (1963): 330, 332–33.

Terdiman, Richard. *Modernity and the Memory Crisis.* Ithaca: Cornell University Press, 1993.

Thiessen, Matthew. "The Form and Function of the Song of Moses (Deuteronomy 32:1-43)." *Journal of Biblical Literature* 123 (2004): 401–24.

Thompson, J. A. *Deuteronomy: An Introduction and Commentary.* Tyndale Old Testament Commentaries. London: InterVarsity, 1974.

Thompson, P. E. S. "The Yahwist Creation Story." *Vetus Testamentum* 21 (1971): 197–208.

Thompson, Thomas L. *The Historicity of the Patriarchal Narratives: The Quest for the Historical Abraham.* Berlin: Walter de Gruyter, 1974.

_____. *The Mythic Past: Biblical Archaeology and the Myth of Israel.* London, Basic Books, 1999.

Tigay, Jeffrey. *Deuteronomy.* The JPS Torah Commentary. Philadelphia: Jewish Publication Society, 1996.

Tov, Emmanuel, Editor in chief. *Discoveries in the Judaean Desert.* 31 vols. Oxford: Clarendon, 1955–.

Tur-Sinai, Naphtali H. "ʾôt." Pages 183–84 in vol. 1 of *ʾEnṣîqlōppedia Miqraʾit.* Edited by B. Mazer et al. 9 vols. Jerusalem: Bialik, 1950–88 (Hebrew).

Ullendorff, Edward. "Thought Categories in the Hebrew Bible." Pages 52–67 in *Is Biblical Hebrew a Language? Studies in Semitic Languages and Civilizations.* Edited by E. Ullendorff. Wiesbaden: Otto Harrassowitz, 1977.

Van der Toorn, Karel. "The Exodus as Charter Myth." Pages 113–27 in *Religious Identity and the Invention of Tradition: Papers read at a NOSTER Conference in Soesterberg, January 4–6, 1999.* Edited by J. W. Van Henten and A. Houtepen. STAR 3. Assen: Royal Van Gorcum, 2001.

Van Gennep, Arnold. *The Rites of Passage.* Chicago: University of Chicago Press, 1960. Repr., London: Routledge, 2004.

Van Seters, John. *The Life of Moses: The Yahwist as Historian in Exodus–Numbers.* Louisville: Westminster John Knox, 1994.

______. *In Search of History: Historiography in the Ancient World and the Origins of Biblical History*. New Haven: Yale University Press, 1983. Repr., Winona Lake, IN: Eisenbrauns, 1997.

Vogt, Peter T. *Deuteronomic Theology and the Significance of* Torah: *A Reappraisal*. Winona Lake, IN: Eisenbrauns, 2006.

Warburton, William. *The Divine Legislation of Moses Demonstrated: to which is prefixed, a discourse by way of general preface: containing some account of, the life, writings and character of the author. By Richard Hurd*. London: Millar & Tonson, 1788. 10th ed. London: Thomas Tegg, 1846.

Watts, James W. "Ritual Legitimacy and Scriptural Authority." *Journal of Biblical Literature* 124 (2005): 401–17.

Weckman, George. "Understanding Initiation." *History of Religions* 10 (1970): 62–79.

Weinfeld, Moshe. "בְּרִית, *berîth*." Pages 253–79 in vol. 2 of *Theological Dictionary of the Old Testament*. Edited by G. J. Botterweck and H. Ringgren. Translated by J. T. Willis, G. W. Bromiley, and D. E. Green. 14 vols. Grand Rapids: Eerdmans, 1974–.

______. "*B^e^rît:* Covenant vs. Obligation." *Biblica* 56 (1975): 120–28.

______. "The Covenant of Grant in the Old Testament and Ancient Near East." *Journal of the American Oriental Society* 90 (1970): 184–203.

______. "Deuteronomy, Book of." Pages 168–83 in vol. 2 of *The Anchor Bible Dictionary*. Edited by D. N. Freedman. 6 vols. New York: Doubleday, 1992.

______. *Deuteronomy and the Deuteronomic School*. Oxford: Clarendon, 1972. Repr., Winona Lake, IN: Eisenbrauns, 1992.

______. *Deuteronomy 1–11*. Anchor Bible 5. New York: Doubleday, 1991.

______. "Theological Trends in the Books of the Torah." Pages 401–13 in *Studies in Biblical History*. Edited by M. Cogan. Jerusalem: The Zalman Shazar Center for Jewish History, 1997 (Hebrew).

Weitzman, Steven. "Sensory Reform in Deuteronomy." Pages 123–39 in *Religion and the Self in Antiquity*. Edited by D. Brakke, M. L. Satlow, and S. Weitzman. Bloomington: Indiana University Press, 2005.

Wellhausen, Julius. *Prolegomena to the History of Israel*. Atlanta: Scholars, 1994. Reprint of Edinburgh: 1885 ed.

Wenham, Gordon J. *Genesis 1–15*. Word Biblical Commentary 1. Waco, TX: Word, 1987.

Westermann, Claus. *Genesis 1–11: A Commentary*. Translated by J. J. Scullion. Minneapolis: Augsburg Press, 1984–86.

_____. *The Promises to the Fathers: Studies on the Patriarchal Narratives.* Translated by D. E. Green. Philadelphia: Fortress Press, 1980. Originally published as *Die Verheissungen an die Väter.* Göttingen: Vandenhoeck & Ruprecht, 1976.

Wevers, John Williams, ed. *Septuaginta: Vetus Testamentum Graecum.* Auctoritate Academiae Scientiarum Gottingensis Editum. 21 vols. Göttingen: Vandenhoeck & Ruprecht, 1977.

Whitehouse, Harvey. "Apparitions, Orations, and Rings: Experiences of Spirits in Dadul." Pages 173–94 in *Spirits in Culture, History and Mind.* Edited by J. M. Mageo and A. Howard. New York: Routledge, 1996.

_____. *Arguments and Icons: Divergent Modes of Religiosity.* Oxford: Oxford University Press, 2000.

_____. *Inside the Cult: Religious Innovation and Transmission in Papua New Guinea.* Oxford: Clarendon, 1995.

_____. *Modes of Religiosity: A Cognitive Theory of Religious Transmission.* Walnut Creek, CA: AltaMira, 2004.

_____. "Rites of Terror: Emotion, Metaphor and Memory in Melanesian Initiation Cults." Pages 133–48 in *Religion and Emotion: Approaches and Interpretations.* Edited by J. Corrigan. New York: Oxford University Press, 2004. Repr., from *Journal of the Royal Anthropological Institute* 2 (1996): 703–15.

Whitehouse, Harvey, and James Laidlaw, eds. *Ritual and Memory: Toward a Comparative Anthropology of Religion.* Walnut Creek, CA: AltaMira, 2004.

Whitehouse, Harvey, and Luther H. Martin, eds. *Theorizing Religions Past: Archaeology, History, and Cognition.* Walnut Creek, CA: AltaMira, 2004.

Wiebe, Donald. "Critical Reflections on the Modes of Religiosity Argument." Pages 197–213 in H. Whitehouse and L. M. Martin, eds. *Theorizing Religions Past: Archeology, History and Cognition.* Edited by H. Whitehouse and L.M. Martin. Walnut Creek, CA: AltaMira, 2004.

Willander, Johan, and Maria Larsson. "Smell Your Way Back to Childhood: Autobiographical Odor Memory." *Psychonomic Bulletin and Review* 13 (2006): 240–44.

Williams, F. E. *Orokaiva Magic.* London: Humphrey Milford, 1928.

_____. *The Vailala Madness and the Destruction of Native Ceremonies in the Gulf Division.* Port Moresby: Territory of Papua. *Anthropology Report* 4 (1928).

Wilson, Anthony. "Revitalization Movements." *American Anthropologist.* New Series 58 (1956): 264–81.

Wilson, Robert R. *Prophecy and Society in Ancient Israel.* Philadelphia: Fortress Press, 1980.

Wright, David P. "Ritual Theory, Ritual Texts and the Priestly-Holiness Writings in the Pentateuch." Pages 195–216 in *Social Theory and the Study of Israelite Religion: Essays in Retrospect and Prospect.* Edited by S. M. Olyan. Atlanta: Society of Biblical Literature, 2102.

Wright, G. Ernest. "The Lawsuit of God: A Form-Critical Study of Deuteronomy 32." Pages 26–67 in *Israel's Prophetic Heritage: Essays in Honor of James Muilenburg.* Edited by B. W. Anderson and W. Harrelson. New York: Harper & Brothers, 1962.

Yalon, Hanoch. "The terms: ידע, למד." *Tarbiz* 36 (1967): 396–400 (Hebrew).

Yates, Frances. *The Art of Memory.* Chicago: University of Chicago Press, 1966.

Yerushalmi, Yosef Hayim. *Zakhor: Jewish History and Jewish Memory.* Seattle: University of Washington Press, 1982.

Yeshurun, Yaara, Hadas Lapid, Yadin Dudai, and Noam Sobel. "The Privileged Brain Representation of First Olfactory Associations." *Current Biology* 19 (2009): 1869–74.

Youngblood, Ronald. "The Abrahamic Covenant: Conditional or Unconditional?" Pages 31–46 in *The Living and Active Word of God: Studies in Honor of Samuel J. Schultz.* Edited by M. Inch and R. Youngblood. Winona Lake, IN: Eisenbrauns, 1983.

Zakovitch, Yair. "The Book of the Covenant Interprets the Book of the Covenant: The 'Boomerang' Phenomenon." Pages *59–64 in *Texts, Temples and Traditions: A Tribute to Menahem Haran.* Edited by M. V. Fox et al. Winona Lake, IN: Eisenbrauns, 1996 (Hebrew).

Zuesse, Evan M. "Ritual." Pages 405–22 in vol. 12 of *The Encyclopedia of Religion.* Edited by M. Eliade. 16 vols. New York: Macmillan, 1987.

Index of Subjects and Names

170, 171 (*see also* individual practices under ritual); priests in, 84, 90; signs in, 70–71, *161n1*; theology, 4, 6, 7, 10, 27, 49, 77–78; *ṭôṭāpōt,* 158; wisdom and, 79–80, 103; women in, *11n20*, 90–91, *91n47*
Deuteronomy, book of, xi, 4, *5n5, 6n7*, 8, 9, *10n17*, 11, 13, *13n28*, 15, 16, *16n36*, 17, *17n40*, 20, 21, 22, 23, 25, *25n73*, 27, 28, 29, 30, 31, 34, *34n6*, 41, 43, 45, 46, 47, 60, *60n24*, 61, *63n30*, 64, 65, *65n38, 66n41, 66n43*, 67, 71–72, 75–104, *75n1, 77n8, 78n11, 85n33, 86n35, 88n40, 91n47, 92n62, 98n65, 99n68, 103n72, 113n29, 124n2, 136n32,* 151, *151n9, 157n28*, 158, *161n1*, 170, 171
Divergent Modes of Religiosity, Theory of, *14n29*, 25, 52, *52n15*, 129, *138n35*
Documentary Hypothesis, *5n5, 9n13*

Eliade, M., *24n68*, 41, *130n20, 130n22, 134n28*
Eliezer, 23, 126
Enuma Elish, 36, 38
Exodus, Book of, 5, 81, 92, 93, 123, *133n25, 136nn32–33*

festival(s), 3, 15–16, 63, 75, *76n6*, 81, 91, 92, 114, 123, 148, *149n4,* 151, 152, *153n17, 154n20,* 155, 156, 166, 170 (*see also* pilgrimage); of Booths, 3, 76, 90, 91, *133n26*; of Unleavened Bread, 3, 54, 91, *93n50,* 132, 152–54, *154n19,* 156, 157 (*see also maṣṣōt*); of Weeks, 76, *84n30* (*see also Bikkurîm*)
Fisch, H., *97n63*
forget[ting], 3, 51, 60, *60n22,* 61–62, *62n29,* 63, 75, 78, *78n12,* 87, 89, 90, 94–96, *97n63,* 101, 103, 170; as an act of rebellion, 62, *62n28,* 66, 101; God does not forget, 46, 54, *54n17*; God forgets, 5, 19, 38, *39n20*; terms for, 61–62, 101

Geertz, C., 25, 27
Geller, S. A., xi, xii, *5n5, 116n37, 127n12, 144n45, 163n5,* 165, 168
Genesis, Book of, xi, 5, *5n5,* 6, 7, 9, 23, 29, 33, 34, 35–47, 71
Greenberg, M., 4–5, 83
Gerstenberger, E. S., *69n54*
Gilgamesh, 36, 38
Goldstein, B., *149n4*
Greenstein, E., xii, 20, 21

Halbwachs, M., 50–51
Halpern, B., 18
Haran, M., *68n53*, 107, *108nn10–11*, 111
Heilsgeschichte, 15, *15n36*
Hendel, R., xii, 18, 109–10
Hezekiah, 10, *10n15,* 91
Holiness tradition (H), 9, *9n13,* 12, 13, 30–31, 54, 59, 61, 62, *64n37, 69n56, 82n23, 93n49,* 125, 147–60, 162, 164, 166, 167; Holiness Code, *84n30, 120n46*
Horeb, 4, 23, 65, 77, 81, 86, *86n35*, 103, 104, 135
Hosea, 78, *78n13,* 119
Hwang, J., 20–21, *23n65*

incense, 68–69, 107, 111, 115–16, 117, 125–26, *126n7,* 127, 137, *137n33,* 139, 169
initiation, 128–30, *130n17, 133n24,* 134, *134n27*

J (Yahwist) source, 23, *36n9,* 39–40, *39n23*
Josiah/Josianic, 10, *10n15*, *10n18*, 11, *11n19,* 91

Index of Biblical References and Rabbinic Texts

HEBREW BIBLE

Genesis

Joshua

NEW TESTAMENT AND APOCRYPHA

MISHNA AND TALMUD

CPSIA information can be obtained
at www.ICGtesting.com
Printed in the USA
BVHW01s0219240118
506161BV00020B/394/P

9 781451 465617